City at
the Water's Edge

A Natural History
of New York

Betsy McCully

City

at the Water's Edge

Rivergate Books

An imprint of Rutgers University Press

New Brunswick, New Jersey, and London

Library of Congress Cataloging-in-Publication Data

McCully, Betsy, 1950–

City at the water's edge : a natural history of New York / Betsy McCully.

   p. cm.

Includes bibliographical references and index.

ISBN-13: 978-0-8135-3915-7 (hardcover : alk. paper)

1. Natural history—New York (State) I. Title.

QH105.N7M385 2006

508.747'1—dc22   2006007084

A British Cataloging-in-Publication record for this book is available from the British Library.

Designed by Karolina Harris

Manufactured in the United States of America

Contents

Acknowledgments

This book is the culmination of a fifteen-year project. It could not have been completed without the help of many people.

I thank my first reader, Kirkpatrick Sale, whose book *Dwellers in the Land* inspired me, and whose belief in my project encouraged me to go forward. The urban bioregionalist Peter Berg was an invaluable resource of ideas and materials on the sustainable city. I also wish to acknowledge Charles Merguerian of Hofstra University, who read and corrected a first draft of the geology chapter, and Robert Grumet, who read and commented on an early draft of the chapter on the Lenapes.

I thank my colleagues at Kingsborough Community College who have expressed confidence in my endeavor and enthusiasm for the project. I especially wish to acknowledge Gene McQuillan, Tara Weiss, Robert Singer, Len Green, Lea Fridman, Norah Chase, and Bonne August. I could not have completed the book without generous research grants from the Professional Staff Congress of the City University of New York during the years 2003 to 2005.

I spent many hours researching materials at the excellent libraries of New York City, including the library of the American Museum of Natural History, the rare book room of the Brooklyn Botanic Garden, and the New York Public Library.

In the final stages of writing my book, the meticulous editing of Audra Wolfe, senior science editor at Rutgers University Press, has made me a better writer and I believe made a better book. I am also grateful to Steven Handel of Rutgers University, who generously sent me materials on habitat restoration projects in New York City.

I wish to express special thanks to my son, Ben Cooper, who has supported me in untold ways. He has trekked with me in the wilds of New York City, as we explored its many parks and snapped countless pictures of the plants and animals which inhabit them. A professional photographer, Ben has taken several of the photos that appear in this book.

Finally, my deepest gratitude goes to my husband, Joe Giunta, whose unflagging support, extraordinary patience, understanding, and love have seen me through the long and complex process of writing a book. He has been my constant walking companion in all my forays into the natural places of the New York region. A gifted naturalist and birder, he has taught me much of what I know in the field.

Introduction

Coming Home

I chose not to go to the woods. I prefer the company of my fellows and like the colorful jumble of rooftops I view from my window. I like the smooth sidewalks and black-topped streets, especially when they glisten with rain. I take pleasure in walking to the store, in selecting fruits and vegetables from the greengrocer, fresh fish from the fishmonger, or a fresh cut of meat from the butcher. I am an urban dweller by choice and inclination, and my life is as natural as breathing.

I live in a community tucked away in the southwest corner of an island off the Atlantic Coastal Plain, where salt and fresh waters commingle at the Great River's drowned mouth, the ocean surging upriver at high tide, and the river draining at ebb. Here in Lower New York Bay, barges, freighters, fishing boats and ocean liners ply the waters that Verrazano and Hudson once explored. The Lower Hudson Bioregion is a place of salt marshes and estuaries, sand dunes and barrier islands, bays and inlets and broad sandy beaches. The confluence of fresh and salt waters in the Lower Hudson estuary now provide a geologically rare habitat that supports a diversity of species, including our own.

Tens of millennia ago, glacial cliffs towered over a vast plain, and the Hudson roared through a deep gorge to spill into the Atlantic. When the last glacier receded, it left in its wake a boulder-strewn landscape of moraines and kettle holes, drift and outwash. As the climate warmed, the ocean rose and flooded the low-lying coastal lands, drowning the Hudson canyon and creating an archipelago. Humans began to settle here ten to twelve thousand years ago, efficiently exploiting the rich resources of woodland, wetland, grassland, and maritime habitats that characterize the region. This is the site of New York City.

I am an urban dweller by choice, but I also have a deeply ingrained respect for nature. I am appalled to see how megacities like New York overrun the land, depleting resources, destroying habitats, polluting water, air, and soil. This doesn't lead me to conclude, however, that the city is an environmental scourge diametrically opposed to nature; rather, I blame a mind-set that shows no regard for nature whether one lives in city, suburb, or country.

We tend to view nature and city in opposition. The city is always the place to escape from, and nature the place to escape to. Yearning for space, we harried town folk flee to the country. We viscerally react to feeling crowded—too many people, too many cars, too many featureless buildings blocking out the light. We are packed into subways and buses, clogged bumper-to-bumper on the highways, jostled in supermarket aisles. Space is at such a premium we rush to fill it—on the highway, on line at the supermarket, in the subway car—before someone else grabs it. We become aggressive and nasty in our jockeying for space, intent on claiming our bits and pieces of territory, and guarding them from the infringement of "the other guy."

In our desperate search for more space and breathing room, we pile into our cars and clog the highways, doing five miles an hour in our race to get away. We spill out of our cities into prefab suburbs to gain that little patch of lawn or fringe of woods that gives us an illusion of nature. And in our continued drive to return to the land, we gouge the landscape and bulldoze woods and farms so that we can entertain our various fantasies of country living.

And what have we gained? Not a quiet, spacious haven if getting there means commuting through heavy weekend traffic to spend one or two nights "in the country." Not an open vista if we fill up space with cars and housing developments and malls. Not unspoiled nature if we destroy piece by piece the very landscape that drew us there. Our desire to escape the city has ironically only contributed to the ongoing degradation of the environment, as sprawl consumes what's left of nature.

A more sustainable way to connect to nature is, paradoxically, by coming home to the city.

When I came to New York City at the age of thirty-four, my vision of a vibrant, magical city with a glittering skyline soon gave way to an ugly reality of ubiquitous garbage, a crumbling infrastructure, and the sense of crowding that creates tension, even violence. Yet, I chose to affirm this urban landscape as my home ground.

Doing so required that I change the way I perceive the city. I needed to see New York not as a material dream fallen on hard times (though it is), not as something opposed to nature (though it often acts that way), but as a human community that is part of a bioregion. The fates of New York City and its bioregion are inextricably bound: both hinge on our willingness to re-imagine the nature of New York, to reconfigure its boundaries to include the Lower Hudson Bioregion in which it is embedded.

To view our home place as a bioregion, however urbanized, is to nurture a love for the land we inhabit. The love grows from an intimate knowledge of place, one rooted in its ecology and natural history. Every place has its story. Understanding how the land came to be, knowing how geological and biological forces have shaped and continue to shape it, connects us to the place where we live. Science and history give us windows into deep time that puts cities in perspective. We see the concrete city as a recent human habi-tat, a thin veneer overlying the earth's ancient strata.

The history of New York City's growth at the expense of its land is an ex-treme example of the mentality that sets up a dichotomy between nature and culture. According to this paradigm, the city is seen as a marvel of human in-genuity, a testament to our capacity to master nature. The technological imagi-nation is always challenged to solve the problems posed by nature: to redirect the flow of the river, to dam the stream, to break the force of the tide, to blast the rock, to drain the marsh, to clear and level the land — literally to move mountains and part waters. We erect our soaring towers of steel and glass as triumphs of man over nature, yet such a triumph is a Pyrrhic victory. Only when we see our city as the habitat of one species in a larger ecosystem — stripped of the false assumption of human superiority — can we clearly see the unsustainable losses we have sustained in such a war. We cannot destroy the earth that gives us life; we cannot destroy our own home.

The difficulty of such a paradigm shift, of course, is in reconciling our sense of place as bioregion with the concrete city we encounter every day. Some advocates for nature view the modern "megacity" as analogous to a parasite that kills its host. Historian Kirkpatrick Sale, for instance, contends that the megacity has "gone beyond the ecological balance point at which it is able to sustain its own resources. . . . It is an uncontrollable experiment, a violation of the laws of human and biotic nature that cannot be safely main-tained, at least not on the scale we know today."[1] Scaling down the megacity and bringing it into balance with the bioregion is a daunting prospect. Urban ecologist Peter Berg offers constructive proposals for "reinhabiting" the city: "People are part of a life-place, as dependent on natural systems as native plants and animals. Green City proposals aren't based on simply cleaning up the environment but rather on securing reciprocity between the urban way of life and the natural life-web that supports it."[2] Such a vision requires us to transcend the artificially constructed boundaries of the city, and to see ourselves as urban dwellers within the more fluid natural boundaries of the watershed region.

As I drive along the Brooklyn-Queens Expressway at night, the city's columns and spires shining across the water remind me of Oz. Is it all sham and delusion, this material city packaged and sold in dreams? Then, like a hologram, the image shifts. I see the river reflecting the city. I think of the rivers that have flowed through this region for millennia, before cities were dreamt of. I think of the first humans who came to this place and stayed because they found the waters and land enough to sustain them for millennia. I think of how the city's rise has brought about the demise of habitats and species. It saddens me to know how irreversible such losses are — but all is not lost. Habitats can be restored, polluted waters and lands cleaned up, and species brought back from the brink of extinction.

This book tells the story of a place — its ancient history, its evolving habitats and inhabitants, including the human species. It tells the story of creation and destruction through both natural and human forces, and recounts human efforts to restore what we have degraded and preserve what's left of nature in an increasingly urbanized region. It is the author's hope that the story will inspire urbanites to see themselves as dwellers in the land, and as such, to commit themselves to live in more sustainable ways.

City at
the Water's Edge

Bedrock New York

A cold day in January is a good time to walk the beach. Only hardy, beach-loving souls are out here on Coney Island, drawn to the shining expanse of the Atlantic lit by the low winter sun as it arcs across the southern sky. A few gulls warm their breasts in the sun, a dog races ecstatically along the water's edge distantly trailed by his bundled-up owner, and a human scavenger sweeps her metal-detector across the sand. I search for what the tide has disgorged — an interesting piece of driftwood, an unbroken conch shell — and a jagged piece of rock that glints and glitters when the sun strikes it catches my eye. I pick it up and turn the rough, flaking stone in my hand, knowing I am touching the bedrock of New York City.

This rock connects me to both the natural and human history of this place. The jetties that protect beaches and homes from the ocean's direct onslaught are comprised of ripped-up bedrock, called rip-rap. These were quarried during Manhattan's great building boom at the turn of the last century, the by-products of subways and skyscrapers. The rock I hold in my hand is a piece of Manhattan schist, one of three layers of rock that form the bedrock of New York City. The rocks bear testimony to the rich geological history of the city, a story that takes us back a billion years. Imagine a Manhattan skyline of jagged mountain peaks.[1]

This piece of schist tells me that around 450 million years ago, volcanoes erupted off the northeastern coast, spewing lava that cooled and gradually formed a volcanic island arc. Winds blew volcanic ash into a shallow marine basin, where sediments accumulated in mineral-rich layers that were gradually compressed into shale. The sediment-laden oceanic crust slid beneath the lighter continental crust in a process known as subduction, and the volcanic island arc accreted to the continent. The mica-rich shale, subjected to the intense heat of the earth's mantle, was recrystallized and transformed into the schist I hold today, plucked out of the sands of Coney Island.

Most of New York City is built on three layers of strata known as Manhattan Schist, Inwood Marble, and Fordham Gneiss. The exception is Staten

Island, where a northeast-trending ridge of Serpentinite erupts to the surface in the island's middle, peaking at 540-foot-tall Todt Hill, the highest point in New York City. Schist forms the spine of Manhattan from the Henry Hudson Bridge on its north end to the Battery on its southern tip; it dips abruptly several hundred feet below ground at Washington Square, and makes a gradual ascent beginning at Chambers Street. These dips and rises account for

Fig. 1.1. W. W. Mather, Geological map of Long and Staten Islands with the environs of New York, 1842. (Courtesy of The Lionel Pincus and Princess Firyal Map Division, The New York Public Library, Astor, Lenox and Tilden Foundations.)

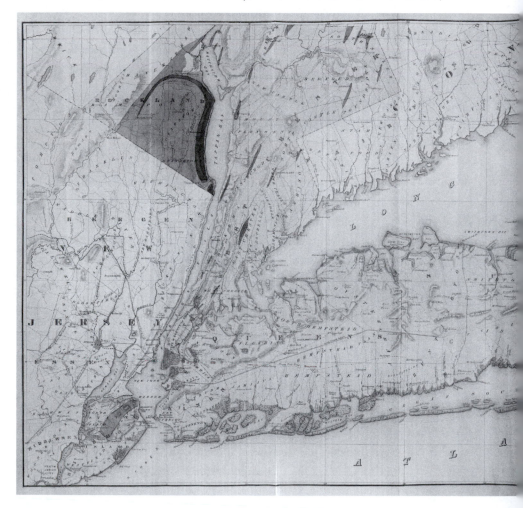

the gap between "midtown" and "downtown" in the Manhattan skyline, since tall buildings had to be anchored on solid bedrock, and not on the glacial till that fills the valleys. The contemporaneous Inwood Marble, metamorphosed from limestone, forms beds 150 to 500 feet thick beneath the Harlem River and adjacent regions known to geologists as Inwood Lowland; it underlies the East River and the Harlem Lowland and above ground forms a ridge from Dyckman Street on the upper west side northward to Marble Hill. The billion-year-old Fordham Gneiss erupts to the surface in the Bronx, forming the Riverdale and Grand Concourse ridges. The three strata of schist,

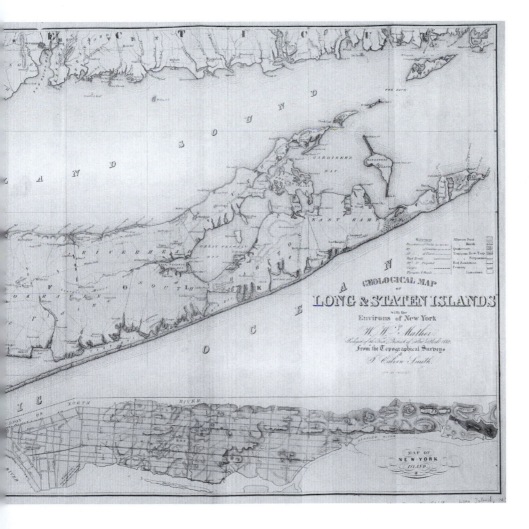

Table 1.1 Geologic Time Chart

(with selected major geologic events from southeastern New York and vicinity)

Era Periods (Epochs)	Years (Ma)	Selected Major Events
Cenozoic		
(Holocene)	0.1	Rising sea forms Hudson Estuary, Long Island Sound, and other bays. Barrier islands form and migrate.
(Pleistocene)	1.6	Melting of last glaciers forms large lakes. Drainage from Great Lakes overflows into Hudson Valley.
		Dam at The Narrows suddenly breached and flood waters erode Hudson shelf valley.
		Repeated continental glaciation with five (?) glaciers flowing from NW and NE form moraine ridges on Long Island.
(Pliocene)	6.2	Regional uplift, tilting and erosion of coastal-plain strata; sea level drops. Depression eroded that later becomes Long Island Sound.
(Miocene)	26.2	Fans spread E and SE from Appalachians and push back sea. Last widespread marine unit in coastal-plain strata.
Mesozoic	66.5	
(Cretaceous)	96	Passive eastern margin of North American plate subsides and sediments (the coastal-plain strata) accumulate.
	131	(Passive-margin sequence II).
(Jurassic)	190	Baltimore Canyon Trough forms and fills with 8,000 feet of pre-Cretaceous sediments. Atlantic Ocean starts to open. Newark basins deformed, arched, eroded.
	200	Continued filling of subsiding Newark basins and mafic igneous activity both extrusive and intrusive.
(Triassic)		Newark basins form and fill with nonmarine sediments.
Paleozoic	245	
(Permian)		Pre-Newark erosion surface formed.
	260	Appalachian Orogeny. (Terminal stage.) Folding, overthrusting, and metamorphism of Rhode Island coal basins; granites intruded.

Era Periods (Epochs)	Years (Ma)	Selected Major Events
(Carboniferous)	320	Faulting, folding, and metamorphism in New York City area. Southeastern New York undergoes continued uplift and erosion.
(Devonian)	365	Acadian Orogeny. Deep burial of sedimentary strata. Faulting, folding, and metamorphism in New York City area. Peekskill Granite and Acadian granites intruded.
(Ordovician)	440	Taconic Orogeny. Intense deformation and metamorphism. Ultramafic rocks (oceanic lithosphere) sliced off and transported above deposits of continental shelf.
	450	Cortlandt Complex and related rocks intrude Taconian suture zone. (Cameron's Line). Arc-continent collision. Great overthrusting from ocean toward continent. Taconic deep-water strata thrust above shallow-water strata.
(Cambrian)	510	(Passive-margin sequence I). Shallow-water clastics and carbonates accumulate in west of basin (= Sauk Sequence; protoliths of the Lowerre Quartzite, Inwood Marble, part of Manhattan Schist Formation). Deep-water terrigenous silts form to east. (= Taconic Sequence; protoliths of Hartland Formation, parts of Manhattan Schist Fm.).
Proterozoic		
	570	Period of uplift and erosion followed by subsidence of margin.
(Z)	600	Rifting with rift sediments, volcanism, and intrusive activity. (Ned Mountain, Pound Ridge, and Yonkers gneiss protoliths).
(Y)	1100	Grenville Orogeny. Sediments and volcanics deposited, compressive deformation, intrusive activity, and granulite facies metamorphism. (Fordham Gneiss, Hudson Highlands, and related rocks.)
Archeozoic		
	2600	No record in New York.
	4600	Solar system (including Earth) forms.

marble, and gneiss are complexly interfolded. Each layer tells its own story from which we can reconstruct the geological map of New York City, one that delineates a continental mosaic of ever-shifting boundaries.

The boundary where North America's eastern edge fused with the volcanic island arc is an extensive thrust fault zone known as Cameron's Line, which trends southwest to northeast from Staten Island into western Connecticut. East of Cameron's Line, in western Connecticut and southeastern New York, lies the Hartland Formation, first mapped by geologist Charles Merguerian of Hofstra University in 1983. This strata was metamorphosed from shale, graywacke, and volcanic rock that had formed in deep ocean water during the early Paleozoic period. West of Cameron's Line lies the Manhattan Prong, composed of metamorphosed rocks of shallow water origin — Fordham Gneiss, Inwood Marble, Manhattan Schist, and Lowerre Quartzite (metamorphosed sandstone). The east-west division is hardly a neat one. A recent map of Manhattan drawn by Charles Merguerian and his son Mickey Merguerian of Duke Geological Laboratory depict the deep-water schist unit of the Hartland Formation as the bedrock of Manhattan south of Eightieth Street. Cameron's Line zigs and zags across Central Park. The presence of the Hartland Formation in Manhattan tells the story of a violent east-to-west overthrusting of the older schist unit onto younger schist strata during the Taconic orogeny, or mountain-building episode. Prior to Merguerian's discovery, all of the schist on Manhattan was designated as "Manhattan Schist"; now, Manhattan Schist refers to the younger layer to distinguish it from the older Hartland Schist.[2] The schist, marble, and gneiss strata of Manhattan are by no means arranged in simple layers like the leaves of a book; over hundreds of millions of years, they were intensely folded, pushed up into mountains, eroded and weathered, buried under thousands of feet of sediment, and exposed by glacial scouring.

On Staten Island, the serpentinite formation was originally formed 450 million years ago in deep water, probably at an oceanic trench, and is considered an igneous rock (derived from the earth's mantle). During the Taconic orogeny, a sliver of this deep oceanic strata was broken off and thrust westward over existing continental bedrock. Millions of years later, during the ice age, glaciation scoured and sculpted the strata into roche moutonee outcrops, a geological term that describes the rounded shape (*moutonee* is French for sheep).[3]

Cameron's Line marks the "suture" boundary where the North American

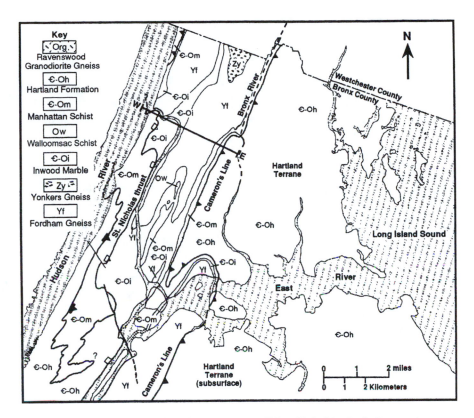

Fig. 1.2. Geological map of northern segment of New York City, including portions of Manhattan, Queens, and the Bronx. (Courtesy of Charles Merguerian, Hofstra University, 2004.)

plate on its eastern edge collided with the oceanic plate. It testifies to great earth-moving forces that are hardly dormant. Indeed, a number of faults criss-cross Manhattan. One northwest-trending fault underlies 125th Street. South of 125th Street two more faults slice through the island, one at 14th Street; north of 125th Street five additional faults veer northwestward, as mapped by Charles Merguerian in water tunnels between 1983 and 1985. These north-west-trending faults transect the northeast-trending faults, cutting up Man-hattan into blocks that are by no means stable. Climbing down into the water tunnel beneath Amsterdam Avenue at 125th Street, Merguerian was startled to find a ninety-degree rotation of "highly fractured Manhattan Schist," indicating strike-slip motion along the 125th Street fault. In fact, Merguerian

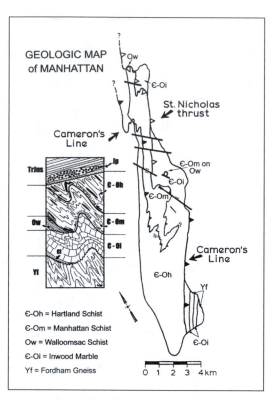

Fig. 1.3. Bedrock map of Manhattan showing the three schist units. (Charles Merguerian, Hofstra University, and Mickey Merguerian, Duke Geological Laboratory, 2004.)

notes, a magnitude 4.0 earthquake on October 19, 1985, centered in West-chester County (known as the Ardsley quake), "was related to episodic slip along a fault with a northwest trend." The last earthquake before that was in 1884—a magnitude 5.0 centered offshore to the south of Brooklyn, and felt as far away as Philadelphia and Hartford. Could it happen again? Absolutely, Merguerian assures us, and with far more damage, considering the extensive construction over landfill that has taken place in the last few decades in New York City.[4] After conducting extensive mapping of the new Queens water tunnel between 1998 and 2000, Merguerian concluded:

> Ground-breaking rupture and seismic activity cannot and certainly should not be ruled out for this region. Because large magnitude earthquakes have struck NYC in 1737, 1783, and 1884, this new data identifies a potential failure surface along which earthquake energy could be released. Given the population, cultural development, infrastructure, and financial investment

concentrated in New York City, the specter of a massive earthquake must be considered in revising existing building code designs and emergency preparedness procedures. Unfortunately, despite the scientific community's pleas for action, severely limited emergency planning exists at the present time. Clearly, this should be changed, as pre-emptive urban seismic planning is an absolute necessity in New York City.[5]

New York City is located, after all, at a site where continental plates collided and broke apart—cataclysmic events written in the rocks. According to plate tectonic theory, the earth's surface is composed of crustal blocks, or plates, that "float" on a deeper layer of plastic rock acting like a conveyor belt. The continental and oceanic plates are continually moving around, crashing into each other (what geologists call "docking") or rifting. Half a billion years ago, the North American continent was tipped over on its eastern side and bisected by the equator, placing the New York region in a subtropical zone south of the equator. The continent then was much smaller in area, and New York was part of the submerged continental shelf. Between roughly 450 and 250 million years ago, a series of continental collisions known collectively as the Appalachian orogeny culminated in the creation of the supercontinent Pangaea. The first of these mountain-building episodes, the Taconic orogeny, pushed up the Taconic mountains in eastern New York as North America collided with an offshore volcanic island arc. During this event, marine shales and limestones metamorphosed, or melted and recrystallized, into Manhattan Schist and Inwood Marble. The same event thrust a layer of billion-year-old Fordham Gneiss (metamorphosed during the earlier Grenville orogeny) onto the schist and marble strata, forming what geologists call the Manhattan Prong, an ancient ridge that extends from New England to its southernmost point beneath Manhattan. The second event, the Acadian orogeny that took place between 375 and 335 million years ago, pushed up alpine mountains in New England. Sediments that flushed westward from these mountains buried the eroded stumps of the Taconics and created the Catskill Delta. The climax event, the Alleghenian orogeny of 250 million years ago, was a huge continent-continent collision that uplifted colossal mountains. The Appalachians formed the backbone of Pangaea, comprised of the earth's continents like pieces of a jigsaw puzzle. It stood its ground for 50 million years.

During this period, the mountains were being steadily eroded, their sediments flushed by streams and rivers into alluvial fans and lakes. Over time, the sediments cemented into layers of sandstone and siltstone, forming the great Permo-Triassic red beds such as those in the Connecticut River Valley and New Jersey's Newark Basin. The superabundance of oxygen in the earth's atmosphere at that time oxidized the sediments, in effect rusting them.

Two hundred million years ago, the earth began to move again. A plume of molten rock from the earth's mantle erupted with such cataclysmic force that it tore a gash in the crust. Rifting, volcanic eruptions, floods, and crustal slumping marked the breakup of Pangaea, as North America pulled away from Africa. The earth's crust was being stretched and splintered into fault blocks, which dropped down, creating basins. The basins, or rift valleys, filled with sediments and sank further, in the process tilting up ranges like the Watchung of New Jersey, west of the Newark Basin. (You can see the same basin-and-range conformation in northwest Africa, like two matching pieces in a geological puzzle.) Lava erupted and flowed through rift valleys, hardening into basalt that capped the redbeds. Where the lava intruded instead of flowing over the layers, it hardened to form blocks of dolerite encased in sandstone. Over time, the rock layers were tilted and exposed, and the sandstone envelope eroded, leaving great vertical blocks of diabase sill that extend in a 1,000-foot bed from Haverstraw, New Jersey, to Staten Island. The dramatic maroon columns of the Palisades, 400-foot-tall cliffs overlooking the west side of the Hudson River, testify to the great forces that broke apart Pangaea.

On Coney Island, a walk on the jetties here offers a chance to touch the three strata of New York City's bedrock: Manhattan Schist, Inwood Marble, and Fordham Gneiss. The whitish marble blocks are granular like sugar, many streaked with yellow and red derived from iron minerals. If you look closely, you may discern the original limestone layers of the metamorphosed rock. Both the schist and gneiss glint with mineral grains such as biotite mica. Schist is a coarse, flaky rock that separates easily along cleavage planes and may show a wavy structure. Gneiss is a denser rock, with buff bands of feldspar crystals alternating with charcoal bands of biotite mica. Both schist and gneiss may be veined with quartz and studded with garnet.

Holding a rock that I know has been pushed deep within the earth's crust and thrust high in an ancient mountain, I am humbled by the forces that shape our planet. Plate tectonics yields a moving map of the world, a dizzying dance of the continents. One can never be sure where "here" is: this rock was not formed "here" but "there," when eastern North America was south of the equator, and the continent was flirting with Africa. It could not have been formed without being subjected to the intense pressure and heat of the lower crust, and it got there only by sliding down into it, as the heavier oceanic crust was subducted beneath the lighter continental crust. This picture of the earth consuming itself revives the ancient myth that depicts the world as a snake swallowing its tail. Envision thick sea-bottom sediments compressing into shale, sliding into the earth's mantle, metamorphosing into schist. When North America bumped into Africa, the schist strata were folded and uptilted into jagged mountains. As these mountains eroded, the weight of their sediments ultimately buried their own roots. They were inundated by a sea, exposed again when the sea regressed, and eventually became the bedrock of the archipelago that forms New York City. And I hold this rock in my hand, turning it in the light, only because humans — who settled here in the last instant of time — blasted it out of the bedrock when they wanted a subway, and transported it here when they wanted seawalls and jetties to protect their homes from the eroding onslaught of the ocean on the land they had reclaimed from the sea.

To break out of the textbook terminology of New York's complex geology, I must walk the terrain and touch the rock. Manhattan is one of the best places to explore the island's rocky past.

Twenty thousand years ago, a glacier scoured the island's surface to expose beautiful outcrops of schist. Both Hartland and Manhattan schist can be seen in Central Park. Hartland schist is exposed in the southern part of the park, while Manhattan schist crops out in the northern end. A famous example of Hartland schist is Umpire Rock, a huge hump of rock located at the school playground in the west side of the park around Sixty-third Street. Two northeast-trending brittle faults cut through the rock, and on its northwest edge, northwest-trending glacial troughs bear witness to torrents of glacial meltwater that once gouged out channels and scoured the bedrock. Although most Manhattan Schist outcrops are exposed in the park's northern half, an example in the southern half can be seen just west of the Carousel off Sixty-fifth Street, distinguished from the gray-weathering Hartland Schist by its rustier coloring.

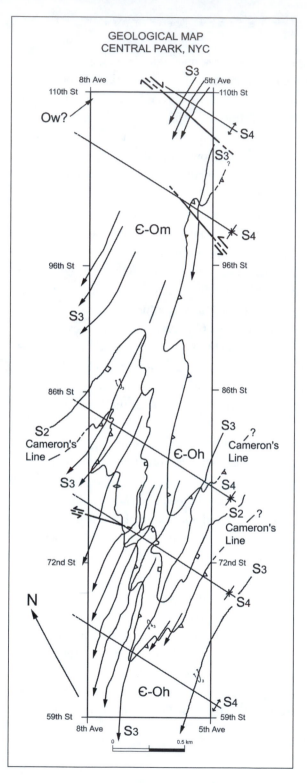

GEOLOGICAL MAP
CENTRAL PARK, NYC

Fig. 1.4. Geological map of Central Park. (Merguerian and Merguerian 2004.)

One of the best places to see all three strata of New York City's bedrock is at the northern tip of Manhattan. Inwood Hill Park affords dramatic views of a ridge of Fordham Gneiss, just across Spuyten Duyvil Creek in the Bronx. Within the park, beautiful outcrops of Manhattan Schist are exposed, and just across the street from the park, Inwood Marble erupts to the surface. The park is located on a high schist ridge that rises 200 feet above the Hudson River on its west side, with the Harlem River to its east. The park may be reached by subway (the A train to 207th Street and Broadway), but a drive and walk allows me to experience the dips and rises of the ancient mountain terrain. Driving west on 181st Street, I turn north onto Broadway. On the west side, the forested ridge shadows the bustling neighborhood of densely built low-rise apartment buildings. Shoppers throng the hilly sidewalks of the main business district, and cars, trucks, and buses thread their way through the streets. Where Broadway crosses Dyckman Street, the terrain flattens out. This is the so-called Dyckman Street Gap, a lowland underlain by Inwood Marble. Typically, Inwood Marble — softer and more water soluble than schist — is the bedrock of the lowlands and river valleys of northern Manhattan and the Bronx.

From Broadway I turn west at 207th Street, then north onto Seaman Avenue. At Isham Street I park the car and get out to walk around the marble outcrops of the pocket park across from the entrance of Inwood Hill Park. The sugary rock crops out in a sinuous ridge, its colors ranging from white to bluish-gray, weathering to brown. Pegs of quartzite (known by the French word *boudins* for their sausagelike shape) intrude segments of the rock, indicating intense metamorphism. I pick up a broken-off piece and run my thumb over the crumbly texture.

Crossing Seaman Avenue, I enter Inwood Hill Park. I never walk alone so I am joined by my constant walking companion, my husband, Joe Giunta. We follow the path that winds uphill toward Overlook Meadow. A glacial erratic placed on the path bears a plaque that testifies to the alleged sale of Manhattan to Peter Minuet on this spot, where a giant tulip tree once grew. This is known as the Shorakapok Rock, after the name the Lenapes called their village site. North of this rock, a large field slopes down to a tidal marsh that edges Spuyten Duyvil Creek, the waterway that snakes around the island's northern tip connecting the Harlem and Hudson rivers. Inwood Marble underlies this lowland, which once served as planting fields for the Lenapes and later for the Europeans when the area was still rural.

The path takes us up through increasingly dense oak-hickory woodland that has been uncut since the Revolutionary War. The straight massive trunks of tulip trees tower over the canopy, underlain by a rich understory of sassafras, witch hazel, and viburnum. Narrow overgrown trails descend from the main path toward kettle ponds, but their remoteness discourages us from exploring. As we ascend the western ridge, we stop to examine the massive schist outcrops. The wavy structure of one outcrop testifies to the rock's heating during metamorphosis. The outcrops glint with mica flakes and garnet crystals. Muscovite mica looks silvery gray, while biotite mica looks blackish. The schist strata also contain lenses of blackish amphibolite, a metamorphosed igneous rock formed in deep water before the Taconic Orogeny.

We ascend to Overlook Meadow, listening to the roar of cars on the Henry Hudson Parkway below. The forest opens into a clearing where we can look westward across the Hudson to the Palisades. A rusty chain-link fence has been partly peeled away to allow access to the schist ledge overlooking the river gorge. We step gingerly, for the ledge tilts down to a steep drop-off. It is a somewhat hazy day, but the Palisades' sheer maroon cliffs rise across the water, offering us a window into another geological era. Indeed, the Hudson marks the boundary between two geological eras: on its west side the Palisade cliffs date to the breakup of Pangaea that began 200 million years ago; on its east side, the schist ledge dates back 500 million years, when the continents began to clump and fuse into the supercontinent Pangaea. To take us back even further in time, we continue up the path to the northernmost end of the park, where the Henry Hudson Bridge crosses into the Bronx. Looking across Spuyten Duyvil Creek, we can see billion-year-old Fordham Gneiss snaking to the surface as Riverdale Ridge in the Bronx.

Back home, I take a sunset walk along the beach and contemplate what geologists of old called the "testimony of the rocks." Here on Coney Island in Cenozoic time, buildings cluster at the edge of sand and water, themselves made of rock and mineral, worn away by salt and wind and rain and pollution, in various stages of decay. Coney Island rusts; sand drifts under the boardwalk and shapes itself into incipient dunes until bulldozed flat again. The shifting tidal lines along the beach repeat, on a microscale, the shifting boundaries of continents. Mica dust leaves silvery traces like tidal shadows. The shore can teach us about the tenacity of life on the edge and its astounding capacity to transform itself and evolve new forms. Metamorphosis is the recurring theme of nature, whether of rocks or animals. In a few mineralized grains of sand, in a pebble or rock fragment, in the crushed mussel shells that litter the beach, in the barnacles that encrust the jetties, in the microscopic life of a small tide pool — the history of the evolving earth is telescoped.

2

The Teeming Shore

Looking southward across the water on a clear spring day, I can see the low bluffs of Sandy Hook, New Jersey, and the wave-washed barrier beach of Far Rockaway, two spits of land that form the gateway to Lower New York Bay. The bay's relatively warm, shallow waters have for millennia been home to a rich abundance of wildlife.

Receding waves have deposited a shimmering tracery of dark mineral grains that remind me of a Chinese painting of mountains. Phases of the tide demarcate the beach into zones: the littoral, or intertidal zone, between the low and high tide lines; the sublittoral zone, the shallow water region extending from shoreline over the continental shelf; and the supralittoral, or splash zone, above the reach of normal high tide. The zones allow us a glimpse into how life evolved, with creatures adapted for each microhabitat. Because of its somewhat protected location and also because of the jetties (rock barriers extending from the beach into the water), the Coney Island beach harbors creatures of both rocky and sandy shores.

Low tide exposes gleaming blue-black mussels attached to the rocks by strong threads spun from their foot. Try prying one of them from the rock and you will be amazed at their tenacious hold. When exposed to air, these mollusks clamp down their shells, but when the tide sweeps over them, they open their shells and unfurl their cilia to strain the seawater for plankton. A little further up in the intertidal zone, northern rock barnacles encrust the rocks, their white calcareous shells protecting their soft crustacean bodies from the ravages of the surf. The smaller bay barnacle attaches its cone to rocks at the low-tide line and to pilings and the shells of other animals in deeper water, while the little gray barnacle forms uncrowded colonies near the high-tide line. The shells of both mussels and barnacles are designed to protect them, but they are not foolproof. Among the barnacles lurks the predatory Atlantic dogwinkle, a marine snail that envelops the barnacle's cone, forces open its valves, stuns the creature with a narcotic chemical, then dines on the succulent flesh within. Some dogwinkles prefer mussels, their choice of food reflected in their darker coloring.[1]

Briefly exposed at low tide, masses of rockweed cling to the rocks by means of holdfasts. Also known as bladderwrack, this brown seaweed can survive for limited periods out of water because of its bubble-like sacs that store water. Branching colonies of hydroids, whose wine-glass-shaped heads are encircled by delicate feeding tentacles like glass stamens, attach themselves to the rockweeds. Smooth periwinkles graze on algae in their branches. Atlantic tube worms cement themselves to the submerged rocks by secreting limy tubes. Through these twisty white tubes they unfurl graceful branched plumes of purple, red, orange, or yellow tentacles to sweep food from the water into their toothed mouths.

Below the intertidal zone, blue crabs, lady crabs, and transparent sand shrimp forage in the sandy bottoms. As waves wash over the intertidal zone, hordes of inch-long Atlantic mole crabs with their stalked eyes emerge from their burrows and scurry upslope and down, unfurling their feathery feeding antennae into the backwash of a receding wave.

Single-celled animals called protists may dwell between the grains of sand in the sublittoral zone. Dinoflagellates, for instance, are comprised of numerous species inhabiting both salt and fresh waters. Fossils of these microscopic organisms have been found in rocks dating to the Silurian, over 400 million years ago. Around half the species of dinoflagellates are photosynthetic, acting like tiny solar-energy cells. Some species are able to produce their own light, glowing like fireflies on the water surface as it gets dark. Stirred up in the wake of a boat, they will glow more intensely. The dinoflagellate is a strange hybrid of a creature sometimes behaving like a plant, and sometimes like an animal. Like a plant, it "roots" itself on the seafloor, but like an animal it can become mobile, attacking other organisms by stunning them with a toxin and then digesting them. During the warm summer months, dinoflagellates may "bloom," their numbers swelling to such density as to stain the water golden or red in what is known as a red tide. Some species emit neurotoxins that kill the fish and shellfish that ingest them. Humans who eat those toxic shellfish may get paralytic shellfish poisoning, or PSP.[2]

At certain seasons, hordes of jellyfish wash up on shore and sting the feet of the unwary beachgoer. Moon jellies, whose pale gelatinous bodies can be up to sixteen inches wide, float in great numbers offshore, washing up on the beach after storms and high tides. Though less common, the quivering, iridescent blue and purple body of the Portuguese man-of-war may be among them.

The Portuguese man-of-war is a stray from the Gulf Stream, where fishermen at sea have often seen them swimming in colonies, or "fleets." They lift their gas-filled floats like purple sails, trailing forty- to fifty-foot-long feeding tentacles that stun their prey by injecting deadly toxin.[3]

In the berm above the intertidal zone, ghost crabs emerge at dusk to hunt, their coloration blending with the sand. Strong legs enable them to move swiftly, and powerful saw-toothed pincers equip them to capture prey. If you're out on the beach on a spring night, you might hear the male crab rubbing his serrated pincer against his body like an instrument to attract a female. On a summer night at full moon, you might observe them facing the moon. During winter, these crabs hibernate in their sand burrows. Also inhabiting the berm is the ghost crab's fellow crustacean, the beach flea, an inch-long creature that can leap a foot if it cares to. Beach fleas scavenge at night during low tide, feeding on organic beach debris the tide has discarded; by daylight, they retreat to the high-tide line and dig their deep burrows, where they will hide until darkness and an ebbing tide draw them out again.

The sea wrack deposited by the ocean at high tide also teems with life, day and night. The predatory rove beetle and the orange and black flower beetle pursue scavenging earwigs and ants. Flies and midges that are the bane of beachgoers lay their eggs in the wrack so their larvae may feed on the decaying flesh of washed-up marine animals.

The rough periwinkle, tough cousin to the smooth periwinkle, lives on the rocks above high tide, called the splash zone. Both periwinkles are descended from marine ancestors. A vegetarian, the rough periwinkle uses its chitinous radula with its rows of minute, sharp teeth to "graze" the rocks for algae, wearing down the rocks over time. Algae, the descendants of the cyanobacteria that colonized the surfaces of the pre-Cambrian seas, stain the rocks above high tide.

All the creatures of the upper shore must have access to water in some fashion, and they have devised ingenious adaptations to conserve the water they need. Ghost crabs, for instance, possess gills and a means of storing seawater, which enables them to withstand the hot, dry environment of the upper beach, but they must return to the water to fill up from time to time. Females must return to release their spawn, for crabs are also metamorphosing creatures whose early lives as larvae begin in the sea. Rough periwinkles breathe by means of a gill-like membrane, but unlike other marine organisms do not depend on the sea to reproduce; they hold their developing embryos in egg capsules inside their shells until the young are ready to emerge as miniature adults. Plants, too, have evolved water-conserving features: for example, the blue-green algae that inhabit the berm are covered by slick, rubbery sheaths that prevent them from drying out. If you step on a wet, algae-coated rock, you'll find it quite slippery.

During the warmer months of the year, the waters of spring tides burgeon with life. Spring tides occur twice a month at full and new moon, when they attain their most extreme lows and highs. Just offshore, millions upon millions of larvae float or swim on tidal currents in search of favorable sites for anchorage, secrete their protective shells, and metamorphose into adults that will spawn and begin the cycle anew. Nearly all these creatures, whether sand or rock dwellers as adults, must spend part of their lives in the sea. Oyster, mussel, and clam larvae float on the surface as plankton. The larvae of hydroids, called medusae, swim until they find a solid anchorhold where they can form new adult colonies. Most marine animals go through several metamorphoses. The barnacle, for instance, swims for three months in its larval stage near the surface of the sea before sinking and metamorphosing into a creature resembling an adult ostracod, with a bivalved shell and six pairs of walking legs that enable it to explore its new terrain. When it finds the perfect place to cement itself, it metamorphoses again into the adult barnacle. Rachel Carson compares this last metamorphosis of the barnacle to that of the larval butterfly, a twelve-hour process that involves "a complete and drastic reorganization," during which it exudes six calcareous plates that form a cone protecting its soft body, and four smaller plates at the top that function like a valve, opening to feed. When the sea washes over it at high tide, it opens its valve to feed, gracefully extending its feathery appendage to sweep food from the water; as the tide recedes, it draws in its plumes and closes shop, until the next high tide.[4]

The metamorphoses of these shore creatures from shallow marine origins recall the stages of life's evolution. Life on earth evolved in water, possibly in the mud of a tidal flat, or the muck at the bottom of a pond, or at the edge of a hydrothermal vent. Whether triggered by ultraviolet radiation or lightning or a molecular catalyst, the simple organic chemicals carbon and hydrogen combined into more complex organic compounds, forming nucleotides, amino acids, and proteins — the building blocks of life. A primordial strand of nucleotides, called RNA, matched up to a similar strand, amino acids linked to amino acids, and soon proteins were created, which in turn manufactured more RNA. At some point, a long twisted chain of nucleotides formed into DNA. In the ferment of these chemical combinations and permutations, strands of DNA and RNA intertwined into the familiar double helix that we view as the blueprint of life.[5]

A number of organisms that inhabit the eastern shore of North America today are remarkably similar to those that proliferated at the dawn of the Phanerozoic age, when multicellular animals of modern design first made their appearance at least 570 million years ago. Indeed, the configuration of the East Coast today, with its broad continental platform and so-called passive margin (unmarked by active tectonic events) is strikingly similar to that of early Cambrian time. The New York City region was then part of the submerged continental shelf.[6]

The Phanerozoic age began with a bang, the so-called Cambrian explosion that marks the sudden appearance of diverse multicellular, hard-bodied organisms. In the words of the late paleontologist Stephen Jay Gould, the fossils of these organisms display the "anatomical blueprints" that underlie all modern life.[7] These "shelly fauna" had evolved the capacity to take a waste product of cell metabolism — calcium — and turn it into a hard body part that would eventually serve as protection in the form of chitinous "armor" or structural support in the form of a calcareous skeleton. Once equipped with a means of protection and support, animals were prepared to make the transition to land.

For over 100 million years, hard-bodied animals proliferated in warm shallow seas like the one at the edge of eastern North America (which was then south of the equator in a subtropical zone). They included all four arthropod lines: six hundred genera of trilobites, a now extinct line of arthropods that dominated the Cambrian seas, scavenging the muddy seafloor; and the ancestors of our three modern arthropod groups. The modern groups are crustaceans (including crabs, lobsters, and shrimp), chelicerates (including horseshoe crabs, mites, scorpions, and spiders), and uniramias (including insects, millipedes, and centipedes). In addition, says Gould, there were a myriad of species that don't fit into any modern phyla, perhaps fifteen or twenty that "ought to rank as a separate phylum."[8] A number of them defy classification, their weird combination of features making them at home in a medieval bestiary. Marianne Collins illustrated several of these creatures based on the fossils of the Burgess Shale. The shielded head and segmented body of *Nectocaris*, for example, suggest an arthropod, but its finlike structures running the length of the upper and lower body suggest a primitive chordate. Another weird creature, *Dinomischus*, was an inch-long animal rooted to the sea bottom, swaying on a long stalk that ended in a "calyx" containing both mouth and anus—looking for all the world like a hothouse flower (Protea comes to my mind) with its rayed "petals" pointing upward cupping the "calyx." All these creatures of the Cambrian era, both weird and familiar, are extinct, but the anatomical designs of the familiar types lived on, most fitting into the thirty modern phyla used to classify animals today.[9]

The Cambrian era ended when the sea regressed from the continents some 485 million years ago, and the Ordovician era was ushered in when the sea once again flooded the continental craton. Both these events were associated with plate tectonic episodes. In the New York region, the continent's eastern edge switched from being a passive to an active margin. These catastrophic events triggered a long period of evolutionary experimentation: some forms of life died out while new forms arose, or older forms rose to dominance. The Ordovician fauna differed radically from the Cambrian, although the basic anatomical designs were preserved. The trilobites that had dominated the Cambrian seas declined, while brachiopods and bryozoans flourished, and cephalopods, gastropods, sponges, echinoderms, crinoids, and corals continued to evolve and diversify. Extensive graptolite colonies, microscopic plankton that rapidly evolved and spread over the planet, floated on the sea's surface. They just as rapidly disappeared, their chitinous bodies preserved in black shales serving as convenient "index fossils" for paleontologists to mark the Ordovician strata.[10]

In 1893, thirty-five-year-old Yale paleontologist Charles Emerson Beecher discovered a rich trove of well-preserved Ordovician fossils in a shale deposit near Rome, New York. As a young man, Beecher was an avid fossil collector, amassing over twenty thousand specimens of Devonian invertebrate fossils by the time he was appointed as Yale's first invertebrate paleontologist in 1891. By 1899, he had built a private collection of one hundred thousand fossils which he had meticulously extracted, prepared, illustrated, and classified.[11] His descriptions and illustrations illuminate James Hall's classic *Paleontology of New York*. The fossils of what is known as Beecher's Trilobite Beds reveal that 450 million years ago a deep sea covered the region, harboring in its waters a wealth of invertebrate species. Many species of trilobites hunted and scavenged on the seafloor; worms and clams burrowed in the mud; brachiopods attached themselves to the shells that littered the seafloor, opening their valves to filter the water for food; colorful crinoids (sea lilies) waved their flowerlike stalks in the sea currents; predatory starfish patrolled the muddy bottom; squidlike nautoloids propelled themselves through the water with their long tentacles, seeking prey; and coelenterate polyps built their coral houses on the seafloor while zooids built huge graptolite colonies that floated on the surface.[12]

At the onset of the Devonian around 418 million years ago, plants and animals began to colonize the land. A shallow, warm sea covered much of New York during that time. Around 365 million years ago, the northeastern edge of North America was being pushed up into mountains during the Acadian orogeny. Sediments were flushed from these mountains, creating the Catskill Delta, a huge drainage system that fanned from New York and Pennsylvania southward into Ohio, Maryland, and Virginia. In New York, thick layers of sediments formed the Catskill Mountains. Schoharie Creek originates in the Catskills and descends toward Gilboa, where it cuts a narrow gorge. Now the site of a reservoir that provides drinking water for New York City, in Devonian times Gilboa marked the marshy edge of an ancient inland sea. It was here that fossils of some of the earliest land plants and animals were discovered.[13]

Patricia Bonamo, in her book *The Gilboa Fossils*, relates the history of the Devonian fossil finds. Between 1852 and 1854, Samuel Lockwood, pastor at

Fig. 2.1. Trilobite (*Basidechenella rowi*) from Middle Devonian period, Ludlowville Formation at York, Livingston County, New York. (Collection of Karl A. Wilson, SUNY at Binghamton.)

the Reformed Church of Gilboa and an avid fossil collector, found a fossil tree stump embedded in Schoharie Creek. It was the first North American find of a Devonian tree. In 1869, workmen uncovered two more stumps from a rock quarry near the creek. Several years later, state paleontologist James Hall paid a personal visit to the site and determined that the trees had grown where they were found. Three specimens of the stumps were removed and sent to the New York State Museum in Albany. Hall consulted with Canadian paleontologist William Dawson, who concluded that the stumps were fossils of two species of tree ferns. Decades later, beginning in 1919, the New York State Geological Survey conducted an investigation of Devonian fossil deposits in the state, with particular focus on Gilboa. Work had already begun on the Gilboa dam, so time was of the essence. Again, in a rock quarry not far from where the 1869 discovery had been made, workmen uncovered eighteen more fossil tree stumps, including the largest specimen yet, eleven feet wide at the base. In addition, collectors dispatched by the New York State Geological Survey found what appeared to be fossil fern seeds embedded in shale just below the falls of Manorkill Creek, which empties into Schoharie Creek.

Among the field scientists was Winifred Goldring, who later became State Paleontologist. Piecing together all the fossil evidence collected over the years from the Gilboa region, Goldring imaginatively reconstructed what she believed to be early seed-fern forests. Her exquisite illustration of the "Gilboa tree," named *Eospermatopteris erianus*, depicts a straight trunk rising twenty to forty feet from a swollen base to a crown of feathery six-foot fronds. Some years later, in 1935, German paleobotanists Richard Krausel and Herman Weyland claimed that Goldring's seeds were in fact sporangia, and therefore the trees were not seed ferns. They also concluded that the stumps represented one, not two species of trees, and the fossilized leaves and branches were from a separate plant. So what tree the stumps represent is still a scientific puzzle that awaits the discovery of more fossils, hopefully of a complete tree.[14]

Despite the damming of Schoharie Creek, the Gilboa area has continued to be a fossil hot spot. Harlan Parker Banks devoted much of his professional life as a paleobotanist to the study and identification of Devonian plants of New York State. Since the 1960s, he and his students have painstakingly examined fossil herbaceous lycopods that had been collected from Gilboa and preserved as specimens since the mid-1800s. In 1963, Banks and his student James D. Grierson published *Lycopods of the Devonian of New York State.* Lycopods have persisted nearly unchanged for 400 million years. For example, the "shining club moss" of modern temperate forests bears leaves in a spiral pattern strikingly similar to those of the Devonian era. Both herbaceous, or ground-hugging, and arborescent, or tree-size, lycopods grew in the Gilboa forests. By the Late Devonian, some attained gigantic size: one group of arborescent lycopods, known as Lepidodendrons, towered up to one hundred feet over the canopy. In 1977, a protégé of Banks, Patricia Bonamo, discovered the first progymnosperm, or precursor of seed-bearing plants, found in North America.[15]

While unearthing fossil lycopods, Patricia Bonamo and Doug Grierson stumbled upon the microscopic remains of fossilized arthropods. Among the insects identified in the 380-million-year-old strata were *Trigonotarbids*, affectionately nicknamed "trig" by fossil hunters. These early insects had features that place them as precursors to spiders, except that they lacked poison fangs and spinnerets and had complex rather than simple eyes. In addition to trigs, their team found one of the oldest known fossilized spiders, *Attercopus*, and a spinneret; one of the oldest known centipedes, *Devonobius delta*, minute myrapod precursors of the six-foot-long millipede-like insects that rose to dominance in the Carboniferous; and the oldest known pseudoscorpion, or false scorpion, *Dragochela*, or "dragon pincer," for its open pincerlike jaws. All were predatory animals that may have pursued their vegetarian prey onto land. Among the Gilboa fauna were detritus-eating *Arthropleurids*, similar to modern millipedes, which were likely prey. Insects like *Arthropleurids*, which fed on decayed plant material, were probably the first to colonize land.[16]

The first vertebrates to appear in the fossil record date to the Ordivician era. Ostracoderms (literally "shield skin") were jawless fish with suckerlike mouths, gills, and, in some species, bony head shields and scaly armor. Ancestors of modern lamprey and hagfish, these bottom dwellers fed on algae and other plankton eaters. By the Devonian, fish had colonized both salt and fresh waters. The now-extinct placoderms ("plate skin") were fifteen-foot-long predatory fish with jaws, teeth, thick-plated skulls, and cartilaginous skeletons. Ancestors to modern sharks, they flourished for 50 million years in the Devonian. Fishes with bony skeletons also evolved during this period.

Around 300 million years ago, ray-finned fishes (actinopterygians) appeared, named for the feature of their flexible thin fins. They were progenitors of the teleosts, or true bony fishes that would emerge during the Cretaceous 100 million years ago and evolve into the twenty-five thousand species that dominate the world's seas today. Coelecanths and lungfishes — our closest living fish relatives — made their first appearance around 385 million years ago. The Coelecanth is a lobe-finned fish whose single most important feature is a fused bone connecting paired fins with the shoulder and pelvic girdle — a feature that would evolve into limbs that would enable animals to support themselves on land. Lungfishes possess the ability to survive long periods of drought by burrowing into muddy bottoms. Both are considered "living fossils," having changed little in the last 300 million years.[17]

Seed-fern forests dominated the landscape in the Carboniferous era. These forests extended in vast lowland tracts away from the marshy edges of the sea. For 100 million years, seed ferns formed the understory to a canopy of giant club-mosses and horsetails. The club-moss *Lepidodendron*, for instance, grew up to 150 feet tall.[18] Gull-sized dragonflies darted through the canopy, while man-sized millipedes foraged in the leaf litter. These colossal forests were drowned by the sea and compressed by continental movements, events that transformed their decayed remains into the great coal seams of eastern North America, Europe, and Asia.

The first amphibians crawled onto land during the Carboniferous. Eryops, a bony-plated, six-foot-long carnivore, inhabited the swamps. Among the creatures of the late Carboniferous forests were the first vertebrates to reproduce on land. Tetrapods (literally "four-footed," the generic name for all land vertebrates) had evolved the feature of the amniote egg, which enclosed the embryo in a watery environment, thus freeing animals from dependence on water to reproduce. These reptiles included therapsids, mammal-like reptiles that would survive the great Permian Extinction and evolve into mammals and ultimately ourselves.[19]

In the seas, ammonites rapidly branched out into four hundred genera; during the Triassic, they just as rapidly collapsed to a single one. By the Cretaceous, this single line had evolved into twelve hundred genera, only to become extinct at the close of the Mesozoic, serving as a signature fossil of the era.

The great Permian extinction that closed the Paleozoic era obliterated 96 percent of marine life, and decimated land species as well. Three out of four orders of amphibians, forty-nine out of fifty genera of reptiles, every species of tabulate and rugose corals, all three orders of crinoids, and nearly all species of brachiopods and ammonoids went extinct. What happened to cause extinction on such a vast scale? A drastic change in global environmental conditions, to be sure, but what exactly happened remains unknown. The catastrophic events associated with the formation of Pangaea during the Paleozoic era most likely would have caused local rather than global extinctions. Globally, the level of oxygen in the atmosphere dropped by as much as 15 percent, which may have been a factor in the die-out. Possibly, the worldwide shrinking of warm, shallow-sea habitats triggered the demise of marine life, while the uptilting of continents during the formation of Pangaea created new upland habitats for land-dwelling species.[20]

Between 250 and 200 million years ago, when the continents were joined into the supercontinent Pangaea, eastern North America bumped up against the bulge of North Africa. Our region was an arid interior land of rugged mountains and fault-formed valleys. Rainy seasons alternated with dry seasons; heavy rains flushed sediments down the flanks of mountains into rivers and rift valley lakes called playas. When dry season came, the playas shrank and the muds baked in the subtropical sun. Across these lake beds the earliest known dinosaurs — small, meat-eating reptiles — left their three-toed bipedal tracks.[21]

The Mesozoic era is known as the Age of Reptiles. Dinosaurs evolved by late Triassic time and came to dominate the animal kingdom during the Jurassic and Cretaceous periods.

In 1909, William Mather of the Museum of Natural History unearthed a small fossil dinosaur of Triassic age in a sandstone formation beneath basalt at the base of the Palisades. He identified it as a phytosaur, a crocodile-like dinosaur he named *Rutiodon manhattanensis*.[22] The Palisades marks the site where Pangaea broke apart during the global extinction event known as the Triassic-Jurassic boundary. Perhaps the extinction event opened a niche for the dinosaurs, because they soon became the dominant species on earth. By the Jurassic, some dinosaurs had evolved into the monsters we like to fantasize about. Long-necked, herbivorous sauropods and sharp-toothed carnivorous allosaurs dominated the Jurassic, and the thundering giants Tyrannosaurus and Gorgosaurus dominated the Cretaceous. Dinosaurs are grouped into two lineages. The saurischians, or lizard-hipped dinosaurs, included both

predatory meat eaters such as tyrannosaurs and plant eaters like the sauropods. One branch of the saurischians is the theropod group, which included
fast-running, carnivorous dinosoaurs like the maniraptors, believed to be ancestors to birds. The other major group of dinosaurs is the ornithischians, or
bird-hipped dinosaurs, which never attained the gargantuan sizes of some of
the saurischians. Despite their name, the ornithischians were not the ancestors of birds. These herbivores included the duck-billed hadrosaur adapted to
swampy habitats, the triceratops with its ponderous head and neck shield,
and the stegosaurus with its spiked tail and row of armored plates along its
spine.[23]

Fossilized tracks of saurischians are preserved in the Triassic-Jurassic red
beds of the Connecticut River Valley and New Jersey's Newark Basin. No
fossil evidence has been unearthed in our region for the Late Jurassic giants,
but earlier dinosaurs left footprints now exposed at the Roseland Quarry in
Essex County, New Jersey, and at Dinosaur State Park in Rocky Hill, Connecticut, south of Hartford. The oldest known dinosaur fossil bone found in
New Jersey Cretaceous formations was dug from a clay pit at Roebling, in
Burlington County. It is a 100-million-year-old fragment of a foot resembling

Fig. 2.2. Dinosaur footprint
from the Jurassic period,
New Jersey. (Photo by
Otto S. Zapecza.)

that of a small tyrannosaur. The only known Cretaceous footprints were found in the Hampton Cutter Pits at Woodbridge, New Jersey, embedded in the so-called Raritan Formation strata dating to 90 million years ago. This fossil footprint is preserved in the Rutgers Geological Museum in New Brunswick.[24]

New Jersey has been the site of several historical dinosaur discoveries. In 1858, William Parker Foulke, a member of the Academy of Natural Sciences, unearthed the first nearly complete dinosaur skeleton. In an old marl pit in Haddonfield, New Jersey, he painstakingly excavated forty-nine bones and the teeth of a hadrosaur. Hadrosaurs are duck-billed dinosaurs believed to inhabit tidewater environments for at least part of their lives, since their bones are usually associated with marine strata. Marl is composed primarily of fossil shells. Foulke's bones were identified by dinosaur expert Dr. Joseph Leidy, who named the specimen *Hadrosaurus foulkii,* "Foulke's bulky lizard." The marl pits of Haddonfield became known as a fossil hot spot. Another fossil collector, Edward Drinker Cope, actually moved to Haddonfield in 1868 in order to be close to the marl pits and keep tabs on fossil bones the miners dredged up from the pits. From the workers he obtained fossils of many extinct vertebrates, including the femur of a hadrosaur. His most exciting discovery was of a predatory dinosaur later named *Dryptosaurus.* Cope nicknamed it "eagle-clawed terrible leaper," envisioning the animal as fierce and agile, an image that broke with the stereotype of dinosaurs as sluggish creatures.[25]

During the reign of the dinosaurs, land plants continued to evolve. Gingkos, cycads, and conifers grew abundantly as early as the Triassic; by the middle Cretaceous, flowering plants added their bright blooms to the floral tapestry. Having coevolved with pollen-bearing insects, these spread rapidly over the landscape. In 1996, the American Museum of Natural History dispatched an expedition to an undisclosed site in central New Jersey. There, scientists David Grimaldi, curator of entomology at the museum, and colleagues Kevin Nixon and William Crepet, both of Cornell University, made a groundbreaking discovery. Excavating in deep clay deposits of Cretaceous age, they unearthed eighty pounds of amber from veins of peat. Trapped in the 90- to 94-million-year-old fossilized sap were one hundred species of plants and animals hitherto unknown to science. The insects include the oldest known mosquito, and the oldest amber-preserved moth, bee, and biting black fly. The amber also preserved the oldest known flowering plant specimen, a 90-million-year-old cluster of tiny oak tree flowers. Especially notable was the feather of a terrestrial bird, possibly the oldest such find in North America.[26]

The reign of the dinosaurs ended abruptly with their mass extinction 65 million years ago. What dealt the fatal blow? One of the most popular explanations is Walter Alvarez's theory of an extraterrestrial impact. While this once seemed far-fetched, an enormous crater off Mexico's Yucatan Peninsula is evidence that a five-mile-wide meteor struck the earth. The impact unleashed an enormous tsunami that instantly obliterated life within its periphery, blasted tons of debris into the atmosphere, blocked out light, and triggered a kind of nuclear winter. According to one scenario, such enormous quantities of sulphur dioxide were released that it brought on a radical cooling of earth; another scenario envisions a global warming caused by the vaporizing of carbon dioxide when the meteor crashed into the thick limestone bed of the Yucatan. Whatever the scenario, life-as-it-was ceased. You can see the division, known as the K-T boundary, as a line in geological strata marked by a local layer of disturbed sediments, including tectites, overlain by a global iridium layer (an element concentrated in meteorites but rare on earth), which is overlain with a fossil layer of new species. This marked the end of the Mesozoic and onset of the Cenozoic era — the Age of Mammals.[27]

I return to the shore, where I began my meditation on the history of life. Here where land meets water, I am reminded of our human place within the larger scheme of life — and how our sense of dominance is so grandly out of scale. It is humbling to think that the bacteria that inhabit the terrain of our bodies are descendants of those that inhabited the primeval earth, persisting through extinction after extinction; that we have evolved only in the last blink of time, in conditions that may prove to be temporary; and that we are far outnumbered by arthropods like the horseshoe crab, whose precursors swam in the Cambrian seas before life had colonized the land and air, transforming the earth into the familiar green planet we know today.

Often in my walks along the beach, I encounter the upturned body of a dead horseshoe crab, its segmented triangular abdomen and five pairs of "walking legs" (the sixth pair are the pincers) exposed to the sky, half-eaten by the gulls. He may have been stranded at the high tide line after mating, an event that occurs only once a year. In May, as the spring sun warms the water and a full moon pulls the tide to its highest point, horseshoes by the

Fig. 2.3. Horsehoe crab, ventral view. (Photo by Betsy McCully.)

thousands catch incoming waves and lumber onto sandy shores to mate. The male mounts the female, who is at least twice his size, clutching her abdomen with his thick round walking legs in slow copulation. The female scoops holes in the sand just above the low tide line and lays her five hundred or so greenish eggs — caviar for the birds who descend in hordes for the feast, fueling themselves for their migratory journeys north. Red knots, sandpipers, and ruddy turnstones gorge themselves on the egg masses when the tide recedes.[28]

The larvae of the horseshoe crab so closely resemble early Cambrian trilobites that they are called living fossils. The notion that the adult horseshoe crab is a "living fossil," however, is incorrect, according to Stephen Jay Gould. Paleozoic ancestors of horseshoe crabs date back 400 million years, but the four species that are distributed worldwide today have existed for 20 million years in their present form and not 200 million as is commonly thought, still a respectable survival record.[29] The horseshoe crab is not a crab at all, but an arthropod, related to mites and spiders. It stands in a class by itself, *Merostomata*, which translates as "legs attached to the mouth," referring to its peculiar anatomy. Its common name derives from its horseshoe-shaped carapace. The Latin name for the species of our region is *Limulus polyphemus*, an appropriate appellation for this near-mythical creature with ten eyes.

It's hard to believe that a species that has evolved over hundreds of millions of years is now endangered. These creatures that had lumbered onto the shore by the thousands in spring mating rites have been decimated. For decades, they have been used by fisherman as conch bait and by farmers as fertilizer; more recently, they have been harvested for their medicinal value, once it was discovered that their blood contained a substance used in hospitals to test for bacterial toxins in patients undergoing surgery. As their numbers have plummeted, several shorebird species that have depended on horseshoe eggs to fuel their migratory journeys northward have also experienced drastic reduction in numbers. Red knots, in particular, have been severely reduced. Restrictions on harvesting horseshoes have been imposed in hopes they will recover, but overharvesting combined with pollution of the shallow in-shore waters where their larvae hatch may prove to be the demise of these ancient creatures and the birds who depend on them. Or maybe — as they have done through the ages — they will outlive us all.[30]

We are vertebrates, hominids who evolved only in the last one hundred thousand or so years.[31] The birds have been around longer, linking back to the age of the dinosaurs. I watch them going about their business. A sandpiper weaves in and out with the tide, poking its slender beak into the wet sand for tiny crustaceans. Wheeling in the air, a herring gull drops a clam shell onto the rocks below, trying to break it open, and another fights over a crab that one of the gulls has grabbed during its brief exposure at low tide. Offshore, diving ducks such as grebes and mergansers disappear beneath the surface when they dive for food, reappearing a few moments later. Above the water flies a squadron of geese in V-formation, heading toward Jamaica Bay, and an occasional tern swoops down with the agility of a swallow. Other vertebrates inhabit this shore: among the rocks of the jetty and beneath the esplanade crawl Norwegian rats, no doubt scavenging the garbage left by fishermen or dead organisms disgorged by the sea; in turn, these rodents are pursued by another introduced species — feral cats. And here I stand, another vertebrate, two-legged like the birds, a placental mammal like the rats and cats, and, like all the animals and plants of the shore, a complex assemblage of cells that re-create in their watery medium the ancient seas where life first evolved.

3

At the Glacier's Edge

Following a winter snowstorm, I set out to walk the beach. A bitterly cold wind burns my face. My boots crunch through a knee-high crust of ice that looks like a miniature glacier, reminding me of a not-so-distant time when much of the New York region was buried under ice. Twenty-two thousand years ago, in the deep freeze of the last ice age, the shoreline was seventy miles distant, and the place where I now stand was part of a vast outwash plain at the glacier's edge. A massive river of ice ground over the land, carved out valleys, and plucked boulders from bedrock to scatter like calling cards. Moving like a conveyor belt, the ice sheet ferried thousands of tons of debris, which melted out at the glacier's margin to form towering moraines. Torrents of meltwater dissected the plain, depositing layers of sand and gravel as outwash. Now, as I stand on the outwash plain, waves crashing on the beach, I can almost hear the thundering crack of an ice lobe as the glacier gives way and surges forward, crushing forests in its path. The glacial episode is a recent event — a mere microsecond on the geological timescale — yet our human existence may ultimately prove less durable than the glacier's scratches on a boulder.

During the Wisconsin ice age, which lasted 140,000 years, successive ice sheets flowed southward from Canada into the United States. Several of these reached New York, as ice lobes surged down the Connecticut and Hudson river valleys. Between twenty thousand and thirteen thousand years ago, the most recent glacier, known as the Woodfordian, completely mantled Manhattan Island and the Upper New York Bay, and covered the northern tip of Staten Island and parts of Queens and Brooklyn in Long Island. Sea level was 350 feet lower than today, and from Cape Cod southward, the coastal plain jutted out fifty to one hundred miles farther than the present-day shoreline, almost to the edge of the continental shelf. Draining the waters of the Connecticut, Housatonic, Passaic, and Hackensack rivers, the Hudson cut a deep gorge through the coastal plain and emptied into the waters of the Atlantic.[1]

Only the most tenacious species of plants and animals could tolerate the harsh conditions of the glacial plain. Dwarf and shrub willows, birches, sedges, grasses, and tundra herbs provided forage for grazing herds of woolly mammoth, musk ox, and caribou. Mastodons, elk, and white-tailed deer browsed in patches of pine forests and black spruce swamps, while moose and giant beavers frequented glacial lakes and bogs. These herbivores were the prey of such carnivores as the timber wolf, dire wolf, bobcat, cougar, lynx, and giant short-faced bear — and at least by twelve thousand years ago, the omnivorous human hunter.[2]

We are able to reconstruct the story of ice age New York because of the painstaking work of geologists, paleoecologists, and other scientists who attempt to piece together the puzzle presented by grooves and scratches on exposed bedrock, the erratic wanderings of rocks that do not belong here, and sediments piled on sediments sometimes in neat layer-cake fashion, but more often mixed and swirled like a marble cake. How to account for the changes from layer to layer, and the forces that seemed to move mountains and carve up landscapes?

In 1828, when geology was still a young science, physician and amateur geologist L. D. Gale conducted a street-by-street survey of Manhattan's geological features before the island would be completely altered by anticipated development. His diary became an invaluable reference for subsequent New York City geological surveys. The island's topography was one of rolling hills and valleys, many of which would be cut down and filled in to lay out streets and grade sites for building. At that time, the population was confined mostly to the west side up to Fourteenth Street, but the uptown streets had already been laid out. Beginning at Fourteenth Street, Gale walked up Tenth Avenue, which was then close to the river shoreline. He noted drifts of gravel and sand yielding to boulders of "greenstone, granite, and sandstone." Between Thirty-second and Thirty-seventh streets he described a hill of "some forty to fifty feet in height," and between Thirty-seventh and Forty-second streets a valley containing "many huge granite boulders in its course from Tenth Avenue to the river." Deep drifts of sand, pebbles, and boulders — often "piled up in conical hills" — filled the valleys. He remarked how boulders of greenstone were "worn, rounded and polished," while boulders of granite were "rough and angular." At Seventieth Street, an outcrop of what he mistakenly thought was gneiss (it was in fact schist) "exhibits distinct drift

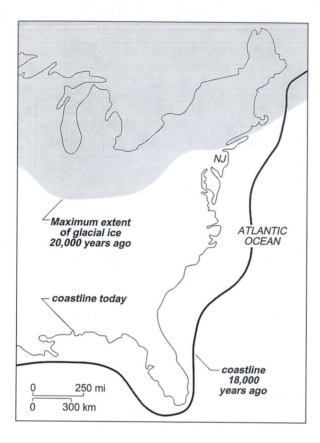

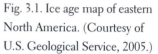

Fig. 3.1. Ice age map of eastern North America. (Courtesy of U.S. Geological Service, 2005.)

grooves and scratches in abundance." The grooves were intriguing, and worth examining more closely. Boulders strewn in the region of Seventy-seventh Street showed northwest-trending "drift scratches . . . extending almost everywhere." The grooves ranged in size from "the finest scratches" to four inches deep and eighteen inches wide, several more like troughs two feet wide and eight inches deep — all "running in the same direction." He was struck by the correspondence between the direction of the grooves and the northwest to southeast trending direction of a valley that cut from Manhattanville (around 119th Street) on the west side to Harlem on the east side.[3]

What made the grooves? Summing up his survey in 1839, Gale attributed them to a flood event: "Diluvial grooves and scratches have been found in every section of the island, from Sixteenth street on the south to 200th-street on the north . . . and from the banks of the Hudson on the west, to Harlem

river on the east." They were most distinct on northwestern slopes, he continued, and far less so on eastern slopes; most trended northwest to southeast, ranging from north forty-five degrees west to north forty-eighty degrees
west, with the predominant direction north forty-five degrees west. Rocks he
examined on the opposite shore, in New Jersey, revealed similar direction of
the grooves. He came up with a rather convoluted explanation for the range
of degrees: "Hence it appears, that the diluvial current which once swept
over this island from northwest to southeast, on reaching the western shore,
was deflected southward, as by the action of some force at a right or some
other angle to its course, and that the same current, before it reached the
middle of the island, again assumed a southeasterly direction, but was again
diverted southerly on approaching the eastern shore."[4]

At the time Gale surveyed the streets of Manhattan, most geologists assumed that drifts and grooves were relics of a great flood. Indeed, most people
believed in a "young earth," certainly no older than the biblical six thousand
years. Geologists who read the rocks as pages in a history that extended back
eons were often labeled as heretics. Even stranger was the idea that much of
the earth was once covered by ice, not water. In a series of popular lectures
at Harvard in the 1840s, paleontologist Louis Agassiz first proposed his glaciation theory to explain the different sets of fossils found in rock strata. A creationist but not a "young earth" proponent, he believed that "the testimony
of the rocks" gave evidence of a series of creations (he proposed fifty), each
following a global catastrophe, that led up to the creation of man. The ice
age in his view was one such catastrophic event. While most geologists dismissed his creationist theory, most came to accept the idea of an ice age. When
William W. Mather published Gale's survey in 1843, he cited Agassiz's glacial theory to explain the drift and groove phenomena Gale observed. In the
same volume, titled *Geology of New York*, Mather published the first geological map of New York City, which was largely based on Gale's survey as
well as his own survey of Manhattan. He also included his notes on Long Island's glacial geology, noting its southern plain to be all sand, gravel, and
loam up to its hills, which contained boulders of greenstone, granite, hornblende, gneiss, red sandstone, and serpentine — rocks transported from someplace else.[5]

Gale assumed that a single flood event transported the boulders and outwash to the region, and he explained variations in groove direction by variations in the current. Following in his footsteps, nineteenth-century glaciologists assumed a single ice event carved out the topography of New York City, and that separate ice lobes of the same glacier caused variations in groove directions. This view is no longer the prevailing one. Based on studies of ancient pollen, radiocarbon dating of rocks and shells, and examinations of groove directions and glacial erratics, most contemporary local geologists believe that the New York City region was shaped by multiple glacial events, but they disagree about the number and dates of the episodes.

The late geologist Les Sirkin proposed two events, with a younger glacier reaching our region by 22,000 years ago, and an older one occurring between 40,000 and 140,000 years ago. The date is difficult to pinpoint because radiocarbon dating goes back only 40,000 years, and most of the older till and outwash was ripped up by the younger glacier. According to Sirkin's scenario, the last glacier created two moraines that define Long Island's topography. The Harbor Hill Moraine was created when the Hudson Lobe surged down the Hudson River Valley to the southern tip of Staten Island and spread westward to northern New Jersey and eastward across Long Island. The Ronkonkoma Moraine was formed when the Connecticut Lobe flowed down the Connecticut River Valley and spread at its margin. The "interlobate region" where they merged is in the Manetto Hills of central Long Island.[6]

Geologists John Sanders and Charles Merguerian of Hofstra University came up with a radically different theory. In 1974, the late John Sanders proposed that four glaciers reached our region over a period of several hundred thousand years. Two of the glaciers terminated at Long Island Sound, including the last glacier, while two older glaciers surged over the Sound and pushed debris into the moraines of Long Island. The earliest of the two older glaciers built the Ronkonkoma Moraine while the later one built the Harbor Hill Moraine. In 1990, Sanders and Merguerian supported this scenario with evidence from their studies of Long Island's stratigraphy and engineering borings. They also cited Gale's notes on the direction of grooves and valley trends. They theorized that the last glacier flowed down the Hudson, Hackensack, and other northeast to southwest trending valleys, terminating at the Connecticut shore of Long Island Sound. In contrast, the older glaciers flowed northwest to southeast across the Hudson and Hackensack valleys. Each of these glaciers deposited till. The color of the till in most places east of the Hudson indicates the origin: the older reddish brown till came from the redbeds of the Newark Basin to the west, and was transported by a glacier that flowed across the Hudson Valley; the younger yellowish brown or gray till originated farther north and was transported by a glacier that flowed down the Hudson Valley. The Harbor Hill Moraine, for instance, is composed of reddish brown till. They note that most of Long Island, except at the eastern and western ends, is composed of outwash, not till.[7]

The ridges and valleys of the region are testaments to the glacier's power to move earth. Glaciers literally created Long Island. In their wake, the receding ice sheets left a hilly, boulder-strewn, and pockmarked landscape of moraines, lakes, kettle holes, peat bogs, meltwater streams, channel-carved valleys, and wetlands. Terminal moraines acted like dams that impounded huge glacial meltwater lakes. One of those lakes was Lake Albany, created by the damming of the Hudson River by the two-hundred-foot-high Harbor Hill Moraine. Sometime between thirteen thousand and twelve thousand years ago, rising waters breached the morainal dam in what must have been a catastrophic flood. The suddenly released waters gushed through the breach at what is now the Verrazano Narrows, carving out a deep gorge. No longer obstructed by the moraine, the Hudson River flowed into its present-day channel, a fault-formed valley dating back to the rifting of Pangaea. The ice age canyon carved by the glacial Hudson River was drowned and is now known to fishermen as the Mudhole, abundant in deep-water fish like tuna. As the sea continued to encroach, reaching its present level a mere six thousand years ago, the archipelago of New York City emerged.[8]

The close of the Pleistocene, marking the end of the last ice age, and the onset of the Holocene (our modern era) was a time of extreme and rapid climatic change. With worldwide global warming, ice sheets melted and the seas rose, flooding continental shelves, destroying old habitats and creating new ones.

In our region, tundra was replaced in a patchwork pattern by spruce forest, extensive cranberry bogs, and pine barrens. Huge dust storms kicked up by glacial winds spread thick sediments rich in pollen and seeds, known as loess, over the glacial deposits; soil formed quickly on water-retentive glacial till, or slowly on outwash or ice-scoured bedrock. Where permafrost persisted, trees could not take root and tundra plants prevailed. Where permafrost thawed, black spruce flourished in glacial till, dominating the landscape from nineteen thousand years ago until ten thousand years ago, when a

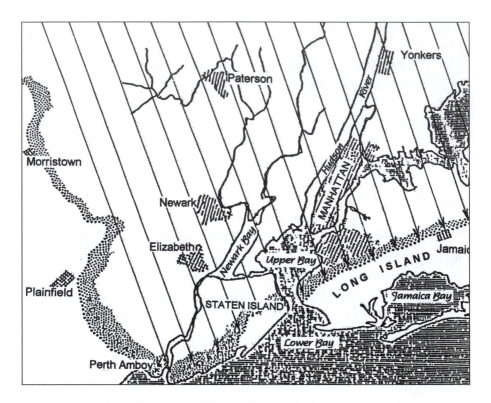

Fig. 3.2. Inferred flow pattern of glacier older than the latest Wisconsin glaciation across Hudson and Hackensack lowlands. (Charles Merguerian, Hofstra University 2004.)

warmer and drier climate favored the spread of pine forest on glacial out-wash and sandy lake and river bottoms. The denser pine forest was composed of red pine, eastern white pine, and jack pine, as well as balsam firs and a few deciduous trees, especially elms, birches and oaks.[9]

Apparently, global warming accelerated ten thousand years ago, triggering rapid changes in plant and animal life. It is possible that Paleo-Indian hunters witnessed the changeover from spruce to pine forest in a single lifetime.[10] As pines thickly colonized the region, tundra disappeared, and with it the mammals that grazed on it. By ten thousand years ago, the glacier had retreated from the Great Lakes region, and a pine forest stretched from Wisconsin to New York, bordered on the south by a warm-temperate forest of oak-hickory and mixed hardwoods. On sandy outwash, jack pine — a pioneer species that is the first to colonize dry sandy soil — was replaced by pitch

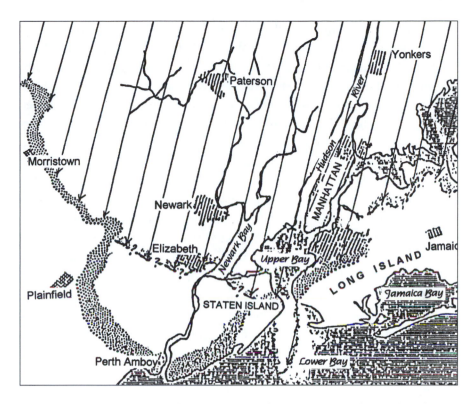

Fig. 3.3. Inferred flow pattern of latest Wisconsin glaciation down Hudson and Hackensack lowlands. (Charles Merguerian, Hofstra University 2004.)

pine. A beautiful remnant of this forest is the Pine Barrens on the South Fork of eastern Long Island. One of only three such dwarf pine barrens in the world, it took root eight thousand years ago at the edge of the Ronkonkoma Moraine in a thin glacial deposit of white quartz sand.[11]

With continued warming, a deciduous forest dominated by oak, chestnut, and hickory established itself on fertile glacial till. In contrast to the less varied forests existing before the ice age, the deciduous forests of the postglacial era were distinguished by a diverse understory. Berry-laden bushes such as viburnums, heaths, and hollies; understory trees such as witch hazel, sassafras, shadblow, and dogwood; and fruiting trees such as wild cherry, crab apple, plum, hazelnut, and hawthorn—all brightened the woodland and provided forage for a number of species.[12]

Some of the mammals that had thrived at the edge of the ice, caribou and elk among them, shifted northward with their habitats, but many others died out in what is termed the "Great Wave of Extinctions." Worldwide, thirty-five to forty species of large mammals and a few smaller species became extinct. Most of the extinctions were in North America.[13]

What caused the mass extinction? A controversial explanation was proposed by paleontologist Paul Martin in 1967. He suggested that when the Paleo-indians entered a new world, they encountered a bounty of big-game mammals that had not learned to fear humans; once they designed a more lethal weapon, the fluted Clovis spear point, they committed overkill. Critics of the overkill hypothesis note that it does not explain those extinctions that took place in Africa and Eurasia at the same time, continents long inhabited by humans. Martin counters by pointing out that most of the extinctions occurred in North and South America and Australia, areas only recently inhabited by humans, and that the extinctions on these continents were far more sudden. (He attributes the early date for the Australian extinctions — twenty-six thousand years ago — to the fact that humans entered that continent forty thousand years ago.) The overkill theory also does not explain why all the game humans hunted — deer, elk, moose, bison, bighorn sheep — did not go extinct. Another argument against the overkill hypothesis asserts that the human population in North America at that time was too small — a few scattered bands distributed across the continent — to have had much of an impact. Moreover, although some may have faced starvation with the loss of their main quarry, the population of Paleoindians actually increased and expanded as they exploited new regions recently freed from the ice.[14]

In contrast to the overkill hypothesis, the environmental theory looks at the extreme climate changes that marked the end of the Pleistocene. As ice sheets rapidly melted and sea levels rose, coastal plains were drowned. Tundra gave way to spruce forests, which gave way to pine and then deciduous forests in a patchwork pattern as the temperate zone shifted northward. The great mammals that had long been adapted to an ice age environment could not adapt fast enough to the changes, and died out. The environmental theory does not explain why mass extinctions did not occur during the Wisconsin glaciation, which was also marked by extreme climate fluctuations and habitat change as glaciers advanced and receded. Nor does it explain why many mammals that had grazed on the tundra and plains did survive the end of the ice age, other than to say that perhaps size does matter![15]

Perhaps overhunting, loss of habitat, and environmental stresses combined to drive the animals to extinction, as suggested by anthropologist Brian Fagan.[16] Whatever the cause or set of causes, the extinction event was a catastrophe. The great beasts that had dominated the ice age landscape were forever gone. Only fossil remains are left to tease our imaginations. Mastodon bones have been unearthed in peat deposits of the Harlem River and twenty-two feet below ground at Broadway and Dyckman Street in upper Manhattan, and mastodon and mammoth teeth have been trawled by fishermen from undersea banks off the Atlantic Coast.[17]

The best place to experience the glacial terrain of New York City is Long Island. A ridge-and-valley glacial topography defines the northern half, and an outwash plain forms the flat southern half. Meltwater from the receding glacier sculpted the necks and incised bays of Long Island's North Shore as it cut channels and stream valleys through moraines. The Nissequogue and Connectquot rivers, for example, were originally meltwater channels that cut through the Ronkonkoma Moraine. Freshwater lakes formed between the receding ice front and terminal moraines. Long Island Sound itself is a drowned valley first excavated by earlier glaciers, then gradually filled in by glacial lakes until a rising sea breached the moraine and saltwater flowed into the sound. As the ice front retreated and stopped, retreated and stopped, it deposited a series of recessional moraines, including those of Sands Point, Oyster Bay, Northport, Stony Brook, and Mount Sinai. Between the terminal and recessional moraines, outwash filled the valleys. In many places, blocks of ice were left stranded by the receding glacier, creating boggy depressions or kettle holes as the giant ice cubes melted. Lake Success and Lake Ronkonkoma are examples of kettle ponds. On the South Shore, Valley Stream is a remnant of a glacial meltwater channel, winding southward from New Hyde Park through Franklin Square and into Valley Stream Park. It's easy to miss, since development has buried so much of it. Yet it still flows through a culvert beneath Sunrise Highway and emerges as a tidal stream that joins the Hook Creek estuary.

Moraine ridges can be walked at Forest Park, in Queens, where the highest elevation is 180 feet, and at Prospect Park, in Brooklyn, where the elevation rises to 188 feet. Alley Pond Park, located on Little Neck Bay in Queens, affords a beautiful example of a classic ridge-and-valley glacial terrain. The name "Alley" may refer to its glacially sculpted valley. You can hike the crest of the moraine through mature oak-hickory and beech woodland, and look downslope into kettle ponds that reflect the trees. I have taken walks with my husband here in several seasons, but fall is my favorite. By late November, winds have stripped away the leaves to reveal the trunks and branches of its great towering trees, and sunlight reaches down to the forest floor, glinting off the kettle ponds. A skim of ice may cover the ponds. You can take a brisk walk through a thick carpet of tan oak, yellow beech, and purple sweet gum leaves. If you're lucky, you might happen upon a small flock of wintering fox sparrows foraging in the leaves by Turtle Pond, or spy a hermit thrush on a branch low to the ground. Note how the sparrow's rusty feathers and the thrush's gray back and cinnamon tail blend beautifully with the tawny colors of oak leaves, pond cattails, and marsh grasses.[18]

Fig. 3.4. Kettle pond, Alley Pond Park. (Photo by Ben Cooper.)

The defunct sand and gravel mine of Port Washington on Long Island's North Shore, now closed off and developed, was once frequented by geologists and their students to study the "two-drift" exposures of glacial till. This site was a favorite of Les Sirkin, who led his students from Adelphi University on field trips here to examine the layer-cake stratigraphy of its morainal bluffs. He described the site in his book on western Long Island geology. At Billy Goat Hill, the lower bed was composed of twenty feet of "tan, gravelly outwash" overlain by "six feet of compact gray-brown till" rich in cobbles and boulders; the younger, upper bed was composed of twenty-five feet of outwash overlain by ten feet of a reddish brown till (so-called Roslyn Till). These beds were underlain by a thick layer of 95-million-year-old Cretaceous-age sand and clay that had been scooped up and redeposited by the older glacier from Long Island Sound. The Cretaceous sediments date to a time when the North American continent drifted away from the spreading mid-Atlantic ridge as Pangaea broke apart. Sediments were eroded and flushed seaward from the Appalachians, gradually extending the continental edge. A twenty-thousand-foot-thick layer of stratified sediments was deposited in a shallow sea over millions of years, creating the Long Island Platform that underlies Long Island. The glacier shoveled these Cretaceous deposits into a pile forty feet thick at the north end of the mines. The Port Washington mines also exposed a bedding "sequence of peat, marine clays, and masses of oyster reef within the upper outwash," relics of a warm interval between the last two glaciations. According to the pollen found in the sediments, radiocarbon-dated at between 43,800 years ago and 21,750 years ago, the region experienced a period of intense cold followed by a warm interval followed by another cold period (the latest glaciation). As the climate alternated between icehouse and greenhouse modes, the vegetation changed from tundra to spruce forests to oak-hickory forests and back to spruce.[19]

Sirkin also described several good exposures of glacial till on western Long Island's North Shore that are open to the public. The beach bluffs at Garvies Point Museum and Preserve reveal a clay-and-sand Cretaceous layer the glacier had excavated from the valley of Long Island Sound, overlain by a thick layer of pebbly outwash, capped by reddish till. The 126-foot-high bluffs of Caumsett State Park at Lloyds Point offer beautiful exposures of pink-and-white sands and red clays of Cretaceous age. The low eroding cliffs of Target Rock National Wildlife Refuge expose Cretaceous sands beneath ascending layers of reddish brown till, yellowish outwash, brownish till, and loess (wind-blown deposits); in the higher bluffs you can see rippled layers of clay and fine sand deposited at the bottom of a lake that had formed between the receding glacier and its moraine.[20]

North Shore beaches were once littered with glacial erratics, boulders ferried by the glacier and left behind as the ice melted. Unfortunately, many of these ice age relics were removed when residents wanted a nice sand beach. But there are several places preserved from development and privatization, such as Target Rock National Refuge and Garvies Point Preserve, where they may be found. At Garvies Point, one can see crystalline basement rocks of gneiss from the Adirondacks and basalt boulders quarried from the Palisades. Smaller erratics include rounded Cretaceous-age concretions known as "Indian paint pots," presumably because the red clay enclosed in the iron oxide crusts was used by the early Americans for pigment. The sea continues to wash out more glacial debris as it encroaches and erodes the bluffs.

Glacial boulders are also scattered throughout our woodlands, the larger ones often marking important places or events. At Pelham Bay Park, for example, Glover's Rock marks the place where Colonel John Glover and his men fought off the British in the Battle of Pell's Point in 1776. Located by Turtle Cove just off City Island Road, the huge white boulder bears a bronze plaque that commemorates the battle. Split Rock, an important marker for the Siwanoy Indians, stands in the northern corner of the same park, at the intersection of the Hutchinson River Parkway and the New England Thruway. According to legend, colonist Ann Hutchinson and her children hid in the crevice of this rock, where Indians attacked and killed them during the Indian Wars of the mid-1600s. Another great rock, now mostly buried by fill near the cove at Orchard Beach's north end, was known to the Siwanoy as "Mishow," their conference rock. These great rocks served as markers and silent witnesses and recorders of human events, sacred in the memory of both Indians and Europeans. Sometimes they stand in mute witness, sometimes they bear plaques with the legend of what they mark, and sometimes they are carved with symbols whose meaning is largely lost to us. A granite boulder housed in the Watson Building lobby of the New York Botanical Garden today testifies to the presence of the ancient inhabitants of these lands: a thousand-year-old petroglyph of a swimming turtle with a symbol on its back speaks to us from a distant time.[21]

4

Land of the Lenapes

According to an old Lenape legend, as retold by Hitakonanu'laxk (Tree Beard), there was a time long ago when the game animals disappeared from the Land of the Lenapes. When the chiefs dispatched their best hunters to find them, they discovered the animals had gone to the Land of the Giants, in the far north, where the spruce trees grow. The hunters reported back to the chiefs, who then dispatched a band of warriors to rescue the animals. But the warriors would discover that the animals were quite unconcerned about their situation. When the War Chief asked the Chief of the animals, a large elk, why they seemed so unconcerned, Elk replied, "You think we are here against our wishes, but this is not so! We wish to remain here and we are content. The Giants have treated us better than you ever did when we lived in your lands! . . . You have wasted our flesh; desecrated our forest homes, and our bones; you have dishonored us and yourselves." When the War Chief asked Chief Elk how they could make things right with the animals, Chief Elk replied, "Honor and respect our lives, our beings, in life and death. Do what you have failed to do before. Stop doing what offends our Spirits." The War Chief gave his promise, and the animals returned with the warriors to the Lenape homeland. That is why, as the storyteller concludes, "Ever since that time we Lenape have always offered tobacco and shown the utmost respect when hunting or upon killing an animal for food. We never took more than we needed, and we used as much of the animal's remains as we could."[1]

Paleoindians entered the Hudson Valley sometime after retreat of the glacier, at least 12,000 years ago. Dutchess Quarry Cave, a site near Monroe, New York, has been dated by archaeologists to 12,580 years ago. There may well have been earlier coastal settlements, but any evidence would have been submerged by the advancing sea. The vast coastal plain was a mosaic of habitats. Patches of tundra, extensive black spruce woodlands, peat bogs, huge glacial lakes, and rushing rivers offered abundant resources for humans to exploit.[2]

New York City became free of ice by eighteen thousand years ago, although it would not be until around six thousand years ago that the sea would reach

Fig. 4.1. Eastern box turtle. (Photo by Ben Cooper.)

its present-day level. Sometime during that interval, at least twelve thousand years ago, Paleoindians set up camp on several sites in the region. At that time, New York City was located a considerable distance from the Atlantic, but this inland region was brimming with glacial meltwater streams and lakes, and was rich in plant and animal resources. Artifacts suggest that these ancient New Yorkers were skilled hunters, fishers, and gatherers who efficiently exploited the maritime, riverine, and woodland environments of the region.

By 11,200 years ago, Paleoindians had perfected a new technology that enabled them to become more efficient hunters. The Clovis point was a razor-sharp, three- to four-inch-long fluted projectile point fashioned from fine-grained stones like chert, obsidian, or chalcedony. The highly prized stone used to manufacture the points was obtained from far-flung quarries, indicating an extensive trading network. These skilled hunters and stoneworkers spanned an entire continent in just a few centuries, as evidenced by the Clovis points they left behind like "archaeological footprints." They pursued mammoth and bison across the Great Plains and set up camp at sites along waterholes where the mammals were known to visit. Excavated kill sites in Arizona, New Mexico, Wyoming, and elsewhere reveal Clovis points along with butchering tools embedded in mammoth and bison carcasses. A single mammoth kill was more than enough to feed a small hunting party, usually a family group of twenty to forty, who ate some of the meat fresh but preserved most for long-term use. Often, mammoth carcasses were only partially butchered, leaving the rest to scavengers like the vulturelike teratorns. Still, little was wasted: hides and pelts provided clothing, bones and tusks were worked into tools, and internal organs were rendered for fat. Because what is known of Clovis culture is based on what has been found at their kill sites, the picture of these hunters is somewhat distorted. They may well have supplemented their diet with small game, fish, and plants.[3] Indeed, recent archaeological excavations in the Northeast reveal a diet that included small game, fish, seal, plants, and nuts.[4]

The Clovis culture spread to New York City by 11,000 years ago. At Port Mobil, an industrial zone on Staten Island's west shore overlooking Arthur's Kill, amateur archaeologists Albert Anderson and his son Robert discovered twenty-one Clovis points among oil tanks, pipelines, and refuse in the late 1950s. Archaeologist Herbert Kraft, an expert on the Lenapes, was called in to assess the site. Using peat borings from the continental shelf and surrounding region, Kraft painstakingly pieced together a somewhat fragmentary picture of the Clovis hunters and their habitat. At that time (11,000 years ago), the exposed continental shelf was still home to mammoths, mastodons, giant beavers and ground sloths, deer, caribou, and elk as well as smaller fauna, which browsed and foraged in the patchwork of tundra, grassland, bogs, and spruce forests that characterized the postglacial region. Archaeologists surmise that the Port Mobil site was a temporary camp chosen by hunters for its height (then around 75 feet above sea level), which afforded them excellent views of the surrounding country and their quarry below while they fashioned their hunting spears and prepared for the hunt.[5]

A mere thousand years later, the great mammals were gone. With the demise of their traditional game, the Clovis hunters must have experienced a crisis. The animals had provided them not only with food, but with tools, clothing, and shelter: a whole way of life, both material and spiritual, had centered on these animals. Faced with their loss, one can speculate that Paleoindian bands may have disintegrated and whole cultures become unraveled.

As the ice receded, those animals that survived the mass extinction, including herds of caribou and elk, migrated northward with their habitats. A few Paleoindian bands probably pursued the herds northward; others remained, adapting to their changed habitat, while still others migrated into new habitats.

Despite the loss of game and radical environmental change, the human population of North America expanded. During the postglacial age, maritime and woodland hunting-gathering cultures established themselves and thrived in eastern North America. Surely their ability to adapt to change, and to diversify, was the key to their survival. They "traveled lightly," as the saying goes. They had not become locked into a particular ecological niche nor become overspecialized; they were able to devise a number of strategies for survival and continuance, whether as seminomadic hunter-gatherers or (later) village horticulturalists.[6]

One can trace the cultural evolution of the early Americans by examining the archaeological record. Archaeologists have divided the cultures of postglacial North Americans into periods based on technological innovations and changes in lifeways. These are termed the Early (10,000 to 8,000 B.P.), Middle (8,000 to 6,000 B.P.), and Late (6,000 to 3,700 B.P.) Archaic periods. My description focuses on the cultures of eastern North America.[7]

The Early Archaic peoples of the Northeast pursued a seminomadic way of life. As hunter-gatherers, they returned year after year to favored sites, usually located near rock outcrops of chert, and always near water. In the New York region, a number of sites dating back as far as the Early Archaic have been excavated in Staten Island, southern New Jersey, Great Meadows, the upper Delaware Valley, and the Lower Hudson. From these sites we can piece together the lives of these ancient Americans. Skilled hunters and fishers, they lived primarily off deer, but also ate bear and elk, smaller game such as rabbit and squirrel, and birds such as turkey and passenger pigeon. The freshwaters yielded catfish, drumfish, and mussels. The oak-hickory woodlands provided plenty of forage. In the woods they gathered acorns, boiled them to leach out bitterness, then dried and ground the nut meat into meal. Along streams and forest edges they gathered berries and wild greens as well as root vegetables, which they ate fresh or preserved for winter consumption. Excavations at the Shawnee-Minisink site in the Delaware Water Gap, occupied between 13,000 and 9,000 years ago, reveal that the inhabitants gathered and ate goosefoot, wild lettuce, smartweed, pokeweed, ground cherry, blackberry, hawthorn plum, hackberry, and wild grape.[8]

The close of the ice age was followed by a period of rapid global warming that peaked around 4,000 years ago before a temporary cooling trend set in. A rising sea flooded estuaries, and rivers began accumulating silt and forming oxbows and backwater swamps. The nutrient-enriched flood plains of the Midwest, Southeast, and Mid-Atlantic regions of North America encouraged the proliferation of aquatic fauna, which in turn offered "fixed-place" resources for human groups. Hunter-gatherers began exploiting more localized food sources on river flood plains, staying longer and returning annually to favored sites. They were gradually shifting from what archaeologists term a "free wandering" culture to a "centrally based wandering" one, a shift that marked the transition into the Late Archaic period. Populations expanded, and families hived off into new territories. Hunter-gatherers began to modify their seminomadic lifestyle as they relied more on local resources and adapted to local conditions. By 8,000 years ago, according to archaeologist Dean Snow, the coastal plains cultures diverged from the oak-chestnut-hickory cultures. In the Mid-Atlantic region, coastal plains peoples set up "base camps" along river mouths and tidewater streams.[9]

During the Middle Archaic, the Eastern Woodland peoples began to use fire to clear trees and hollow out canoes, and to use more refined woodworking tools. The sedimentary and metamorphic stones that once served as hammerstones and net sinkers were now shaped into axes, adzes, and gouges. Spear points were manufactured from a variety of stones quarried from somewhat distant sites, including argillite and shale from north-central New Jersey, quartzites from southwestern New Jersey, rhyolite from Maryland and Pennsylvania, chert from the Hudson Valley, and jasper from Pennsylvania.

Larger camp sites and new grinding tools such as millstones, grinding mullers, mortars, and pestles characterize the Late Archaic. Judging from the great size of the oysters found in shell middens, people were apparently harvesting and consuming these for the first time. Shell middens have been found at Tottenville, Staten Island; Tuckerton, New Jersey; on the lower Hudson and as far north up the Hudson as Croton. One such midden was found in Washington Heights, on the site of the old Hudson River Railroad tracks; another is at Inwood Park, adjacent to a rock shelter. An older shell midden, dating to the Middle Archaic, has been uncovered at Dogan's Point, a site 30 miles north of New York City, on the Hudson.[10] The existence of thick shell middens indicates a more sedentary lifeway, and the appearance of new grinding tools points to more intensive collection and processing of wild seed-bearing plants such as goosefoot.

Archaeobotanists have dated the origins of wild plant domestication in eastern North America to between 4,000 and 3,000 years ago. As populations grew, limiting the foraging territories of hunter-gatherer bands, the necessity of finding more localized food sources led, as early as 4,000 years ago, to the small-scale cultivation of native seed-bearing plants. Goosefoot (*Chenopodium*), sumpweed or marsh elder (*Iva annua*), gourds (*Cucurbita pepo*), and sunflowers (both *Helianthus annuus*, the common sunflower, and *Helianthus tuberosus*, also known as Jerusalem artichoke) were harvested, processed, stored, and replanted. Over time, the women, who were the principal food gatherers, would have learned to distinguish edible or useful plants from "weeds," and begun to weed out unwanted plants and thereby maintain a favorable habitat for the useful plants. From there, it would have been a short step to the planting of harvested seeds — and the birth of horticulture. By 2,000 years ago, maygrass (*Phalaris carolinia*), knotweed (*Polygonum erectum*), and little barley (*Hordeum pusillum*) were also harvested, and the eventual domestication of these plants constituted, in the words of archaeologist Bruce Smith, a kind of "pre-maize husbandry."[11] Together, these cultivars provided a pantry that spanned spring to fall: the seeds of maygrass and little barley matured in spring, while those of sunflower, goosefoot, and knotweed were fall maturing; these plants provided a nutritious diversity of starchy and oily seeds, and moreover, goosefoot provided nutritious spring greens. Between twelve hundred and nine hundred years ago, the Indians of the Eastern Woodlands adopted maize and beans (*Phaseolus vulgaris*) — both domesticated plants from the southwest.[12]

The use of soapstone vessels for cooking marks the major innovation of the Terminal Archaic (3650–2700 B.P.). Before soapstone, women cooked in bark containers or animal skin pouches heated with a hot stone. The flat-bottomed soapstone bowls were manufactured at quarry sites in southern New England, southeastern Pennsylvania, and Maryland, suggesting an extensive trade network in the highly valued containers. Pottery came into use in the Northeast around 2,700 years ago, although as early as 4,500 years ago, pottery was being manufactured on the coastal plain of South Carolina. It may have spread north and west along trade routes or it may have evolved independently, as suggested by the marked difference in style in the thin-walled, corded pottery of the Northeast. Bruce Smith refers to the appearance of pottery as the "container revolution," for it enabled people to better store and process plant foods and was indicative of a more sedentary way of life.[13]

Pottery manufacture and the emergence of farming economies characterize the Early Horticultural period (c. 2700 B.P. to 1000 B.P.). The cultivation of maize, beans, and squash — all migrants from Central and South
America — effected the transition from a primarily hunting-gathering way of
life to a village-agricultural way of life.

The success of the ancient North Americans is a testament to the human
propensity to adapt and survive during times of great climatic change. These
early Americans adapted their lifeways to changing conditions, diversified
their food sources, and exploited a variety of habitats. These were the seed
groups of the later Native American cultures that, in all their astonishing diversity, would take root and flower in the soil of North America. Among these
cultures were the Lenapes, who came to inhabit the New York City region.

The Lenapes, loosely translated as "the common people," lived in Lenapehoking, an arcing swath of land from the Lower Hudson region to Delaware
Bay that includes portions of New York, New Jersey, Pennsylvania, and Delaware. Their time of arrival in the region and point of origin are unknown,
since archaeological evidence gives few clues to the identities of the groups
who settled here. Archaeologist Herbert Kraft believes the Lenape ancestors
migrated to the New York City region from the coastal southeast and Appala-
chia during the early Archaic (10,000 to 8,000 B.P.), based on evidence from
sites in southern New Jersey, Staten Island, the lower Hudson, and the Upper
Delaware River Valley. The Shawnee-Minisink site in the Delaware River
Gap, which is the historic heart of Lenape lands, has been dated to between
9,000 and 13,000 years ago. Tools and weapons found at this site include stone
scrapers, wedges, drills, and spear points; bone awls and needles; and wood
spear shafts, foreshafts, and handles. Ethnologist Robert Grumet believes
that the Lenapes came to this region around 3,000 years ago (at the beginning of the Late Woodland period) from points westward.[14]

Among Algonquins — Indians of diverse tribes who are united by a common
root language — the Lenapes are "the Grandfathers," the first Algonquin-
speaking people from whom all others are descended. According to oral traditions, as reconstructed by Lenape chief Hitakonanu'laxk (Tree Beard), the
Lenapes came from the north, where the climate had grown sharply colder,
forcing them to seek a warmer home in the south. They migrated south and
east, finally arriving at the confluence of the Mississippi and Ohio rivers, where
they joined forces with the Iroquois and defeated the hostile inhabitants

(Cherokee). The Lenapes and Iroquois divided up the land, with the Iroquois taking the northern portion and the Lenapes taking the southern portion. Some Lenapes did not engage in battle, but settled west of the Mississippi; some settled in the lands that were won in battle; and some pushed on eastward until they came to the land between the two great rivers of the Delaware and Hudson, which became the heart of the Lenape Nation. And so these three related groups lived for millennia until the coming of the white man.[15]

The group that settled in the New York City region were the Munsee, so-named because of the particular Algonquin dialect they spoke. The heart of the Munsee territory was Minisink, in the Delaware River Gap. They called the Delaware river Lenapewihitak, or River of the Lenapes. Because of their association with the Delaware River, the Lenapes were named by Euro-Americans the Delaware, after Sir Thomas West, Baron de la Warr, who governed the English colony of Virginia in the early 1600s.[16]

Much of what we know about the Lenapes is pieced together from archaeological evidence, written accounts by the first Europeans who encountered them, and the Lenapes' own oral traditions.

According to the archaeological accounts, the Lenape culture was less sophisticated and more egalitarian than the Adena (3000 B.P.–1900 B.P.), Hopewell (2200 B.P.–1600 B.P.), and Mississippian (1200 B.P.–500 B.P.) cultural complexes to the west and south. These cultures were distinguished by large-scale agriculture, elaborate burial rites, social hierarchies, and highly stylized decorative arts. Although the Lenapes may well have had contact with these cultures, they retained their traditional hunting and gathering economy, efficiently exploiting the rich natural resources of the region. In time, they supplemented their diet with maize, but they never adopted the large-scale agriculture of their neighbors.[17]

Lenape men stalked deer and bear year-round. In fall, however, hunting parties of as many as two hundred to three hundred — women as well as men — organized deer drives. They caught deer by first setting fire to a portion of the forest (creating a "fire surround"), and then driving them into traps or snares. They hunted fowl such as cormorants, geese, swans, grouse, pigeons, partridges, and turkeys by means of nets or arrows. They fished using lances, lines with hooks of bone or bird claw, long drag nets woven from hemp, and weirs constructed of hundreds of wooden stakes set across estuaries and streams (particularly effective at spring spawning). Dutch colonist David de Vries described how the Indians would braid purse seines "from seventy to eighty fathoms in length," which they weighted with stones. They also wove smaller nets that they set on sticks in the rivers. In this manner they caught striped bass, herring, and sturgeon as the fish swam upstream by the thousands to spawn.[18] Both men and women fished and gathered shellfish. Rivers and streams, ponds and bays teemed with salmon, shad, sturgeon, striped bass, haddock, flounder, and herring. Estuaries abounded with oysters, clams, mussels, and crabs. Fish and shellfish could be cooked fresh, or smoked for winter use.[19]

Nature provided all the materials the Lenapes needed to manufacture containers, tools, weapons, clothing, and houses. Women and old men wove baskets and mats from rushes, cornhusks, and ash splints; and braided cordage from wild hemp, nettle, and elm bast. Women gathered clay, tempered it with grit, rolled pieces into coils to form the walls of the vessel, smoothed the walls with shells, and stamped them with geometric designs before drying and firing them. Using bone needles and awls, they sewed clothing from the skins of deer and elk—breechcloths for men and wraparound skirts for women, as well as sashes, leggings, and moccasins for both. They decorated the clothing with colorful dyed porcupine quills, seeds, and shells. The men made all their own tools and weapons. They fashioned bows of painted witch hazel and arrows of elder or ironwood; they strung the bows with sinew, and attached arrowheads shaped from fine-grained stone. They felled the trunks of "whitewood" (possibly *Liriodendron tulipifera*) and cedar, then turned the fire-hollowed trunks into large dugout canoes; they constructed smaller canoes of elm bark. They carved wooden bowls from maple, buckeye, and elm wood, and designed pipes of stone, clay, horn, or copper.[20]

Because the Lenapes tended to move from one site to another, season to season, they made "disposable" tools, such as horseshoe crab shells for scoops and clam shells for hoes. They also furnished their wigwams and longhouses with portable articles such as sleeping mats and skins. During the summer months, families tended to live in separate dwellings called wigwams, constructed out of poles that were set into the ground, bent to form a dome shape, and lashed together at the top. These ribbed structures were put up by the men but finished by the women, who covered them with squares of bark or mats made of woven grasses and lined the interiors with decorative mats, perhaps embroidered with dyed porcupine quills, or painted them. In winter, the structures were left in place but stripped of their mats, which were taken along with other essentials to the winter camp. In the winter camps, they constructed bark-covered longhouses that served as multifamily dwellings and ceremonial centers.[21]

For millennia, the Lenapes had practiced small-scale cultivation of native plants. Around a thousand years ago, some Lenape groups began to cultivate maize, beans, and squash. Maize is a demanding crop, so the decision of a community whether or not to adopt a maize-centered horticulture probably had to do with the soil they had to work with and the consequent degree of growing success. The alluvial soil of river bottoms, for example, is highly conducive to growing crops, while stony morainal soil is not. In the New York City region, we know from farmers today that the sandy soil of Long Island's south shore — the glacial outwash plain — is ideal for growing crops.

Fig. 4.2. Reconstructed bark wigwam. Pelham Bay Park on Siwanoy Trail. (Photo by Betsy McCully.)

And we also know from Contact-era accounts as well as the Lenapes' own oral traditions that some groups of Lenapes here practiced small-scale farming, growing the revered "three sisters" crops of maize, beans, and squash.[22]

The shift to a maize-centered agriculture profoundly affected the relationship between the people and the land. They no longer depended solely on the availability of resources; now they became managers of the land. Although they may have long used fire to trap deer by the "fire-surround" method, they now used fire on a regular basis to clear fields, burn woodland undergrowth, and keep down weeds in abandoned fields. The Indian practice of annual controlled burning of woods and meadows prevented growth of underbrush, encouraged growth of grasses, and improved the soil. It also created "edge" habitats between woods and grassland that attracted game animals such as deer and encouraged the growth of strawberries and raspberries in the old burn areas. As William Cronon concluded in his study of New England ecology, the Indians not only reaped the bounties of nature, they created them.[23]

The increasing emphasis on farming also affected the social organization of Lenape society. Women, in their essential role as cultivators, held high status. Indeed, the Corn Spirit is feminine: *Kahesana Xaskwim*, or Mother Corn (*xaskwim* is the Lenape word for corn).[24] The women managed small plots in which they cultivated the fields of maize, beans, and squash. Only the growing of tobacco was reserved for men and older women (past menopause). The women owned (in trust for the clan) the fields and houses, and the eldest woman of the village chose leaders according to descent along maternal lines. The women, equal with the men, could be civil as well as spiritual leaders, shamans, and medical practitioners.[25]

Preparing the planting fields involved intensive work that was shared by men and women. They timed planting according to the leafing out of certain trees and the arrival of alewives (a type of herring) in the rivers. The men cleared the fields by several methods. According to the slash-and-burn method, they first chopped down trees with stone axes known as celts, then burned the fallen trees and undergrowth. They mixed the ash into the topsoil to enrich it. According to the girdling method, they cut an incision through the bark all around the trunk, then stripped the deadened bark, leaving the tree to die. After girdling the tree, they would wrap the upper part of the tree in wet binding and set fire to the lower trunk in order to fell the tree. The preserved trunk would then be hollowed out for use as a canoe. When the fields had been prepared, the women planted seeds in hills set between the stumps. They would plant three or four kernels of maize to a hill, followed by beans and squash when the corn was a finger high; the cornstalks provided support for the bean plants. Over the growing season, women and girls carefully tended the plants. At harvest, they dried most of the produce to store for long-term use. An account by Henry Hudson describes an Indian house "which contained a great quantity of maize, and beans of last year's growth, and there lay near the house for the purpose of drying enough to load three ships, besides what was growing in the fields."[26]

According to evidence from archaeological sites, the Lenapes grew a northern variety of corn known as *maiz de ocho*, which was about four inches long with eight rows of kernels. By the time the Europeans arrived, according to colonial accounts, the Indians had "white, red, blue, flesh-colored, brown, yellow and spotted ears," and a number of varieties of maize, each "adapted to particular localities." The extraordinarily prolific grain thrived in the sandy soils of the Atlantic coastal plain.[27]

Maize could be eaten fresh or dried, green or fully ripe. The women roasted green ears wrapped in their husks in ashes and cooked ripe maize with beans in a succotash. Even small low-yield stalks did not go to waste: young and old alike loved to suck their sugary juices. After harvest, the women braided the unshucked maize and hung them from rafters to dry. They shucked and shelled the dried maize and stored the kernels in baskets, which they buried in pits lined with mats. They prepared dried maize by pounding it in a wooden mortar, sieving the meal through a finely woven basket, mixing the meal with water to make a dough, wrapping the dough in a grape or maize leaf, then baking it in ashes to produce a bread. They might add berries to sweeten the corn cake. They also ground dry kernels into a coarse grain to make gruel, or *sa'panmush*, or soaked the dried ears with ash to release the hulls and make hominy. The winter larder contained not only dried maize, but dried beans, dried squash and pumpkin rings, smoked and dried fish and shellfish, and smoke-cured meat.[28]

The community moved to different sites according to the season and the activity. They migrated from summer villages by the coast, where they grew their crops and gathered shellfish, to fall and winter hunting camps in the mixed deciduous forests where deer could be taken, to spring fishing camps where salmon and other fish spawned. Their way of life was based on the cyclical rhythms of the seasons and was, for them, an ancient pattern rooted in nature.

Food gathering, like food growing, was always timed to the seasons. In the Northeast, wild food plants augmented the maize-centered diet. Year-round, the foragers — always women — knew where to find nutritious tubers. In summer, they searched for the little vine of the ground nut (*Apios americana*) growing along woodland streams to gather their walnut-sized tubers. In fall, they sought out the fat arrowhead-shaped leaves of Wapato, or *Sagittaria latifolia*, poking out of the mud along pond edges, to harvest the plant's potatolike tubers called water nuts. In winter, if the ground was not frozen, they dug Jerusalem artichokes (*Helianthus tuberosus*), potato-sized tubers of wild sunflowers that grew abundantly in the fields. In the woodlands of early spring, women harvested the corms of Jack-in-the-pulpit (*Arisaema atrorubens*), dried them, and ground them into a cocoalike flour. They also picked field greens like wild leeks and onions, which were plentiful in spring. In summer, along the shores and in fields, they gathered beach plums, wild grapes, and berries such as blueberries, cranberries, strawberries, serviceberries, and elderberries. In fall, they collected nuts such as chestnuts, hickory nuts, walnuts, and acorns.[29]

Nature was not only the American Indians' pantry but also their pharmacy. Their extensive knowledge of medicinal wild plants is well-documented. As ethnohistorian Gaynell Stone Levine argues, "the empirical curative value of aboriginal herbal medicine is attested by the fact that a majority of substances in the U.S. Pharmacopoeia today stem from these sources."[30] In fact, according to botanists Stephen Foster and James Duke, as of 1990 over 40 percent of prescription drugs sold contain at least one ingredient derived from plants. In their "Acknowledgements" for their *Peterson Field Guide to Medicinal Plants* of Eastern and Central North America, they write: "Tribute must be paid to the 1,100 to 5,000 generations of Native Americans whose experience and evolution with the indigenous native flora ultimately made this book, and a scant two centuries of literature, possible."[31] Mrs. Van Rensselaer, a nineteenth-century descendant of Dutch colonists in New York who wrote about her female forebears, attested to the plant lore of the Lenapes: "The Indians had many medicines made from plants, roots, barks, and herbs. They understood the virtues of stramonium, smut-wheat, golden-rod, elderberry, etc. They would brew catnip tea for the sick or strengthen an invalid with a decoction of strawberry leaves."[32]

Ethnobotanist Barrie Kavasch describes the medicinal uses of a few northeastern herbs. Boneset (*Eupatorium perfolatium*), also called Indian sage, was sought after for its efficacy as a tea in treating "break-bone fever," now known as influenza. It was also used as a cold remedy and to relieve the pain of rheumatism. Its cousin, Joe Pye weed (*Eupatorium purpureum*), was named after the eighteenth-century Algonquin medicine man Joe Pye, who prepared strong teas from the plant to treat a variety of ailments. The milkweeds were also used extensively, and may well have been cultivated. Goldenrods were also renowned for their healing properties, which led Linnaeus to name the genus *Solidago*, which means, "to make whole." These are a mere handful of the hundreds of medicinal herbs they used.[33]

"Green medicine" was the purview of a few who knew the special properties of every native plant. Gifted men or women who received a vision or dream from the spirit world could become *meteinuwak*, or "medicine people," healers and mediators between the spirit world and the everyday world. Collecting of medicinal plants had to be done with respect for proper rituals or the remedies would not be effective. When gathering herbs, the collector stops at the first plant, drops a tobacco offering in a hole dug eastward of the plant, then goes on to pick the next plant of the same kind — but only if "clean and well-formed, with roots free from knotty growths." Bark is stripped only from healthy trees, and only from the sun-facing side. The collector strips bark downward if it is to serve as a cathartic, and upward for an emetic. When preparing decoctions, the herbalist always stirs medicinal brews counterclockwise, "to simulate the direction the sun travels."[34]

According to Barrie Kavasch, plants are viewed in American Indian cosmology as part of the "sacred circle" of life, and are as much imbued with spirit as humans and other animals. Illness is viewed as a case of an individual being out of balance, and the healer's art is to restore the balance not only through the administering of healing botanicals, but through an approach that involves ceremony, ritual, dreamwork, and respect for the healing power of nature: "To replace what you have taken by making a tobacco offering is a recognition or acknowledgement of the life you take, whether it is a tree cut down to make baskets or an animal killed for food," says Schagticoke Elder Trudie Lamb Richmond.[35]

Lenape cosmology reveals an intimate relationship to the natural world. They recognized an indwelling spirit in everything, with no division into living and nonliving. A rock as well as a tree, a cloud as well as a turtle, even a made object such as a bowl or pipe was imbued with spirit. What the Lenapes referred to as *maneto* (plural, *manito'wak*) was the indwelling spirit of all things, and was a word often used to identify anything that was strange or wondrous or beyond comprehension. Hence, the first Europeans, with their firepower and books, were maneto — a word that Europeans in their arrogance or cultural bias took to mean "God." The Lenape Creator God, *Kishelamakank*, lives in the twelfth tier of the universe; the soul must travel twelve days to journey to this tier after death. It is Kishelamakank who created the manito'wak to govern the universe; these included the Earth Mother (*Kukna*), Corn Mother, and the Keeper of the Game (*Misinkhalikan*). Everything in nature possessed maneto, and if offended, the maneto could cause mischief. To placate the spirits, the Lenapes performed such seasonal rituals as the "sacrifice of the first fruits," whereby the fat of the first buck killed was offered

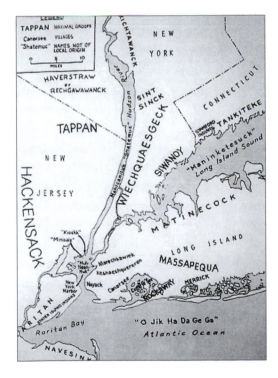

Fig. 4.3. Map of Upper Delawaran Groups of greater New York area. (Courtesy of Robert S. Grumet.)

to the Keeper of the Game. Similarly, burnt offerings of corn were made to the spirits of the deer and bear, of bear meat to the corn spirit, and of fish-shaped bread to the fish spirit. Tobacco (*ksha'te*) was used extensively in spiritual rituals: tobacco smoke would be offered to the crops at planting time, to the game animals before the hunt, to the forest before entering for the purposes of hunting and gathering — all to insure a bountiful outcome and to offer thanks. Failure to perform these rituals was thought to bring terrible consequences.[36]

When the European colonists arrived, the particular Lenape culture they encountered had been established for a thousand years. Despite regional variations in language and customs, the Lenapes thought of themselves as a coherent culture, united by a complex system of kinship that traced their lineage back to common ancestors. There were probably a large number of clans, but only three have been recorded: the turtle, the wolf, and the turkey. At the time of European contact, the Lenapes numbered as many as sixteen to twenty thousand, and were divided into roughly twenty autonomous groups that were closely interconnected through clan membership. The Raritan occupied portions of Staten Island and central New Jersey north to the Raritan River valley. The Haverstraw inhabited the west bank of the Hudson and seemed closely tied to the Hackensack and Tappan of New Jersey. The Wiechquaeskeck dwelled on the east bank of the Hudson, in the southern portion of Bronx and Westchester counties, and had close ties to the Siwanoy, who lived on the north shore of Long Island Sound, including Pelham Bay. The Nayack inhabited the eastern shore of the Narrows and were related to the Hackensack. The Massapequa, Merrick, and Rockaway resided on western Long Island; the Matinecock lived on the north shore of Long Island from Queens to Suffolk County; and the Canarsee and Marechkawieck made Brooklyn their home. As Robert Grumet has emphasized, such confederations and tribal groupings were temporary arrangements in times of crisis, which is surely what the natives faced at the time of the European invasion. It is therefore difficult to ascertain what the demographic patterns were before European contact, as historians have relied on European concepts that grouped the native peoples into "tribes" or "nations" organized under "kings" or *sachems*, often confusing names and places.[37]

For the Lenapes, their identity as a people was not with a nation or tribe but with a clan. Clan lands and dwellings were "owned," or held in trust for the clan, by the women as heads of households. The concept of shared land use was fundamental to Lenape society—and utterly foreign to the European system of land tenure. The ascendancy of the European system in North America would prove devastating to the Lenapes, whose communal identity was rooted in a land of fluid natural boundaries.[38]

5

Staking Claim

Often during my summer walks on the shore, I come upon the desiccated shell of a female blue crab, recognizable by her bluish gray carapace and legs with reddish orange pincers. It's just as savory to gulls as to the humans who go crabbing along the jetties here. Spying a glistening live crab just stranded by the receding wave, a gull swoops down to grab it, then flies off to an isolated spot to dine on the sweet flesh. It was this crab that Dutch colonist David de Vries noted as a propitious sign from the gods: "In the summertime crabs come on the flat shores, of very good taste. Their claws are of the color of the flag of our Prince, orange white and blue, so that the crabs show sufficiently that we ought to people the country, and that it belongs to us."[1]

The land "discovered" and "possessed" by the Dutch in seventeenth-century New Netherland was a place of astonishing plenty, awaiting the arrival of the European to reap her bounty. The waters were teeming with fish, the air with birds, the land covered with a luxuriant growth of trees, fruiting vines, and grasses. To the European with an eye toward settlement, it was the proverbial Land of Plenty.

Henry Hudson, an Englishman sailing under the auspices of the Dutch East India Company, nosed his little ship *The Half Moon* into Lower New York Bay in 1609. Based on Hudson's "discovery," the Dutch staked their claim to the region they named New Netherland, which roughly corresponded with Lenapehoking. As described by Adriaen Van Der Donck, a lawyer who settled here in the 1600s, the colony was bounded by New England on its northeastern side, demarcated by the Connecticut River; Canada to the north, demarcated by the Saint Lawrence River; and Virginia to the south, past the Delaware River. The Dutch claimed control of both the Delaware and the Hudson rivers.[2]

By the time Hudson sailed into the river that would be named after him, the natives had grown used to seeing the strange sailing ships and bearded men. Explorers, traders, fishermen, and pirates had visited the shores of the Atlantic seaboard since the late 1400s, and possibly earlier. Word of the white man would have spread rapidly along trade routes, and the word was not always good. In many instances, Europeans — Spanish, Portuguese, French, English, and Dutch — had dispossessed American Indians of their lands, abducting, enslaving, and killing them. Verrazano, for example, who explored the Lower New York Bay as far as the Narrows in 1524, had abducted a young Indian boy from Delaware to bring back to show the French king.[3] It was in the interest of both Indian and European traders, however, to maintain friendly relations. The Indians desired the Europeans' trade goods, and the Europeans desired access to the Indians' vast trading network. The Dutch, specifically, sought to establish trading outposts on Manhattan and at Fort Orange (now Albany) as gateways to the Hudson trading corridor.

Hudson's voyages opened up the North American fur trade for Dutch merchants. The Dutch West India Company (DWIC), chartered in 1621, was given exclusive North American trade rights. The original intent of the Dutch was to secure control of fur trade routes — the Hudson River being key — and to that end they did not at first seek to establish permanent settlements. Fort Amsterdam was merely a tiny trading outpost, and the fur trade was far down the list of their priorities in the Americas, priorities dominated by the slave trade, sugar production, and imperial aims. As bluntly put by historian Daniel Friedenberg, "Sacking, slaving, and the conquest of Brazil relegated the tiny settlements of Fort Orange (Albany) and Manhattan to a position of little importance."[4]

The fur trade may have been a low priority to the Dutch West India Company, but it was highly lucrative. Beaver was especially profitable. Not only was beaver fur highly esteemed in Russia and Germany, but beaver testicles were believed to have curative powers, and beaver oil was thought "good for dizziness, trembling, rheumatism, lameness, and pain in the stomach."[5] The high European demand for beaver pelts and by-products naturally led to the animal's being overhunted. Beaver may once have numbered as high as 60 million; within decades of European colonization, the animals were extirpated from the Northeast.[6]

No sooner had the Dutch established their trading posts than they actively recruited Algonquin men for market hunting. By the 1640s, they equipped these men with guns to increase their efficiency as hunters, with the result that beaver and other fur-bearing animals were quickly decimated in the region of the Lower Hudson, Delaware, western Long Island, and along the coast of Massachusetts.[7] Commercial hunting was to have a profound impact on Indian culture. Indians had long engaged in subsistence hunting, maintaining edge habitats for deer and other game close to their settlements. The fall deer drive often involved a whole community. As Indian men pursued their increasingly scarce quarry farther inland, they stayed away from their settlements for long periods of time. They were driven by the desire to gain prestige among their people by accumulating European trade goods and wampum (finely crafted shell beads that had long been used to commemorate events and alliances among Indians, but came to be used as currency among American Indians and Europeans). Indian participation in the fur trade radically altered their relationship to animals, transforming not only their hunt-

t' Fort nieüw Amſterdam op de Manhatans

ing practices but their personal values. Trade among Indians once served more than a utilitarian purpose, enhancing village-to-village diplomacy in a traditional exchange of gifts. Now, trade served an international market. No longer were animals being harvested with respect for the animal and with an eye to preserving a species; now, animals were killed on a mass scale for the sake of trade and profit. Competition for control of hunting grounds and trading routes led to conflicts among Indians, known as the Beaver Wars, which was fueled by the firearms Europeans were glad to provide them in exchange for furs, exploiting Indian conflicts as suited their purposes.[8]

The introduction of domestic animals by Europeans further altered the relationship between Indians and animals. In 1625, the Europeans imported

103 heads of horses, cattle, and sheep to Manhattan; by 1675, on Long Island alone, tax lists show counts of 4,293 cattle, 1,564 sheep, 1,344 swine, and 941 horses—these numbers are in proportion to a population of under 5,500 colonists.[9] The colonists treated their animals not only as an important source of food and by-products for home consumption, but as their private property, and on the market, as a commodity. Horses, beef, and pork, for instance, were exported to the West Indies.[10] The idea of animals as property was foreign to the Indians, who did not "own" animals in the European sense, although they managed stocks of deer by creating suitable browsing habitat. They had no domestic animals except dogs. European livestock overran extensive tracts of the Indians' ancestral lands, trampling woodlands, wetlands, meadows, and unfenced Indian planting fields. Hogs that had been turned onto offshore islands to keep them away from the colonists' planting fields rooted for

Fig. 5.1. Frederycks, Kryn, T'Fort Nieuw Amsterdam op de Manhatans, 1626–28, engraving, 1651. (Courtesy of I. N. Phelps Stokes Collection, Miriam and Ira D. Wallace Division of Art, Prints and Photographs, The New York Public Library, Astor, Lenox and Tilden Foundations. Image #55679.)

shellfish such as clams in the mudflats, destroying a primary food source for Indians. The Indians would often kill a stray hog that had done damage to their shellfish grounds.[11] They resented the cattle that were destroying habitats the Indians depended on for foraging and hunting. In 1644, for instance, the killing of cattle by Indians necessitated the building of a palisade and common enclosure on Manhattan "from the Great Bouwery to Emanuel's Plantation."[12]

European colonists sought to exterminate those wild animals they deemed a threat to their livestock. Wolves were particularly reviled. Both the wolf and the bear had been eradicated from England four centuries before, and in North America the practice continued. Again, the colonists recruited the Indians to kill the wolves. In New Jersey, for instance, an ordinance of 1697 offered bounties of ten shillings to Indians and blacks, and twenty shillings to Christians, for each wolf killed. In New York, a similar ordinance in Westchester, dated 1770, explicitly called for the extermination of wolves and offered bounties of ten shillings to Indians and twenty shillings to Christians for each wolf killed.

In seventeenth-century New Netherland, as long as the fur trade was of high priority, relations between the Dutch and Indians were relatively peaceful, as suited each other's purposes. However, once the fur trade diminished in importance, land and long-term settlement became the focus of a new wave of colonists. Conflicts between Indians and settlers over land and resources erupted into a series of bloody wars in the mid-1600s, and ultimately led to the routing of the Indians from the region.

The history of New York City might have taken a different turn had not the original plan for the Dutch West India Company charter of 1621 been defeated. The plan of Willem Usselinx sought to establish a Dutch empire based on Christian values of peace and goodwill, with no slaves, and small farms worked by voluntary labor; there were to be no profits in silver and gold, only in what the soil itself yielded. Unfortunately, Usselinx's agrarian utopia was marred by his own presumption of Christian superiority, for his proposal also suggested that the American Indian would provide the "voluntary" labor for the farms, and one of the aims of the colonists would be to convert the "savages."[13]

The Dutch West India Company administered the colony of New Netherland on behalf of the Dutch government, a role that included acquiring land

and doling out land grants and patents. In 1628, motivated by the need for private investment in the colony, the company granted large land patents to men with plenty of investment capital, supplied them with slaves, and gave them rights to trade and entitlement to all "fruits, flora, minerals, rivers, and springs" found within the land patent. The patroons, as they were called, functioned like absentee landlords, overseeing lands that were worked by tenant farmers, slaves, and indentured servants. The company also allotted smaller tracts of land to freemen as long as they could cultivate it; these tracts were subject to a quitrent (one-tenth of the produce and cattle to be given to the company annually) and could be repossessed by the company if deemed unproductive or when the farmer died. Most of the patroons sold back their lands to the company by the mid-1630s, discouraged no doubt by Indian attacks and the growing unrest of tenant farmers.[14]

In an effort to encourage settlement, the DWIC drew up a more liberal charter in 1640, allotting two-hundred-acre parcels of land and granting local self-government to enterprising individuals who could bring five adult immigrants to the colony. Ultimately, this charter would fail to establish a permanent and profitable Dutch colony, for its effect was to exacerbate the tensions between whites and Indians that would eventually explode into a bloody, protracted war.

The charter contained a clause that conferred "right of dominion" only "after Indian titles had been properly extinguished."[15] Because the DWIC had never received a formal land patent (its primary interest being trade not settlement), titles to large portions of land were still held by Indians. Even where titles had supposedly been "extinguished," Indians continued to occupy their ancestral lands. This was not perceived to be much of a problem as long as European settlements were limited and temporary, but as the population of New Netherland doubled in the years 1638–1643 from one to two thousand, land became a commodity of increasing value.[16]

To accommodate the new influx of immigrants, DWIC director Willem Kieft bought up large tracts of land from the Indians in 1639, in what would become Queens and Brooklyn. In keeping with former practice, the Indians were "allowed" to remain on their lands, retaining rights to hunt, fish, and farm small portions. Hence, the Rockaway remained on their lands, as did the Canarsee. As the DWIC continued to make large land purchases, a curious pattern emerged, reflecting the radical differences between Indian and

European concepts of land use and possession. The Rockaway, for instance, joined in 1643 with the Massapequa and the Merric in a land sale that included a tract of land they had already "sold" to Kieft. Similarly, a tract of land from Norwalk Bay to Hell's Gate, along Long Island Sound, which had been supposedly sold to the Dutch by the Massapequa in 1639, was sold again in smaller parcels by the Matinecock to English settlers in 1676. The Matinecock had repudiated the 1639 land sale and claimed the right "to remain upon the aforesaid land, plant corn, fish, hunt, and make a living." This pattern was repeated throughout the years of the Dutch colony and extended into the time of the English takeover — until the Lenapes were removed altogether from the colony.[17]

Naturally, the failure of Dutch land purchases to "terminate native occupancy" created considerable resentment on the part of the colonists, who referred to the natives as "Indian-givers." The effect was predictable, as the historian Michael Kammen writes: "Rapacious individuals negotiated with the Indians directly, deceived them, or dragged them into the director's presence to have deals officially sanctioned in speedy transactions." The colonists, anxious to be rid of the Indian "nuisance," began to circumvent company bureaucracy altogether, entering directly into land transactions with the Indians, further confusing titles to the land.[18]

Such confusion over land titles stemmed from a fundamental conflict between the American Indian concept of land use and the European concept of land title. According to the Indian concept, land was held in common by the tribe, and frequently was tenanted by other tribes who shared land use, perhaps because of hereditary claim or simply by agreement between tribes. Staten Island, for instance, was shared by the Raritan and Hackensack, and possibly the Canarsee and Rockaway. When the natives made a "sale" to the Europeans, they conceived it as a lease or temporary occupancy. Robert Grumet notes that a land deed was viewed by the Indians as a treaty marking the beginning, not the end of a relationship. Newcomb writes that the "sale" of land "might . . . be almost any mutually satisfactory change in the relationship of two groups of persons subsisting on the land. In the earliest sales, the Indians seem to have intended only to give whites freedom to use the land in conjunction with the native population." When the Lenapes realized that they were expected to vacate the land to which they had forfeited title (in the eyes of the Dutch), they challenged or repudiated former contracts, and attempted to negotiate better deals. But however good a deal they thought they had ultimately gotten, it is unlikely they could have foreseen the devastating impact on their tribes, both present and future: their children had in effect been disinherited, and the tribe — whose identity was so closely bound with place — had lost the foundation that underlay their traditions, customs, values, and way of life.[19]

With Indians and Europeans using the same lands, it was inevitable that they would clash. By 1639, Governor Kieft had adopted a policy toward the natives of removal and extermination. He quickly seized on two unrelated incidents as evidence of an Indian "conspiracy": the Raritans attacked the crew ordered by Kieft to collect tribute from them, and on the same day a native thought to be a Raritan killed several hogs on Long Island (a common occurrence where free-wandering hogs trampled unfenced Indian maize fields). Kieft dispatched an expedition of eighty soldiers and sailors to Staten Island under the command of Cornelius van Tienhoven to attack the Raritan settlement. Van Tienhoven, who had no official sanction to kill the natives, conveniently removed himself at some distance from his men in order to free them to kill and torture as they pleased. One of the men they tortured was the sachem's brother, whom they gouged "in his private parts with a piece of split wood." In revenge, the Raritans attacked several outlying Dutch boweries (farms), including that of David de Vries on Staten Island, where they killed four tenants and burned the house and barn. Kieft became more militant, inciting other Indians to kill Raritans by imposing a bounty of ten belts of wampum (their currency) for every head of a Raritan, double for a murderer. The policy was effective, as Grumet recounts: "On November 2, 1641, Pacham, a chief of the Tankiteke Indians living in Westchester County, brought the severed hand of a Raritan chief on a stick to Fort Amsterdam and presented it with great ceremony to Kieft."[20]

A murder set off a chain of incidents that would unleash the full measure of Kieft's wrath toward the Indians. A drunken Wiechquaeskeck who had gone to trade with an old man in Manhattan killed him with his ax and stole his trade goods. When Kieft demanded satisfaction from the Wiechquaeskeck sachem, demanding him to hand over the murderer, the sachem refused. Incensed by the refusal, on August 28, 1641, Kieft called together the heads of all families living in or near New Amsterdam to discuss the possibility of "a punitive expedition." These men elected a committee of twelve, who advised negotiation before military action, which they felt should be taken only as a last resort. Not wishing to be hampered by what was to him the undue cautiousness of the committee, Kieft dissolved it. The following February, he dispatched another regiment across the Harlem River at night to attack the Wiechquaeskeck, who lived in the Bronx, but the attack was scuttled when his soldiers got lost in the woods and retreated in confusion. Kieft had issued his warning, however, and that spring the Indians sued for peace. Despite their efforts at reconciliation, two more murders were committed the following summer, this time by the son of a Hackensack sachem. Again, Kieft demanded the murderers be handed over; again, he was refused. Events came to a head in February 1643. A band of eighty to ninety Mahican warriors from Fort Orange (Albany) — angry at not getting their annual tribute — attacked the Wiechquaeskeck, killing seventeen, torching their towns, and taking prisoners of women and children. Those who survived — nearly a thousand — sought protection from the Dutch, to whom they twice fled. But their "refuge" was to prove illusory: seeing his chance, Kieft gave his unofficial sanction to an expedition of eighty soldiers who took it in their hands to avenge the murders of the previous summer. On the night of February 25, they surprised the Indians in their sleep, slaughtering the hapless Wiechquaeskeck and Hackensack at Pavonia (in New Jersey) and Corlaer's Hook (in Manhattan). By the end of the night, 120 men, women, and children lay dead and mutilated. Patroon David de Vries described the massacre:

When it was day, the soldiers returned to the fort, having massacred or murdered eighty Indians, and considering they had done a deed of Roman valour, in murdering so many in their sleep; where infants were torn from their mother's breasts, and hacked to pieces in the presence of the parents, and the pieces thrown into the fire and in the water, and other sucklings, being bound to small boards, were cut, stuck and pierced, and miserably massacred in a manner to move a heart of stone. Some were thrown into the river, and when the fathers and mothers endeavored to save them, the soldiers would not let them come on land, but made both parents and children drown — children from five to six years of age, and also some old and decrepit persons. Those who fled from the onslaught, and concealed themselves in the neighboring sedge, and when it was morning, came out to beg a piece of bread, and to be permitted to warm themselves, were murdered in cold blood and tossed into the fire or the water. Some came to our people in the country with their hands, some with their legs cut off, and some holding their entrails in their arms, and others had such horrible cuts and gashes, that worse than they were could never happen.[21]

In revenge, all the natives of the region — having buried the hatchet with one another in order to ally themselves against the Dutch — killed as many farmers and burned as much of the settlers' holdings as they could, including de Vries's own "farm, cattle, corn, barn, tobacco-house, and all the tobacco." Roger Williams, who had come to New Amsterdam to take a ship back to England (after being exiled from the Massachusetts colony), described a holocaust: "Mine Eyes saw . . . flames at their Townes . . . and ye Flights and Hurries of Men, Women & Children." By the end of what came to be known as Kieft's War, nearly sixteen hundred Indians had lost their lives, and hundreds of colonists had lost their lives or farms. Among the dead were Anne Hutchinson and her family (like Roger Williams, banished from the Massachusetts colony), killed when her house near New Rochelle was attacked and burned. Her murderer, the war chief Wampage, took the name of Ann Hook to commemorate his deed.[22]

As a lawyer, Adriaen Van der Donck was impressed with the American Indian's sense of honor, both in respecting the "right of nations" and "the right of nature." His linking of these two "rights" reveals the essential differences between Europeans and Indians in their attitudes toward nature and land ethics. To the Indians, whom the Dutch called *Wilden,* or wild men, "the wind, rivers, woods, plains, sea, beaches, and banks . . . were open and freely accessible to every individual of all the nations with which they are not publicly engaged in quarrels. They may use these freely and enjoy these in as much freedom as though they were born there. They won't abuse or violate this freedom." How strange the Indian concept of nature must have appeared to a man who in the same report outlined the basis for the claim of the Netherlanders to the lands they possessed by right of first "discovery." From Van der Donck's point of view, the Netherlanders had done everything aboveboard, buying estates from the Indians and securing possession of lands through legal channels, so that "it is outright improper and unrighteous that any other nations should assume any right to, or jurisdiction over, these places or to those that are included in it — places that we Netherlanders first took into possession."[23]

Robert Grumet notes the Lenapes and Europeans shared "a number of surprisingly similar ideas about land." For example, the Lenape belief that clans held land in trust for their creator god Kishelmukong was similar to the European idea of "divine right," whereby land was held by their divinely ordained monarch; and the complex system of land transfer, by means of deeds and other documents, is paralleled by the Lenape system of "equally binding oral agreements."[24] While it is true that the concept of land trusts was hardly foreign to the Europeans — even today, the U.S. government holds many lands in a common trust — such similarities are superficial compared to the fundamental difference between the European concept of private property and the Indian concept of communal lands. It was this conceptual difference that undermined the "binding" nature of such agreements. And, as Grumet also notes, once the Lenapes caught on to European concepts of land transfer, they exploited that knowledge to their advantage by delaying sales, pointing would-be buyers to less desirable tracts or lands belonging to other tribes, and even challenging deeds in court.[25]

In most of the early Dutch colonial narratives, the natives are neither idealized as noble savages nor denigrated as subhuman "wild beasts." Rather they are referred to as "the people of the country." As a rule, the Dutch treated them as suited their purpose: first, to secure a monopoly of the fur trade in the region; and second, to secure land for settlement. As long as the Indians were willing to trade or sell, they were left alone, even tolerated — and it may be argued that the Dutch were the most tolerant among Europeans of the time, as indicated in a 1625 document instructing the provisional director Willem Verhulst to "see that no one do the Indians any harm or violence, deceive, mock, contemn them in any way, but that in addition to good treatment they be shown honesty, faithfulness, and sincerity in all contracts, dealings, and intercourse, without being deceived by shortage of measure, weight, or number, and that throughout friendly relations with them be maintained."[26] Unfortunately, the realities of their dealings with the Indians put shame to their ideals.

The greed that characterized the Europeans in their pursuit of land, trade, and profits, coupled with their shameful treatment of the Indians, was severely criticized by Jasper Danckaerts, a Labadist Christian minister who toured the Dutch and English North American colonies in 1679–1680, exploring the feasibility of establishing a religious colony. His journals give us a firsthand, unvarnished account of the colonists' dealings with the Indians. Although his portrayal of the Indians is somewhat idealized, it is worth noting for his comparison of the Indian concept of the commons with the European concept of private property.

Prior to the coming of the Europeans, he wrote, "everything was held in common: lands, fisheries, hunting grounds."[27] Lacking money or private property, the Indians knew neither theft nor avarice. To the charge of laziness, he answered: "And for whom would they have labored? For their children inherited nothing, nor could they inherit anything, because there was nothing but the ground and this was so immense and spacious that it would have been absurd to make oneself the owner of a small plot, and it was all free for them, and freer than a single plot." To support his conclusions about pre-Contact Indian morality, he points to the absence in the Algonquin language of words for theft, drunkenness, or deceit. To his way of thinking, the European import of the concept of private property corrupted the Indian way of life, ushering in a host of biblical sins. Indeed, European materialism was to Danckaerts the sin of civilization. Danckaerts attributed the tragic demise of the Indians to a process of demoralization and depopulation: "For they are melting away rapidly, whether it be because of war with one another, or whether it be because of sickness, especially the smallpox from which many occasionally die at the same time. . . . For I have heard tell by the oldest Netherlanders that there is now not 1/10th the part of the Indians there once were, indeed, not 1/20th or 1/30th; and that now the Europeans are 20 and 30 times as many."

Perhaps Danckaerts was simplistic in his analysis of Indian and European morality, and perhaps he was motivated by a biblical, even fanatical, sense of mission; nonetheless, the details of Indian lifeways and their clash with European ways speak for themselves. And one cannot deny the stark truth of his estimates of population decline among the Indians: conservative estimates of the Lenape population in 1600 range from eight thousand to twelve thousand, although recent studies double these figures; by 1700, the population was reduced to three thousand at most. Diseases — smallpox, malaria, measles, bubonic plague, and many others — unwittingly imported by the white man from the time of Contact took a terrible toll. Between 1633 and 1702, fourteen or more epidemics swept through the villages of the Lenape. Pastorius, in a letter of 1694, wrote: "A great many of these savages have died, even since I came here, so that there are hardly more than a fourth part of the number now existing that were to be seen when I came to the country ten years ago."[28]

Such killer epidemics exacted an even higher toll than the devastating loss of lives in the Lenape's ongoing wars with their enemies the Iroquois to the north and the Dutch to the south. And both together cost them nothing less than their faith in traditional healing practices, trust in the spiritual powers, and sense of security and stability as a people. With the loss of their elders who had been the historians and keepers of tradition, their culture unraveled. And as the Europeans pushed their land claims farther and farther into the American wilderness, the remnant Lenapes — weakened and demoralized by the continuing onslaught of diseases and wars throughout the seventeenth century — finally relinquished any claim to their traditional homeland. The loss of the homeland, Lenapehoking, was the most devastating blow of all, for the identity of the people had been bound up with the land for thousands of years. They now became exiles and wanderers, dependent upon the hospitality — and subject to the hostility — of other tribes. With the severing of their ancient bond to the land, the source of their visions dried up. In the words of a Delaware in the early nineteenth century, "No one can have visions because the earth is no longer clean."[29]

The ancient "people of the country" seem to have vanished, their former presence attested to in multisyllabic place names: Manhattan, Connecticut, Hackensack, Passaic, Weehawken, Mamaroneck, Neponsit, Massapequa, Ronkonkoma, Jamaica, Nesconsett, Syosett, Setauket, Rockaway, Canarsie. . . . Names linger like lost echoes, lost voices. Yet the vanishing is only a myth, and the loss is in fact ours. However fragmented the tribes and dispersed the peoples of the regions, whatever the borrowed strands interwoven into their folklore and religion, the culture and identity of the Native American persists.

Over a period of two hundred years, the Lenapes, now known as the Delaware, dispersed over the continent. By 1760, most Delawares had moved to Ohio. The few who remained were "nomads in their own land."[30] Some worked as servants and farm workers in European households, others as expert whalers, and still others as peddlers plying such wares as splint baskets and brooms. The Massapequa of western Long Island moved eastward to be absorbed into the Poosepatuck and Shinnecock tribes, now confined to reservations on the East End; in the nineteenth century they intermarried with newly freed African slaves.[31] Many of these "removes," or migrations, were forced by the United States government. They fled severe persecution and violence in the 1790s, as they were routed from the Ohio River Valley. Some found refuge in reserves at Moraviantown and Muncy in Ontario, Canada. Most moved west, as their people had repeatedly done since they had been pushed out of their original homeland. By the 1820s, many had settled in Indiana in what would later become the city of Muncie. Continual skirmishes with whites who also desired the fertile river-bottom lands came to a head when the U.S. government backed the white settlers in their land claims, using the Indian Removal Act of 1830 to force the Delaware to move farther west. Ultimately, most settled in the Indian Territory of Oklahoma, where they signed an agreement in 1867 with the Cherokee Nation to reside among them. Since 1989, the Delaware have numbered about thirteen thousand. Perhaps twenty speakers of the old language remain, but that may change as there has been a revival of interest in the old tongue, as well as an attempt to restore religious songs, dances, and ceremonies.[32]

6

Muddied Waters

Looking across the salt marsh of Jamaica Bay, I see the skyscrapers of Manhattan shimmering in the distance, their hard geometry juxtaposed against the soft muddy lines of tidal flats and wavy grasses. The city seems a world away, and a time apart. Dwarfing the Manhattan skyline, a snowy egret stalks its prey at the edge of the marsh, its head cocked, motionless. Here, a bird in the marsh reenacts an ancient scene; there, manmade towers rise like upstarts — hives of concrete and glass that serve as a human habitat.

Before cities were dreamed of, the New York archipelago was created when the last glacier receded, and a rising sea reclaimed the continental shelf. In the glacier's wake, the land slowly rebounded from the weight of the ice, and islands rose from the sea. Over the millennia, the ocean continued to encroach on the land, drowning the mouths of rivers like the Hudson, Connecticut, and Hackensack. The commingling of fresh and salt waters created estuaries, which are tidal rivers — geologically rare ecosystems that form only when sea level reaches a certain point. At high tide, the sea pushes upriver, and at low tide, the sea withdraws — hence the Lenape name given to the Lower Hudson, Mahicanituk, which eighteenth-century Mahican scholar Hendrick Apaumaut translated as "the great waters or sea, which are constantly in motion, either ebbing or flowing."[1] The word "estuary" is derived from the Latin word *aestus,* meaning tide. In the shallow waters of the estuaries, sediments eroded by tidal action are deposited along the shores, building mudflats where cordgrasses take root and grow into salt marshes. The estuaries, bays, and salt marshes of the New York City region have supported a diversity of species, including our own: hunter-gatherers settled along the waterways here, thriving for thousands of years on the abundance of plants and animals that shared their habitat, and gave them the food, shelter, fuel, clothing, and tools they needed.[2]

Hudson River historian Robert Boyle describes the Lower Hudson estuary as "a nutrient trap, a protein plant, a self-perpetuating fertilizer factory" fed by an array of minerals eroded from the land, enriched by the recycled remains of dead plants and animals, and stirred by tidal action. The brackish waters are inhabited by both fresh- and saltwater species of fish, including striped bass, alewives, and shad that swim upriver every spring to spawn; weakfish (sea trout) that spawn in the estuaries; summer flounders (fluke), and bluefish larvae and juveniles that feed in the estuaries in the summer months. Some shellfish — oyster, crab, and clam — spend their whole life cycles in the estuarine ecosystem, while others such as shrimp feed in estuaries during their larval stage.[3]

The salt marshes fringing the shores harbor a diversity of species. Blue crabs molt in the protected waters of salt marsh creeks, and the larvae of crustaceans and mollusks drift on their surface. Along creek banks, fiddler crabs burrow, excavating pellets of sand or mud with their super-sized claws. Little white marsh periwinkles graze on the algae that coats the lower stems of cordgrass, while fish such as menhaden and mullet forage on the decaying stalks. Salt marsh amphipods, tiny shrimplike creatures, emerge at night during low tide, scavenging for decayed plant and animal food; before daylight, they excavate little underground chambers above the high tide line, where they rest by day safe from feeding shorebirds. A host of insect species inhabit the marsh, including dragonflies, beetles, and a number of biting flies, much to the misery of those mammals whose blood females feed on. Throughout the salt marsh in summer months, the ubiquitous golden saltmarsh mosquito abounds, spending its larval stages in the shallow waters. Minnows — mummichog, killifish, stickleback, and sheepshead — feed on the abundant mosquito larvae.[4]

Intertidal sand and mud flats are inhabited by numerous tube-building worms and other burrowers. The ice cream cone worm (once called the trumpet worm, so-named because the wide end of the tube is flared) is one of the most skilled builders. It uses its feeding tentacles to carefully select sand grains of the same size, secreting mucous to cement the grains into a delicate cone house. At low tide you might see the tip of the inverted cone protruding above the wet sand or mud. The worm's pinkish body is splotched with blue and red, and its head sports a pair of red gills on either side. Most remarkable is a pair of golden combs that bristle below the mouth; the worm uses these like pitchforks to excavate the sand. The parchment worm is housed in a U-shaped tube that serves as a water tunnel through which it pumps water at high tide; the cast-off tubes of dead parchment worms may be found on the beach. Near the low tide line, tiny cratered mounds advertise the burrows of the 15-inch long amphitrites, or ornate worms (so-named for their reddish orange bodies and yellowish orange tentacles), which build foot-long tubes of sand or mud below the surface, through which they extend their tentacles to feed. Plumed worms encase themselves in leathery tubes, burrowing just below low tide line; they camouflage their exposed bodies with bits of shell and seaweed — hence its old name of decorator worm.[5]

Mollusks and crustaceans also find safe harbor between tides by burrowing into the wet sand. Ribbed mussels anchor themselves halfway down, while quahog, soft-shell, and razor clams slip deep beneath the surface, breathing through their siphons. When alarmed, the soft-shell clam squirts a jet of water through its siphon. Ghost shrimp (so-named for their colorless, translucent exoskeletons) tunnel several feet down, their pinpoint entrance holes surrounded by pellets.[6]

In the sandy shallows of the bays, winter flounders camouflage themselves, their flattened oval bodies resting on the bottom, their two eyes protruding on their skyward-facing side like a face in a Picasso painting. A hermit crab scavenges for food on shelly bottoms, housing itself in a cast-off snail shell; its elongated tail places it closer to lobsters than to true crabs. Purple

Fig. 6.1. Clam shell in tidal sand flat. (Photo by Betsy McCully.)

sea urchins make their way slowly across the debris by means of suction-cupped feet. Their bristly spines protect them from the predatory mantis shrimp, which lurks just beneath the surface, ready to slash its prey with its spiny, scythelike claw.[7]

All this abundance of aquatic life provides food for other animals: muskrats dine on shellfish and grasses, raccoons dig for clams, otters swim in the creeks, turtles such as the diamondback terrapin forage for worms and mollusks, and numerous birds — migrants on the Atlantic flyway as well as year-round residents — feed, mate, and nest in these waters. Waders stalk their prey in marshy shallows and mud flats. The usually nocturnal black-crowned night heron may hunt by day for minnows and killifish in the shallows, while the great blue heron seeks out amphibians, reptiles, fish, and small rodents along the perimeters of salt marsh pools. The glossy ibis probes its long, down-curved bill into the muds in search of crustaceans, perhaps closely followed by a snowy egret who dines on what the ibis has dredged up. Secreted in the spartina grass, the diminutive sharp-tailed sparrow snacks on amphipods, and the elusive clapper rail, more easily heard than seen, feeds on snails, worms, and crabs. Audubon wrote about this rail: "They have a power of stretching their body to such a degree as frequently to force a passage between two stems so close that one could hardly believe it possible for them to squeeze themselves through." Patrolling overhead, a marsh harrier seeks out its prey of mice and voles, snakes and frogs.[8]

The myriad creatures who inhabit the estuaries have adapted over the millennia to the extreme fluctuations in their environment — from variations in saltiness of the seawater to oscillations in wet and dry, cold and hot conditions. They have devised a number of ways to accomplish this: they may burrow, close their shells, or even alter their body chemistry. Catastrophic changes, however, may cause massive die-offs. The change can be a result of a natural process, such as floodwaters that dilute the salinity of an estuary to such a degree as to decimate marine life. After each flood, the ecosystem reverts to normal conditions, and life returns. Human-caused changes, on the other hand, may render the ecosystem lifeless. All organisms need oxygen, and if pollution triggers a catastrophic decline in oxygen level in the waters, the animals suffocate. Such was the case in Long Island Sound in 1987, as described by Tom Anderson: "Vast blooms of algae had turned the Sound an opaque reddish-brown, oxygen levels were pushing down to zero, toxic hydrogen sulfide was being loosed from the sediments, and fish and lobsters were dying in uncounted numbers." Our wholesale destruction of estuaries and marshes shrinks the available habitat on which the animals depend for part or all of their life cycles.[9]

When the Europeans began settling these shores beginning in the early 1600s, they found an abundance of marine life that astonished them. Seventeenth-century Dutch and English chronicles are replete with superlatives about the size and numbers of animals. Perhaps they exaggerated, but to Europeans whose fisheries had been depleted, American waters in contrast teemed with astounding numbers of fish. Because they had not been overharvested, American fish appeared super-sized. Juet, an officer on Hudson's ship *Half Moon*, wrote in his log that the men caught mullet "a foot and a half long a peace, and a Ray as great as foure men could hale into the ship." In spring, fish were so plentiful in the rivers, it was said, that a man could walk across the river on their backs. Dutch colonist David de Vries described fish swimming up-river to spawn by the hundreds of thousands — alewives, sturgeon, shad, and striped bass among them. English colonist William Wood described ale-wives "in such multitudes as is almost incredible pressing up such shallow waters as will scarce permit them to swim." Dutch traveler Jaspar Danckaerts and colonist Adriaen Van der Donck both described oysters as long as a foot, Van der Donck noting that these were best for roasting, while the smaller ones were excellent raw. The Dutch were familiar with only ten species of fish, so when they encountered unfamiliar species, they resorted to number-ing them: shad was *elft*, striped bass was *twalft*, drum was *dertienen*, and so on, the numbers indicating the order of their seasonal appearances.[10]

All this wonderful abundance was threatened as soon as the Europeans began to colonize the region. The great wetlands that were prime habitat for waterfowl and nurseries for all kinds of fish and shellfish yielded to their hands. The colonists aggressively drained them to create cropland and pasture, polluted them with sewage, rendered them stagnant by blocking stream outlets, and filled them to support roads and buildings.

When the Dutch first encountered the marshy tracts of New Netherland they were undaunted, seeing them as amenable to their hands. In fact, they were reminded of home, where most of the Netherlands was below sea level

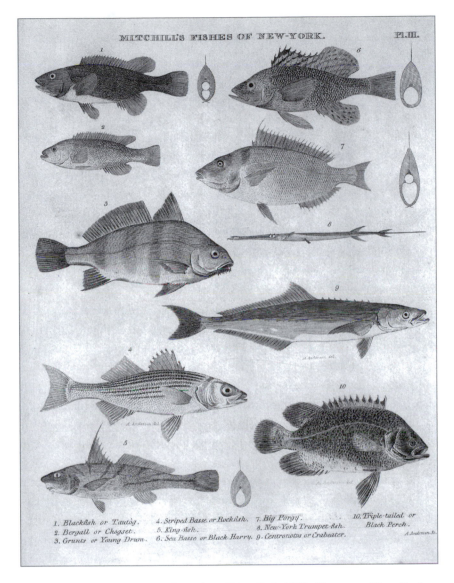

1. *Blackfish or Tautog*.   4. *Striped Basse or Rockfish*.   7. *Big Porgy*.   10. *Triple-tailed or*
2. *Bergall or Chogset*.   5. *King-fish*.   8. *New-York Trumpet-fish*.   *Black Perch*.
3. *Grunts or Young Drum*.   6. *Sea Basse or Black Harry*.   9. *Centronotus or Crabeater*.

Fig. 6.2. Samuel L. Mitchill, *The Fishes of New York*, 1815. (Courtesy of Rare Books Division, The New York Public Library, Astor, Lenox and Tilden Foundations. Image #412984.)

and had been reclaimed from the sea. Van der Donck, surveying the lands of the new colony, could see only potential pasturage and cropland:

> Near the rivers and water sides there are large extensive plains containing several hundred morgens [a morgen is about two acres] . . . which are very convenient for plantations, villages and towns. There also are brook lands and fresh and salt meadows; some so extensive that the eye cannot oversee the same. Those are good for pasturage and hay, although the same are overflowed by the spring tides, particularly near the seaboard. These meadows resemble the lows and outlands of the Netherlands. Most of them could be dyked and cultivated. We also find meadow grounds far inland, which are all fresh and make good hayland. Where the meadows are boggy and wet, such failings are easily remedied by cutting and breaking the bogs in winter and letting off the water in the spring.[11]

The Dutch invention of the wipmolen, or the wind-powered mills that pumped water from wetlands and peat bogs, had enabled Dutch farmers of the seventeenth century to convert large tracts of hitherto unusable land into arable land, pasturage, and urban estates. The Dutch were renowned for their skills in land reclamation and were employed throughout Europe wherever marsh drainage or flood control was needed. In 1630s England, for example, Dutch engineers and workers were employed on drainage projects when the enclosure movement—whereby hitherto public fens or wetlands were privatized and fenced—was well underway.[12]

From the European viewpoint, undomesticated land was wasteland and ill-used. To justify the fen enclosure movement in seventeenth-century England, for example, advocates of drainage and enclosure depicted the fens as "barren and unprofitable," and the fenmen as "a kind of people according to the nature of the place where they dwell rude, uncivil, and envious to all others whom they call Uplandmen."[13] They characterized the fens as places of disease, in contrast to the healthfulness of drained land. The Europeans carried over this attitude to the New World. Isaac de Rasieres, in a letter to Samuel Blommaert in 1626, described the wetlands he found along the East River as having "a great deal of waste reedy land."[14] Jared Eliot, in his *Essays upon Field Husbandry in New England, 1748–1762*, urged his fellow farmers to drain and ditch, because marshy ground was not to be tolerated. He viewed swamps as "frog-ponds," and described them as "ulcers or sores in a man's face," spoiling the "beauty of a field." He described his own methods of converting a low-lying swamp into salt meadow for hay by ditching, his draining of a pond to convert it into pasture of twenty acres, and draining of a forty-acre cranberry bog, which he called a "shaking meadow." He mowed five times a year so as to prevent woody plants like elder bushes from spreading their roots and clogging his drains and ditches. In his pasture he sowed clover and grasses, and in his newly drained cropland he planted maize, flax, barley, Cape-Breton wheat, cotton, indigo seed, licorice roots, and dye woods.[15]

Shellfish that once thrived in New York's waterways were soon threatened by overharvesting and pollution. Oysters in the 1700s were still plentiful in New York waters, but old-timers complained of their diminishment. On the south shore of Long Island, Peter Kalm found an abundance of oysters, crabs, and lobsters. "When the tide is out, it is very easy to fill a whole cart with oysters, which have been driven on shore by one flood. The island is strewn with oyster shells and other shells which the Indians left there; these shells serve now for good manure in the fields."[16] Oysters were highly valued,

Fig. 6.3. Salt marsh, South Shore of Long Island. (Photo by Betsy McCully.)

and a considerable industry grew around harvesting and pickling them for export. The shells were "gathered in great heaps, and burnt into a lime" that served as fertilizer in wheat fields, and in building houses. In colonial times, huge oyster beds extended up the Hudson to Croton Point, and according to an 1839 account, the annual harvest was a good million and a half bushels. Oysters were similarly abundant in the Newark and Raritan Bays of New Jersey; Arthur Kill and Kill Van Kull between Jersey and Staten Island; the Gowanus Canal (originally a creek) and Gravesend Bay in Brooklyn; Flushing Bay in Queens; and Long Island Sound. Such overharvesting was soon to lead to the extirpation of the oysters: by the mid-nineteenth century, wild oysters were gone from New York waters, and oystermen had to seed the old nurseries with domesticated oysters — a practice that temporarily revived the oyster industry — but eventually these too would diminish, unable to thrive in increasingly polluted waters. According to a report in the *New York Times* on May 27, 1877, "the oystermen say that all that they can rake up . . . is from four to eight inches of stinking garbage, and that every oyster, seedling and all, has been killed. The fishing, too, which was formerly excellent, has been irreparably destroyed." By 1900, oysters could be found only south of the Narrows; by 1920, they had disappeared from New York harbor. Outbreaks of typhoid traced to the consumption of New York oysters led to a ban on commercial oyster harvesting in New York waters by 1921, a ban that still holds today. A similar ban on clams was imposed in 1916.[17]

The scale of pollution in New York waterways during the nineteenth and twentieth centuries was staggering. In 1885, pollution of New York waterways by raw sewage had become so critical that the New York State legislature was compelled to pass an act giving the State Board of Health "power to protect from contamination, by suitable regulations, the water supply of the State and their sources." The New York Bay Pollution Commission was established to study the problem, issuing several reports, followed by the Metropolitan Sewerage Commission, which documented the extent of pollution in a series of reports published in 1910, 1912, and 1914. Crude sewage from a population of six million was being discharged into the waters with no purification or regulation, they charged, and New York had the dubious honor of standing alone among the great cities in its failure to provide a sewage treatment and disposal program. A 1929 study by the Regional Plan Association reported that the regional population of ten million were dumping over a billion gallons a day of raw sewage into the waters, reducing the oxygen content as much as 68 percent between 1914 and 1926. In some of the worst places, such as the Harlem River, oxygen had fallen to zero percent, a condition known as anoxia. Dissolved oxygen is critical to marine life; to maintain healthy populations, a minimum of four to five milligrams of dissolved oxygen in a liter of water is required. Bacteria that feed on decomposing matter like sewage use up oxygen; as dissolved oxygen levels fall (a condition known as hypoxia), marine animals die from suffocation, and as these dead animals decompose, more oxygen is depleted until it falls to zero percent.[18] Pollution of the bays and beaches was so bad as to warrant closing the beaches and prohibition against swimming in 1927. Fecal matter polluted the beaches of City Island and Pelham Bay; the Harlem and East rivers, Newtown and Coney Island creeks, and the Gowanus Canal had become cesspools. People were dying of typhoid and dysentery because of eating contaminated shellfish or bathing in the waters; massive fish kills covered the bays. New York had truly become, as a Public Health Committee report declared, "a body of land entirely surrounded by sewerage."[19]

While raw sewage had long posed a threat to the waters of New York, chemical effluents were added to the toxic stew as the region became more and more industrialized. Petroleum refineries and chemical plants were clustered along tidal creeks and rivers, discharging their wastes into the waters. The 1881 issue of *The Sanitarian* exposed the sources of "stenches" emanating from Hunter's Point, across the East River from Manhattan. Here, along a mile and a half stretch of Newtown Creek, an assortment of industries had become concentrated: petroleum refineries; kerosene, ammonia, potash, superphosphate, and cream of tartar works; and traditional "nuisance" industries like tanneries and bone-boiling establishments. The report describes "the hundreds of acres of marsh saturated with the drainage and soakage of filth," and the slime-coated banks of Newtown Creek. This tidal creek, which once meandered through an extensive salt marsh, had now become a toxic cesspool that threatened the health and lives of those, especially children, who lived near it. Despite proclamations by the governor, the practice continued: forty-six years later, the Regional Plan Association found Newtown Creek, Coney Island Creek, and the Gowanus Canal still being used illegally as reservoirs of chemical effluvia.[20]

In the first study of Hudson River water quality, conducted by the U.S. Public Health Service in 1933, the percentage of oxygen in the waters below Albany had dropped to zero. Industries that had sprung up along the river between Albany and Troy included a number of paper mills, two steel mills, a drug company, a chemical company, a textile company, an auto manufacturing plant, a cement plant, and oil storage facilities. Industrial wastes combined with commercial and domestic wastes — a total of 50 million gallons of untreated wastes — were discharged into the river daily, polluting the waters upstream and down. No longer confined to the New York metropolitan region, the problem now concerned the whole watershed.[21]

Dumping, both legal and illegal, also poisoned the waters. In the late nineteenth century, nearly all the refuse produced by the city was dumped directly into the sea a mere 16¾ miles from Long Island's south shore and 21 miles from the Jersey shore — and that was only the legal dumping. Private contractors for beachfront hotels and industries illegally dumped far more: "The Defilements of New York Harbor" were reported in 1880 by a concerned doctor, who declared that even when dumped thirty miles out, the garbage floated back to the shore, carried by tides and prevailing winds. The year before, *Harper's Weekly* had reported on their undercover investigation of illegal offshore dumping, with "barge after barge" going out under cover of darkness and dumping offal and animal matter, which with the incoming tide left the surface of the sea off Coney Island covered with "putrid slime." Landfill had long been the city's favored solution to garbage disposal, and marshes were used as the dumping grounds. Egbert Viele, sanitation engineer in the mid-nineteenth century, noted that landfill blocked Manhattan's natural drainage system, creating large areas of stagnant water and saturated ground that mixed with noxious wastes, giving off "poisonous exhalations." Echoing Viele, an 1883 *New York Times* editorial condemned the city for the practice, which created a "subterranean source of disease and death."[22]

Presaging the massive oil spills of the 1980s, oil began to spread its deadly slick over the waters in the late nineteenth century. Oil was discharged from steamers into the bay, and oil run-off from garages and street surfaces drained directly into the bay, poisoning thousands of shellfish and waterfowl. Not until the passage of the 1888 New York Harbor Act, and the River and Harbor Act of 1899, was such discharging prohibited. But this did little to prevent accidental oil spills or the flaunting of the law. The New York State Conservation Law of 1911 prohibited the pollution of streams by oil refineries, but the prohibition was largely ignored, as indicated by a 1926 report by a state legislative committee that decried the killing by oil of "great quantities of fish and thousands of wild fowl which the state has been trying to conserve." That same year, an International Conference on Oil Pollution was convened in Washington, D.C., with thirteen nations participating; they agreed to prohibit oil discharge into waters within 50 to 150 miles of shore. Still, oil pollution continued to threaten New York waterways. As noted by the Regional Plan Committee, "government regulation alone cannot remedy conditions unless public sentiment is ready to demand a strict enforcement of the necessary laws."[23]

In 1903, the city attempted to tackle the problem of sewage, beginning with the formation of a Sewerage Commission in 1903 and the undertaking of a number of scientific studies of water quality in the region. Sewage plants previously built on Coney Island in 1887 and at Sheepshead Bay in 1891 served as models of how to treat sewage by chemical precipitation. According to this method, after screening the sewage to filter out large particles and debris, lime and perchloride of iron were added to sewage in settling tanks, the sludge was disinfected and deodorized by chlorine, and the effluent was discharged into saltwater. The Sewerage Commission proposed a sewage treatment plan based on the Coney Island and Sheepshead Bay models; this plan was implemented in 1920. By 1927, the Jamaica Bay plant was built, followed by three more plants by 1952. In Norwalk, Connecticut, a sewage treatment facility was built in 1931 using a similar method of chemical precipitation. In 1937, New York City completed its state-of-the-art Ward's Island Treatment Works at Hell Gate, adding an improvement to the method. Instead of discharging the disinfected effluent directly into New York waters, the facility releases the wastewater into an aerating tank that contains a little sludge, where aerobic microorganisms consume most of the remaining organic particles before the wastewater is finally discharged into Long Island Sound. The Ward's Island facility was designed to handle one-sixth of the city's sewage, 180 million gallons a day piped in from Manhattan and the Bronx.[24]

The results of modern sewage treatment in restoring the health of the region's waterways were dramatic. After a sewage treatment plant began operating in 1958 at New Jersey's Raritan Bay, for instance, invertebrate species increased from 6 to 20 within a year. By 1974, the number of species in Raritan Bay and Sandy Hook had increased to 78, although mollusks remained low, a mere 4 species. Compare this number to the 24 mollusk species inventoried the same year in the cleaner waters of Buzzard's Bay and Fisher's Island Sound. In the Mullica River/Great Bay estuary of New Jersey, where the waters were relatively pollution-free, bottom-dwelling invertebrate species numbered 143 species, including 35 mollusk species.[25]

The problem of stopping industrial pollution was more intractable, no doubt due to the power of the industrial purse. Industries continued to flaunt the laws long into the twentieth century, and report after report attested to massive fish kills traced to oil and chemical pollution in the watershed and tidal waterways. In addition, power plants such as the Indian Point nuclear power plant in Buchanan, New York, just twenty-four miles north of New York City on the Hudson, killed millions of fish by sucking them into their turbines and by literally cooking them in heated discharge water. According to Riverkeeper, an environmental watchdog organization, in 1977 the Indian Point nuclear power plant killed 2,215,890 fish — and this figure does not take into account the billions of fish eggs and larvae that were destroyed. Industries were also dumping into the river carcinogenic chemicals such as PCBs, which are polychlorinated biphenyls manufactured since 1929 by Monsanto for industrial uses. While not killing fish outright, PCBs accumulate in the fatty tissue of fish and eventually find their way into the human diet. In 1973, GE admitted to dumping an average of thirty and as much as ninety pounds a day of PCBs into the Hudson at Fort Edward and Hudson Falls forty miles north of Troy, New York, since 1942. In the 1970s, fishermen, environmentalists, and concerned citizens began to organize to clean up the Hudson. The coalition, known as Riverkeeper, aggressively prosecuted GE, Con Ed, and other industries (nearly a hundred) for polluting the Hudson River. Their prosecuting attorney, Robert F. Kennedy, Jr., utilized the nearly forgotten New York Harbor Act of 1888 that had been passed to stop the discharge of oil and other chemicals into New York waterways, as well as the National Environmental Policy Act of 1969. The prosecution argued that the Hudson River belonged to the people as a common natural resource, and not to the industries to pollute at will. Industries should be held liable for their willful pollution of the river. As Hudson River historian Robert Boyle said of the fight against the polluters, "We felt we owned the Hudson. For most of us the Hudson was the largest thing we ever hoped to own. We would be simpletons or fools if we allowed someone to take it from us. If someone pulled a truck up to your backyard and unloaded a tanker full of PCBs, you would sue them. What on earth would stop us from protecting our rights in the river with equal vigor?"[26] Riverkeeper won case after case. Out of the settlement with GE in 1976 came $7 million earmarked for environmental research. Similarly, a 1981 settlement with Con Ed, in which the company's plan to build a new power plant at Storm King was defeated, resulted in $12 million for environmental research, to be administered by the Hudson River Foundation.[27]

The National Environmental Policy Act of 1969 and the subsequent Clean Water Act of 1972 — the first such legislation mandating national environmental standards — resulted in a string of prosecutions and host of regulations that began to reverse the damage done to our regional waters by centuries of pollution. Species that had declined or disappeared, including the striped bass and shad, made a comeback, and today there are plans to restock the Atlantic salmon in the Connecticut River. The Hudson now teems with 209 species of fish, and its spawning stock is intact. The turnaround of the Hudson appears to be an environmental success story.

Unfortunately, things are not so simple. Recently, PCBs have been found in the bottom sediments of the river as well as in the tissue of bald eagles — clear evidence that it is still in the ecosystem. The Comprehensive Environmental Response, Compensation, and Liability Act of 1980 (also known as the Superfund Act) requires industries to clean up their toxic waste disposal sites at their own expense. While some industries have complied, others have dragged their feet in hopes of overturning the laws. GE, for example, is one of the biggest polluters with seventy-nine Superfund sites, nineteen of which it has so far cleaned up. The company erroneously claims that PCBs are not as toxic as once thought, and in any case, break down over time. The EPA and industry scientists haggle over how best to clean up the residues that coat the bottom of the Hudson. Meanwhile, antienvironmental legislators have worked with industry lobbyists to eviscerate if not overturn environmental laws. As recounted in the book *Riverkeepers*, by John Cronin and Robert F. Kennedy, Jr., Speaker of the House Newt Gingrich, Majority Whip Tom Delay, and other antienvironmental Republicans of the 104th Congress, voted into office in 1995, attempted to dismantle the suite of federal environmental regulations. They rewrote the Superfund Act, for instance, to shift the costs of clean-up from the responsible industries to the taxpayers. They proposed legislation to seriously weaken the Clean Water Act, earning the proposal the nickname of Dirty Water Bill. In all, they attached seventeen antienvironmental riders to the bill to renew funding for the Environmental Protection Agency. Environmentalist groups like Riverkeeper rallied to successfully block the reactionary legislation, mobilizing Congress to resoundingly defeat the legislation. But the onslaught on federal and state environmental regulations continues under the two administrations of George W. Bush.[28]

The persistence of toxins like PCB's in New York waterways is attested to by a warning jointly posted in 2004 by the New York State Department of Health and Department of Environmental Conservation. The warning gives guidelines on consuming locally caught fish. From the Lower Hudson to the Upper Bay, American eel, Atlantic needlefish, bluefish, carp, goldfish, large and small-mouthed bass, rainbow smelt, striped bass, walleye, white catfish and white perch should not be eaten more than once a month; from the Lower Bay and other marine waters of the region, striped bass, eel, and bluefish should be consumed no more than once a week — and not at all by children under fifteen or women of childbearing age.[29]

Where are the chemicals coming from? In addition to continued illegal discharging of chemical effluents into the waters by irresponsible industries, there are several other sources. Chemicals from landfills and toxic dump sites, even those that have been capped, continue to leach into groundwater and tidal streams. Sludge (what's left over after sewage treatment) was for decades legally dumped into the bay and offshore waters. Tankers of sludge used to be ferried twelve miles offshore and dumped into the Atlantic, creating dead zones in New York and New Jersey waters. The drowned Hudson River Canyon, known as the "Mud Hole" to fishermen, was one such dump site. Dumping of dredgings, industrial wastes, and sewage sludge into the New York Bight Apex (coastal waters within twenty-five miles of New York Harbor's mouth) was common practice since before the early 1900s, as previously noted, until dumping in the New York Bight was prohibited in 1988. At that point, dumping was simply moved into deeper waters, 106 miles out, at the edge of the continental shelf. Not until 1991 was all ocean dumping prohibited. Now the problem is what to do to cap the ocean dumping sites so that toxic chemicals and heavy metals do not continue leaching into the waters. What to do with the treated sludge, now called "biosolids," is a controversial question. Fertilizer pellets made from treated sludge can and have been applied to agricultural land, for example, but even low concentrations of heavy metals are a concern. De-watered sludge can and has been incinerated or placed in landfills, but leaching and air pollution are a concern. The removal of water from sludge to produce the sludge "cake," or biosolid, poses the problem of wastewater disposal. The water that has been removed contains a high amount of nitrogen, which when discharged into the waterways creates huge algal blooms as the algae feed on the nitrogen. As the algae die and sink to the bottom, aerobic bacteria feeding on the algae use up oxygen.[30] Normally, algal blooms provide essential nutrients for young fish and larval shellfish who feed in the estuaries. But the explosive growth of human population along these shores in the last century has produced excessive amounts of nitrogen in the ecosystem. One source is acid rain, produced by auto exhaust and coal-fired plants that spew nitrogen into the air; in the New York metropolitan region alone, automobiles release into the atmosphere 200,000 tons of nitrogen a year. The largest source of nitrogen in the waterways is from wastewater. Tom Anderson cites statistics on spiking nitrogen levels in Long Island Sound: "Four centuries of increasing development and population had swollen the Sound's burden of nitrogen to 91,000 tons a year, a 128 percent increase over the estimated 40,000 tons that flowed to the Sound before European settlement. The additional 51,300 tons of nitrogen included 29,600 tons from sewage plants and factories, and 8,800 tons from storm water run-off." As of 2002, 1.047 billion gallons of wastewater from eighty-six sewage treatment facilities are discharged daily into Long Island Sound and its tributaries, releasing tons of nitrogen.[31]

Commercial, domestic, and industrial pollution have all taken their toll on the waters and species that have made their homes here for millennia. Added to these stresses are the twin impacts of overharvesting and habitat destruction. To cite one example, one old trapper and his son caught nearly eight hundred muskrats in the Jamaica Bay marshes in 1980, but only thirty-five in 1997. The decline could be attributed to two causes: overharvesting on the part of the trappers, and habitat destruction by the building of John F. Kennedy airport and other developments that encroached on the marshes. In the mid-twentieth century, the Hudson Canyon Mud Hole had been abundant with bluefish, black fish, porgy, cod, and striped and sea bass. Blue-fin tuna once migrated by the thousands every spring from the waters off Spain, Portugal, and France into the New York Bight. Fishermen thrilled to the sight of the tuna's muscular bodies slicing the surface of the water. Commercial fishermen harvested fish by means of drag nets hauled by fifty-foot boats. In the sixties, the advent of a new technology enabled huge trawlers equipped with cameras and sonar to haul up tons of fish at a time. Over the decades, this method of fishing has depleted the old fishing ground — and put the old family-owned dragger boats out of business. Cod, porgy, weakfish, blackfish, and tuna have all been decimated.[32] As noted by John Waldman, "Jamaica Bay once supported forty full-time dragger vessels that fished offshore"; now, they have been reduced to two.[33]

The passage of the federal Clean Water Act of 1972 led to dramatic clean-up of the waters surrounding New York City and helped to restore estuaries as prime habitats for a myriad of animals. Oil spills, such as the Exxon oil spill that saturated the waters and marshes of Arthur Kill in 1990, continue to threaten these waters. Other restoration and conservation efforts are now under-way to save and protect the estuaries and regional wetlands, given impetus — and funds — by the landmark Clean Water/Clean Air Bond Act of New York that was passed in 1997. For example, the Long Island South Shore Estuary Plan and Estuary Reserve Act protects thirty coastal fish and wildlife habitats between the New York City/Nassau County line and Southhampton. A coalition of environmental, business, industrial, and community leaders are implementing a plan to reduce nitrogen levels in Long Island Sound 58.5 percent over the next fifteen years.[34]

Fish and shellfish need clean estuaries and wetlands as nurseries for their young. But anadromous fish require unobstructed waterways so they may swim upstream every year to spawn. Anadromous fish begin their lives in freshwater, migrate to saltwater as adults, then return to freshwater to spawn. Since colonial times, naturalists like Peter Kalm noted how dams blocked fish from swimming upstream during their spring runs. Alewives, for in-stance, once migrated upstream by the hundreds of thousands, an event that marked the Lenapes' planting time. Now they had disappeared. Old hunters claimed that "in their youth, the bays, rivers, and brooks, had such quanti-ties of fish, that at one draught in the morning, they caught as many as a horse was able to carry home. But at present things are greatly altered; and they often work in vain all the night long, with all their fishing tackle."[35] Re-cently, the U.S. Fish and Wildlife Service has been working in partnership with a number of public and private agencies under the rubric of SNEP

(Southern New England–New York Bight Coastal Ecosystems Program) to restore populations of anadromous fish such as alewives, blueback herring, and salmon. SNEP has constructed fish ladders, or fishways, on rivers in Connecticut and Long Island. A dramatic result has been the return of alewives to spawn in Long Island waterways in the spring of 2000, the first season since the colonial era.

After centuries of degrading New York's estuaries and decimating the species that had thrived here for millennia, efforts to restore the region's marine ecosystems are long overdue.

The New Jersey Meadowlands was once a vast sea of grasses that covered 19,730 acres along the lower Hackensack and Passaic rivers. Comprised of salt, brackish, and fresh marshes, and harboring an extensive Atlantic white cedar forest, the ecosystem supported thousands of species, including human hunter-gatherers who harvested shellfish and hunted birds and small game. When the European settlers arrived, they used the Meadowlands in much the same way the Lenapes did, as a rich source of wild animal foods. But there was an essential difference: they privatized the Meadowlands, cutting it up into narrow plots that the owners harvested for salt hay to feed and bed their domestic livestock. To demarcate lots, they dug six-foot-wide and two-foot-deep ditches. This practice continued into the early twentieth century. They also harvested white cedars for the valuable wood, deforesting it by the late 1890s.[36]

Construction projects beginning in the seventeenth century altered the Meadowlands' ecosystem by changing the salinity of the estuary. Since the end of the ice age, a rising sea had gradually made the wetlands more brackish (indeed, as noted before, it created the estuary), but human alterations to the land significantly increased the salinity. Colonists constructed dams on the Passaic and Hackensack rivers to create mill ponds as early as the late 1600s, which reduced the flow of freshwater through the wetlands. From the mid-nineteenth century onward, the Passaic and Hackensack rivers and their tributaries were dammed and pumped, their water diverted into reservoirs that served as municipal water sources. These rivers were also dredged beginning in the late nineteenth century in order to deepen the channels for shipping traffic, a practice that let in more saltwater.

The Meadowlands were also drained in the nineteenth century to create farmland, and by the twentieth century, industrial sites. Geologists who surveyed the area in the late 1800s cited the successful examples set by the

Dutch and the English in reclaiming wetlands for agricultural use. Such land-reclamation efforts in the Meadowlands became more aggressive when engineers began to create uplands from landfill in the first decades of the twentieth century. As the urban population of the New York metropolitan region exploded, the Meadowlands became a convenient site to dump the city's waste. The landfill was composed of a mix of river channel dredgings, rubble from construction sites, and garbage.

By the mid-twentieth century, the Meadowlands had become a dumping ground for toxic waste and garbage — and, as rumors have it, the occasional corpse. In 1957, private contractors replaced New York City garbage collectors to haul commercial waste. A number of these trash collectors operated illegally, dumping toxic waste under cover of darkness. By then, a major turnpike system had been built through the Meadowlands, giving easy access for these "midnight dumpers" to do their dirty work. The dumping became so frequent and flagrant that state officials (not to mention outraged residents) could no longer ignore it. In 1968, they formed the Hackensack Meadowlands Development commission, a state agency designed to centralize control over the region and direct its development. They banned illegal dumping, but irreparable environmental damage had already been done. Today, sixteen hundred acres are landfill, and mercury has leached into its channels and creek beds. Clean-up efforts began in the 1970s, when developers and environmental groups reached a compromise. The Hackensack Meadowlands Development Commission changed its name to the Hackensack Meadowlands Conservation and Development Commission in 1969, and requested developers to restore portions of the wetland in exchange for developing other parts of it. The Meadowlands sports complex was built in 1974 on 750 acres of the wetlands, and permits for filling and developing thirty-two additional acres were granted by the Army Corps of Engineers between 1977 and 1997. In 1982, the DeKorte Environmental Center was opened as a restored wetland habitat on the site of a former landfill. As of 2005, according to Susan Bass Levin, chair of the New Jersey Meadowlands Commission, the plan is to restore eighty-four hundred acres of the wetlands ecosystem. The original Meadowlands covered forty-two square miles, now reduced to thirteen.[37]

Some environmentalists see development as inevitable and compromise as necessary if we are to preserve and restore at least some of the wetlands.

Others are not so sanguine, viewing the compromise as a deal with the devil. They raise concerns about setting a precedent that would overturn the first Bush administration's policy that mandated no net loss of wetlands. But there is hope: despite development, the number of bird species in the Meadowlands has increased by over 25 percent in the past two decades, largely due to clean-up efforts by the Hackensack Development Commission working in cooperation with the New Jersey Audubon Society.[38]

The rivers will never be so crowded with fish that one can walk across them on their backs, but one can celebrate the return of once-threatened species, and the restoration of once-polluted wetlands and estuaries, however fragmentary.

7

Footprints

On a humid late summer day, I stand in a trash-strewn parking lot gazing across a steel mesh fence to see a remnant of the only extensive prairie east of the Alleghenies. Once covering sixty thousand acres on western Long Island, what's left of the Hempstead Plains is now surrounded by concrete fields of malls and highways. As cumulus clouds scud swiftly overhead and dark skies threaten a thunderstorm, I am reminded of the unmowed fields of my midwestern childhood. I would gather wildflowers for a bouquet to bring my mother. Chicory's blue flowers beckoned me to pick them and yielded their aniselike scent when I broke off the stem. The caps of Queen Anne's lace, like giant snowflakes, invited me to stroke their soft, tiny flowers. The assertive colors of black-eyed Susans added sparks of gold to the bouquet. Happily, I brought them all home to place in a vase of water. I did not know then, nor did I care, that some of those flowers had not always grown there, but were instead brought by pioneers who wished to re-create the fields of their childhoods. I delight in what has been preserved of the original Hempstead Plains, but mourn the loss of what was once a vast grassland.

The field where I stand is an eighteen-acre parcel just south of Nassau Community College, saved from development by the Nature Conservancy and lovingly maintained by the Friends of Hempstead Plains, now under the management of Betsy Gulotta. Two other parcels on the eastern edge of Mitchel Field, encompassing part of the Meadowbrook Stream valley, bring the total of preserved prairie to a mere sixty-two acres. The original prairie established itself on glacial outwash after the ice sheet retreated from the region, and was a climax ecosystem — that is, one that evolved over millennia to reach its present grassland state. Prairie grasses have deep, extensive root systems that create a thick sod almost impenetrable to woody plants; however, trees and shrubs would eventually invade the grassland if not for periodic wildfires. These lightning-set fires kill the trees, but the burned grasses are able to regenerate by sending up new green shoots from their roots. Grazing by wild animals such as deer, elk, and bison also keeps down volunteer seedlings of trees and shrubs; in addition, grazing stimulates grasses to grow, much like mowing. Of course, overgrazing by domestic animals will eventually erode a grassland.[1]

When we think of a prairie, we think of grasses, but wildflowers add their colors to the floral tapestry. In the Hempstead Plains preserves, you can still see patches of native wildflowers. The lovely bird's-foot violet (*Viola pedata*), a species once believed to have disappeared from the region, blooms in spring. Its deeply dissected five-part leaves may remind you of a bird's foot. Another spring bloomer is the fringed violet (*Viola fimbriatula*), with blue flowers and spade-shaped leaves. In springs past, before development chewed up the prairie, colonies of violets stained large swaths of the plains purplish blue. If you look closely, you might find yellow stargrass (*Hypoxis hirsuta*) growing a few inches from the ground. Its name refers to its grasslike leaves, but this delicate flower is not a grass but a member of the daffodil family. Its star-shaped, six-petaled flower may remind you of a tiny daffodil. In summer, the yellow pealike flowers of wild indigo (*Baptisia tinctoria*) brighten the field; when the flowers die, the cloverlike leaves blacken as they dry on the branch. Rough goldenrod (*Solidago nemoralis*) and early goldenrod (*Solidago juncea*) sport plumes of tiny, rayed yellow flowers. Stiff aster (*Aster linariifolius*) bristles with needlelike leaves, its erect stem topped with gold-centered lavender flowers. The neon-orange caps of butterfly weed (*Asclepias tuberosa*) add a gaudy note. Most of these plants are on the New York State list of endangered, threatened, or exploitably vulnerable plants.[2]

The grasses that grow here also grow in midwestern tallgrass prairies. They once dominated the vast rolling plain. Big bluestem (*Andropogon gerardii*) grows around four feet tall, bearing paired ears along stiff stems. Little bluestem (*Schizachyrium scoparium*) grows about three feet high and bears bristly spikelets on hairy stalks. In late summer, the grass blooms with frothy white flowers. Six-foot-tall Indian grass (*Sorghastrum nutans*) bears long, feathery, golden-brown ears. Switchgrass (*Panicum virgatum*) grows in clumps, its multiple four-foot stems bearing delicate purplish panicles that shiver in the wind (hence the alternate name, panic grass).

Along the fenced borders of our remnant prairie, nonnatives grow in abundance. Thick stands of Queen Anne's lace (*Daucus carota*), mugwort, and wormwood (artemesias) dominate the border flora; chicory (*Cichorium intybus*), yarrow (*Achillea millefolium*), and common St. John's wort (*Hypericum*

Fig. 7.1. Switch grass (*Panicum virgatum*). (Photo by Betsy McCully.)

perforatum) occasionally pop up; and such lowly weeds as pigweed (*Amaranthus retroflexus*), nightshade (*Solanum nigrum*), and plantain (*Plantago major*) thrive in the meager soil between the parking lot and field. One nonnative flower has jumped the fence: among the prairie grasses, the common mullein (*Verbascum thapsus*) lifts its spike of yellow flowers like a torch.

Where did the alien plants come from? Alfred Crosby, in his book *Ecological Imperialism: The Biological Expansion of Europe*, traces the paths of Eurasian plants across the globe, wherever colonizing Europeans trod. He tells us that plantain, for instance, was once called by the Algonquins "Englishman's foot" — because it seemed to follow in the colonists' footsteps.[3]

When the European colonists arrived on North American shores in the sixteenth and seventeenth centuries, they brought with them — both intentionally and accidentally — numerous plants that rapidly colonized the land. Forbs and Eurasian grasses were in the cattle feed on ships that transported both cattle and humans from Europe to the Americas. John Josselyn, who visited New England in the seventeenth century, found the familiar weeds he knew back home, including dandelion, sow-thistle, shepherd's purse, nettles, nightshade, plantain, mayweed, mullein, and wormwood.[4] Clover and Kentucky bluegrass (a misnamed Eurasian species) were deliberately sown together by English colonists as excellent forage crops; both spread across North America like wildfire. Pioneers entering Kentucky in the late eighteenth century assumed the bluegrass that grew there was native.[5] In the mid-nineteenth century, an inventory on the flora of New York State tallied 161 alien species.[6] By the mid-twentieth century, more than half of the 500 weed species in the United States hailed from the Old World (Eurasia), of which 177 were of European origin.[7]

What is a weed? Weeds are simply opportunistic plants that thrive where other plants don't, rooting in the thinnest or most meager of soils. They are prolific and quick to reproduce. Pigweed (*Chenopodium album*), also known as lamb's quarters and goosefoot, produces 500,000 seeds per plant that are viable after as much as forty years. Each common plantain plant produces 16,000 seeds, but makes up for its small seed production by staying viable up to sixty years. White sweet clover (*Melilotus alba*) is even longer-lived: each plant produces 350,000 seeds that can break dormancy after eighty-one years. To the farmer, weeds are abhorrent. A modern weed guide describes pigweed, for instance, as a noxious weed that steals water from crop plants and, even worse, plays host to viral diseases that can spread to crops.[8]

Nineteenth-century British botanist Joseph Dalton Hooker called weeds "the tramps of our flora."[9] His American contemporary, poet-philosopher Ralph Waldo Emerson, once mused that a weed was "a plant whose virtues have not yet been discovered," but he got it historically wrong: a weed is a plant whose virtues we have forgotten. Prior to the advent of agriculture, many weeds were valued as foods.[10] Once food plants and cattle were domesticated, however, wild plants that competed with crops or posed a toxic threat to cattle were viewed as a scourge. Weeds may well have coevolved with agriculture since they quickly colonize disturbed ground. Forage plants like grasses and clover may have evolved along with grazers, forming a mutually beneficial relationship (indeed, the word forb is derived from a Greek word, *phorbe*, or fodder, derived from the root word *pherbein*, meaning "to graze"). Even before the dawn of agriculture, wild grasses had adapted to the grazing of both Old and New World bovines. On the Great Plains of western

North America, for example, buffalo grass and grama grass had evolved not only to survive but to thrive from the grazing of the buffalo herds. As soon as nineteenth-century American farmers and herders stripped the soil of its native vegetation, Old World weeds took root and spread with astonishing speed. A few, like clover, were welcomed as good forage. But most were just as obnoxious to farmers in the New World as they had been in the Old. They could not see, at the time, that their own agricultural practices were to blame. Their herds ate native plants down to the ground, and their plows tore up the earth — opening the way for weeds to gain a permanent foothold.[11]

In hunting-gathering societies of both the Old World and New, weeds provided excellent nutrition. In North America, as early as four thousand years ago, the Indians of the eastern woodlands were cultivating wild plants such as goosefoot, marsh elder, sunflowers, and gourds. Sunflowers and gourds originated in the West, while goosefoot and marsh elder were floodplain plants indigenous to the Midwest; all thrived on disturbed ground. According to what is known as the Flood Plain Weed Theory, disturbed areas created by hunter-gatherer campsites encouraged not only the colonization but hybridization of opportunistic plants of the midwestern floodplain. These plants literally evolved in the human community. It seems that American weeds, like European weeds, sprang up in the footsteps of the American Indians as they migrated eastward across the Americas.[12]

In 1650, Adriaen Van der Donck, a lawyer-turned-gentleman-farmer in New Netherland, made a list of "the healing herbs" he found here. His jumbling of Latin and common names makes it difficult to identify a few of them, and a number of them are not native at all, indicating that they had quickly naturalized. Native herbs he listed included sweet flag, Solomon's seal, wild indigo, laurel, snakeroot, and jewel-weed; naturalized alien plants included plantain, shepherd's purse, and blessed thistle. He described the medicinal values of the herbs: "The land is full of different kinds of herbs and trees besides those enumerated, among which there undoubtedly are good simplicia, with which discreet persons would do good; for we know that the Indians with roots, bulbs, leaves, &c. cure dangerous wounds and old sores" (simplicia were herbal remedies).[13]

One can speculate that Van der Donck, like many chroniclers of the colonial enterprise, erroneously applied European names to similar American plants. But it is also possible, even probable, that a number of European plants had naturalized by then (thirty years after the arrival of the Dutch), and that the Indians may well have made use of introduced as well as native plants. Surely, herbal knowledge flowed two ways, as Dutch and English herbalists — most likely women — exchanged knowledge with their Indian counterparts. In the 1940s, Carlos Westey lived for two years among the Shinnecock on eastern Long Island, where he found them using thirty-six herbal cures, seventeen of which could be traced to European origin. The leaves of plantain, for instance, were steeped and the water used to bathe "sore eyes," or pounded in a mortar to make a poultice that was applied to sore or inflamed areas of the skin. Both colonists and natives alike smoked the flannel-like leaves of mullein for asthma and bronchitis.[14]

Like their Indian counterparts, Europeans had long turned to nature as their medicine chest. Until the development of synthetic drugs in the twentieth century, in fact, plants were the pharmaceuticals. When Europeans settled in the Americas, it was quite natural to study the plant uses of the Native Americans, since their lives could depend on such knowledge. Sassafras, for instance, was touted as a cure-all, described by Peterson in his field guide of medicinal plants as "a medicine chest locked in the bark of a single plant." Sassafras tea was drunk as a blood tonic, and was used to treat all manner of ailments. It was in such demand in seventeenth-century Europe that it was exported by the ton.[15]

European women of the seventeenth century traditionally gathered or grew medicinal plants for home use. Nicholas Culpeper published his English herbal in the mid-sixteenth century primarily for women, who would be the household physicians, midwives, and herbalists in a predominantly rural society where doctors were scarce. In her history of Dutch colonial women, Mrs. Van Rennsselaer writes:

> Placed on a desert island, a Dutch woman of the seventeenth century was capable of making for herself everything needful to support life. All ordinary cooking was done under her immediate superintendence, but it was her hand alone that prepared delicious dainties of pastry, preserves, and pickles. She drew perfumes from the flowers of her garden by aid of her still; she saw the hops planted, gathered, dried and brewed. She culled herbs and simples, and concocted medicaments, and was always prepared to act as an amateur doctor to her household. She instructed her maids in carding and weaving

the woolen goods for her own and her good-man's clothes, and herself spun
the fine thread of flax that had been grown in her private garden, for linen
shirts, towels, etc., or knit the stockings of the family.[16]

By the nineteenth century, men of medicine and male botanists were the
chief collectors of pharmaceutical plants. Samuel Mitchill, for example, was
a medical doctor, surgeon-general of New York State, professor of botany, zo-
ology and mineralogy, and president of the Lyceum of Natural History of
New York in the early 1800s. He amassed a private collection of wild plants
in the New York City region, listing their known medicinal uses. Major J. Le
Conte collected and listed 450 species in Manhattan in 1812, and the specimens were subsequently housed in the Medical Repository of New York. In
1817, under Mitchill's purview, the lyceum passed a resolution to catalogue
the plants of New York. Botanist John Torrey collected plants within a thirty-
mile radius of New York City, assiduously sorting out native from nonnative
plants, noting their medicinal as well as economic and culinary uses. He explored "the woods from Manhattanville to Bloomingdale, the banks of the
Hudson, and the low grounds near Greenwich." On Long Island, he tramped
in the woods near Brooklyn and searched the shoreline near Bath; in New
Jersey, he ventured into marshes and bogs near Hoboken and Weehawken.[17]
He published his catalogue under the auspices of the lyceum in 1819. On
Manhattan alone, he identified many of the grasses of "meadows, parks,
lawns and roadsides" as naturalized European species, including timothy
grass (*Phleum pratense*), fox-tail (*Alopeuris pratensis*), crab-grass (*Digitaria
sanguinalis*), brome grass (various species), and bermuda grass.[18] He also cata-
logued the flora of New York State in 1843, counting 160 plant species as introduced or naturalized. The count might have been 161 had he known that
clover (*Trifolium repens*) was an alien; he assumed it was a native plant because it "springs up everywhere." In 1832, Lewis D. de Schweinitz inventoried 137 weeds in the northern states for the Lyceum of Natural History of
New York, of which the most aggressive were aliens.[19]

The scientific collection and cataloguing of plants highlights an essential
difference between the attitudes toward nature of the colonial European and
the American Indian. To the educated European of the seventeenth century,
the world was a globe for men of science to explore, map, and catalogue.
Nature was viewed as the realm of matter, not spirit, serving the physical needs

and wants of man. Nature could be tunneled, quarried, mined, leveled, straightened, drained, and diked; wild lands — like wild men — could be subjugated and domesticated. Since the time of Adam, man was the master of plants and animals, holding dominion over nature. Although a pre-Christian nature religion may well have persisted in seventeenth-century Europe, such paganism (as viewed by the church fathers) was suppressed. Writes Lyn White, in his classic 1967 essay on "The Historical Roots of Our Ecological Crisis in Science": "By destroying pagan animism, Christianity made it possible to exploit nature in a mood of indifference to the feelings of natural objects. . . . Man's effective monopoly on spirit in this world was confirmed, and the old inhibitions to the exploitation of nature crumbled."[20] (White acknowledged that this was the dominant Christian worldview; he made an exception for Franciscan Christianity.) We do not know if the Dutch hausfrau or English housewife said a prayer of thanks when she picked the plant, but even if she had, her respect for Mother Earth would have availed little in stopping the ruthless exploitation of the land carried on by colonists driven by a market mentality. Surely no respect for the land was exhibited when the land was stripped of its fertility by single-cropping, when trees were clear-cut, marshes drained or dyked, waters polluted, and habitats destroyed. From the Indian viewpoint, the sacred circle that holds animals and plants, earth and water and sky, had been broken.

The European's invasive technology changed the face of the land, not only letting in alien species but destroying whole ecosystems. As White recounts, the introduction of the furrow plow in the seventh century had radically altered northern European farm practices. It required considerable animal power (eight oxen instead of the two that pulled a scratch plow), and therefore new capital, but it enabled those farmers who could invest in such machinery and animals to produce surpluses for a market. Surpluses enabled urban populations to grow, which in turn pushed the farmer to put more land into crops to supply market demand.

The single-culture crops planted by the colonists simply used up water and nutrients and exhausted the soil. Once the soil could no longer support crops, it was turned to pasturage. Grazing cattle trampled and compacted the soil, which reduced its water-retaining capacity and encouraged opportunistic plants to take over.

Not all colonists were so shortsighted. Several had a sense of stewardship toward the land, if not quite an environmental ethic. Jared Eliot, writing in 1747, placed blame for the failure of the wheat crop in Killingworth, Connecticut, squarely on the English farmers whose practices depleted the soil:

> When our forefathers settled here, they entered a Land which probably had never been ploughed since Creation; the Land being new they depended upon the natural Fertility of the Ground, which served their purpose very well, and when they had worn out one piece they cleared another, without any concern to amend their land, except a little helped by the [Sheep] Fold and Cart-Dung. . . . Our Lands being thus worn out, I suppose to be one Reason why so many are inclined to Remove to new Places that they may raise Wheat.[21]

The history of the Hempstead Plains well illustrates how land-use practices have reflected the prevailing land ethic (if one can so dignify the exploitation of land as an ethic). Carole Neidich, Senior Curator of Life Sciences at the Nassau County Museum, gives us a snapshot history of the Hempstead Plains. The Indians, of course, were the first inhabitants, having lived continuously in the region at least five thousand years, according to archaeological evidence. In 1643, a group of English Dissenters led by Reverend Richard Denton purchased the "Great Plains" (later to be called the Salisbury Plains when New Netherland became New York) from the Dutch, who in turn had bought it from the Indians. Like the Dutch, the English used the prairie as common pasturage. Richard's son, Daniel Denton, writing in 1870, described the pastoral value of the Plains to them: "Toward the middle of Long Island lyeth a plain, sixteen miles long and four broad, upon which plain grows very fine grass that makes excellent good hay, and is very good pasture for sheep and other cattle; where you shall find neither stick nor stone to hinder the horses' heels or endanger them in their races."[22] Most of the Plains was eventually subdivided among different families, who fenced their lots, leaving only seventeen thousand acres as commonland well into the nineteenth century. During this time, because the grassland was so highly valued as pasturage, laws forbade fires to be set on the Plains.

From colonial times to 1961, the Plains was also used extensively for military purposes. Its commons provided an excellent place for soldiers to bivouac and their horses to graze and exercise. Troops were quartered here during the French and Indian War, Revolutionary War, the War of 1812, the Mexican War of 1846, the Civil War, the Spanish-American War, and both world wars. British troops of the colonial period named it Mitchel Field. By the twentieth century, the Plains hosted a number of historical flights in the early days of aviation — hence its name, the "Cradle of Aviation in America." It was natural to convert airfields into military air bases during wartime. Mitchel Field was renamed Hazelhurst Field during World War I, and then Roosevelt Field to honor Teddy Roosevelt's son Quentin after his untimely death in an air crash. But the hazards posed by military aircraft to suburban populations, which had grown during the postwar building boom, forced the bases to close after World War II. As housing developments spread across the Plains, only Mitchel Field retained a significant portion of undeveloped land — until it was bought and built beginning in the 1960s by Hofstra University, Nassau Community College, and the Nassau Veteran's Memorial Coliseum.

Presaging the suburbanization of the Plains, in 1869 the department store magnate Alexander T. Stewart bought seventy-five hundred acres, part of which would be developed by his heirs as Garden City. In the postwar baby and housing boom following World War II, suburban developments sprang up like dandelions across the former prairie, beginning with Levittown. Seventeen thousand houses in this development alone also meant seventeen thousand lawns, which introduced alien grasses and other invasive flora.

Thanks to the efforts of the Nature Conservancy, in cooperation with the New York State Department of Environmental Conservation (NYDEC) and grassroots groups like the Friends of Hempstead Plains, about sixty-two acres have been saved from development in perpetuity. These prairie fragments are considered a Natural Heritage site. In their efforts to restore and maintain the prairie, the most incorrigible problem facing restoration ecologists is aggressive, invasive alien weeds. Anyone who gardens knows how incorrigible weeds can be. We pull them, uproot them, mow, and burn them to allow the native grasses and flowers to flourish. It seems a losing battle, however, because the more disturbed the ground, the more niches open for weeds to take root. Why go to such expense and labor to restore a mere patch of the great prairie that long ago gave way to crops and cattle, airfields and housing developments, lawns and parking lots?

According to the mission statement of the Natural Heritage Program, a joint venture of the Nature Conservancy and the NYSDEC, "Invasive [plant and animal] species contribute to the decline of 46 percent of imperiled or endangered species in the United States." They estimate the costs to agriculture, forestry, fisheries, and the maintenance of open waterways to be $137 billion. The Invasive Plant Council of New York State defines invasive plants as those "that aggressively compete with and displace locally adapted native plant communities." While many invasives are introduced species, a few are not, such as phragmites and black locust. Invasive plants hoard light, steal water and nutrients from desired plants, alter soil chemistry, and reduce diversity. The only greater threat to endangered plants is habitat loss.[23]

In the case of the Hempstead Plains, the preservation of an ancient habitat from further development is the first step; the planting of desirable native plants and eradication of invasive alien weeds the second. As daunting a task as it is, the mission of salvaging or restoring what remains of America's great grasslands is worth the effort.

The Grassland Restoration and Management Project (GRAMP) was founded in 1985, when it was realized that the decline of breeding grassland birds was directly related to the loss of open grassland. Their first project was to restore the no-longer-used airfield of Floyd Bennet Field as grassland, an effort spearheaded by Jean and Ron Bourque of the New York City Audubon Society. Ironically, while it was an airfield, it was mowed on a regular basis — a practice that helped preserve its grassland state by keeping woody plants from taking over. This is true of other airfields, even ones as large as Kennedy International Airport, where regular mowing has allowed the upland sandpiper and other grassland birds to breed successfully. (Of course, mowing has to be avoided during prime breeding season, since many grassland birds nest on the ground.) Once Floyd Bennet Field fell into disuse as an airfield, woody vegetation invaded. It took a Herculean effort by the Park Service and volunteers to cut the brush and manually grub the trees and shrubs. A final clearing was done with the aid of a bulldozer, and continued seasonal mowing keeps the field a grassland. Since this restoration, the northern harrier has returned to breed, and the savannah sparrow breeds here, although the grasshopper sparrow and upland sandpiper have not returned.[24]

It is speculated that disturbance of grassland areas throughout the Northeast and Midwest because of more intensive farming methods — especially early spring mowing that destroys nests — is hastening the decline of grass-

land birds. The Massachusetts Audubon Society posts on its Web site a detailed set of recommendations for farmers who wish to preserve grasslands
on their property. The recommendations include rotational, light grazing;
high, regular mowing outside of nest-building and breeding time; the avoid-
ance of alien grasses and fertilizers; and periodic, rotational burning to reduce buildup of dead vegetation, add nutrients to the soil, and prevent the
spread of woody vegetation. They recommend that 125 to 250 acres be set
aside for grassland birds.[25]

Suburban sprawl further degrades grasslands as farmland is sold and subdivided into suburban tracts and malls. These developments not only destroy
open field habitats, but also introduce alien species through lawn and garden plantings, which are often planted with exotics. The use of chemical
fertilizers and toxic herbicides further degrades the ecosystem, in effect ster-
ilizing it. An emerald green lawn exacts a high cost in terms of the health of
the soil, water, and whole ecosystem, of which humans are a part.

The Fresh Kills landfill on Staten Island offers an instructive example of
the challenges and successes of restoring a severely degraded habitat. To
understand why landfill sites like Fresh Kills, once considered dead zones,
became candidates for habitat restoration, it is helpful to review the history
of changes on Staten Island and its flora. A large island of about sixty-one
square miles, Staten Island is comprised of diverse habitats, including meadows, lowland and upland forests, fresh- and saltwater marshes, and beaches.
Indeed, one of the loveliest remnants of a restored upland meadow in New
York City is at Mount Loretto, in the Tottenville section on the south shore
of the island overlooking Raritan Bay. As long as the island remained fairly
isolated, accessible only by ferry, it resisted the urbanization experienced by
much of New York City in the twentieth century. But it became more developed beginning in 1931 as three bridges were built connecting the island
to the mainland of New Jersey, and the pace of development intensified after
the Verrazano Bridge connecting it to Brooklyn was completed in 1965. The
population jumped from 160,000 in 1931 to 400,000 in 1990. A study of
changes in Staten Island flora during the last century was completed by Steven
Handel, George Robinson, and Mary Yurlina of Rutgers University in 1994.
They calculated a loss of 443 native vascular plant species, compared to an
original 1,082 plant species, and most of these losses have occurred since at
least 1930, when a plant census tallied 950 native plant species. In addition,

100 nonnative plant species have been added to Staten Island's flora. Aggressive alien plants like ailanthus have certainly impacted local native plant populations, but development appears to be the main cause of this extirpation event. Why should we be concerned with the local disappearance of species? As the authors of the study note, "No species loss from Staten Island represents an extinction, in global terms, yet it is the accumulation of such local losses that drive the accelerating number of plant species extinctions across North America."[26]

This study and others prompted Steven Handel, ecology professor at Rutgers, and Steven Clemants, vice president for science at the Brooklyn Botanic Garden to form the Center for Urban Restoration Ecology (CURE) in 2000, a collaboration between Rutgers University and the Brooklyn Botanic Garden. Since 1990, the Brooklyn Botanic Garden's New York Metropolitan Flora Project, under the directorship of Clemants, had been conducting a survey of New York City flora. Handel and colleagues from Rutgers had been studying how to restore closed landfill sites in the Hackensack Meadowlands. The landfills had been capped and topped with soil, but no plants were taking root and thriving. Handel figured out that a deeper layer of topsoil (about two feet) was necessary to anchor native plantings, and plantings needed to be diverse enough to attract the kinds of birds and other animals that would disperse seeds. He also noted how the Meadowlands was cut up by highways and other obstructions, thus preventing easy access by birds and other seed-dispersing animals to the sites. As a result of his research, the topsoil at the Meadowlands landfill was enriched with a thick layer of compost, providing anchor and nourishment for a scrub-type woodland that has since taken root. The choice of a scrub habitat (one composed of native grasses and low-growing trees and shrubs) was determined by the need to keep tree roots fairly shallow so they would not puncture the landfill cap. Fragmentation of the region was a more intractable problem — how do you dismantle highways? Nonetheless, the native plantings took root and thrived. The success of Handel's work in the Meadowlands led to a similar project at the Fresh Kills landfill, a twenty-two-hundred-acre dump site for the city's garbage. In operation since the 1940s, it was closed in March 2001, although a portion of it was reopened to accept debris and human remains from the Twin Towers collapse of September 2001. Since 1989, Handel and his colleagues at Rutgers worked in partnership with scientists of the New York Metropolitan

Project to conduct research of the site's ecological history in order to restore the original plantings and habitats of this tidal wetland ("kill" is derived from the Dutch word for stream or waterway). The City of New York Department of Sanitation, under the supervision of Bill Young and John McLaughlin, undertook the actual site preparation and planting. After capping the land-fill with a compacted clay-shale soil mix to seal the landfill and prevent methane from leaking, workers topped that layer with a sandy mineral sub-strate mixed with leaf mulch. They then planted sumac, shadblow, hackberry, blueberry, blackberry, and beach plum — eighteen species of native shrubs and trees in all. These woody plants were chosen to replicate the scrub for-est once found here and still present on parts of Long Island and coastal New Jersey. The project was not without problems, chief among them the invasion by aggressive alien weeds. Within a year, ailanthus, Japanese honeysuckle (*Lonicera japonica*), multiflora rose (*Rosa multiflora*), and Oriental bitter-sweet (*Celastrus orbiculata*) began to colonize the site, so these had to be controlled. The good news is, despite competition from invasive weeds, the native plants increased by means of seeds carried by birds from wild areas outside the landfill site. The importance of animals to seed dispersal under-scores the need for wildlife corridors, and highlights the fact that habitats are complex ecosystems made up of interdependent species. It may take time to establish itself, but Handel envisions a beautiful twenty-two-hundred-acre park of scrub-type coastal woodland, meadows, and salt marshes.[27]

It is a mistake to think of ecosystems as static, of course. They are chang-ing and evolving in response to climate change, fire, and other natural events. Birds and other animals may disperse seeds into new areas; ocean and wind currents may also be means of dispersal. Humans may be viewed as just an-other species that has migrated across the earth, carrying plants and animals with them, wittingly or not. They are hardly the only species to alter the land. Moreover, land management by humans — particularly through the agency of fire — seems a universal human practice.

It is precisely our land management practices that can lead to healing and restoration of the earth. Let's return to our prairie.

Inside the fenced field, the native staghorn sumac grows in a lush stand along the edge, but just outside, the alien ailanthus tree, with its similar com-pound leaves, threatens to jump the fence. Toward the center of the meadow, grasses dominate: native big bluestem ripples in the wind like a dream of what once was like sea of grass. Growing in profusion around the fenced-off perimeter of the prairie, alien plants seem poised to jump the fence: Queen Anne's lace, cowvetch, Japanese honeysuckle, Russian olive. Artemesias such as mugworts and wormwoods are most abundant. A patch of ground inside the fence has been recently burned over to get rid of the artemesias, and their woody stems raked and bundled for removal. It seems a Sysiphean task, for as the weed guide informs us, each plant produces up to fifty thousand seeds that retain their viability for several years of dormancy.

This little prairie is a mere fragment of grassland in a predominantly urban landscape. All the more reason to restore and manage whatever grassland remains. What the colonists once called "waste reedy land" we now value as an integrated ecosystem. We understand now how the loss of one species leads to the loss of others that depend on it, in a cascading effect. Take away the flower that is host to a particular butterfly, and the butterfly disappears along with the plant. Now, the milkweed pod bursts with seeds, each silken parachute a potential flower. Each milkweed plant that takes root will play host to the returning monarch butterfly, which will lay its eggs upon the underside of a leaf. Each egg that survives will hatch a caterpillar, which will suck the milky sap until it is ready to attach itself to the host plant, grow a milky green chrysalis, and transform itself into a butterfly, which will begin the cycle anew.

8

Forests for Trees

The wooded hill stood in the middle of a leafy suburban New Jersey development. On a beautiful Sunday in September I drove through the neighborhood, enjoying the play of sunlight through the tall trees that shaded the lawns and ranch-style houses. I parked my car in a cul-de-sac at the foot of the hill and got out. I had volunteered to help conduct a census of woody flora in the New York City region for the Brooklyn Botanic Garden Native Flora Project, and I had been assigned a grid in New Jersey. My topographical map showed a place named Bunker Hill. Introducing myself to an elderly man who was raking leaves, I told him my purpose and asked about the trees on the hill. He was interested to know that I was doing a survey for the Brooklyn Botanic Garden, and informed me that he and his neighbors were fighting to preserve the hill from development, trying to get it designated a national historical landmark. "It's the site of a battle dating to the Revolutionary War," he claimed. His voice quivered with passion. "Already the developers are clearin' tracts and startin' to build. It's a desecration! Those trees have been undisturbed since the Revolution."[1]

Once he mentioned the trees, I became excited. My heart beating fast, I trekked up the hill and entered the stand of trees. Tall straight trunks of pignut hickories towered over me, sunlight filtering through their crowns onto the woodland floor, where a few gray squirrels gathered hickory nuts in the thick leafy humus. No understory grew beneath these trees, indicating their age; pignut hickories mature at two hundred years and can live up to four hundred years. Now I understood the tone of reverence in the neighbor's voice, and his passionate desire to preserve this remnant habitat. For me, its historical significance was in its pedigree as old native woodland.

I walked to the crest of the hill, where I saw the source of the old man's distress. A road had been cut through the woodland, and acres already cleared for houses. One house was half constructed.

Closer to my home, in the heart of Prospect Park, a tattered pocket of old native woodland hangs on, despite the encroachment of exotic species like

Fig. 8.1. Cally, after Bessa, Pancrace, Pignut Hickory (*Juglans porcina*), stipple engraving. From *The North American Sylva; or, A Description of the Forest Trees of the United States, Canada, and Nova Scotia, 1841–49.* (Courtesy of General Research Division, The New York Public Library, Astor, Lenox and Tilden Foundations. Image #1263369.)

Norway and sycamore maples that easily take root in the compacted soil. The oldest trees stand in a twenty-acre section of Midwood, between Battle Pass and Binnenwater, where oaks, tulip trees, hickories, black birches, and sweet gums shade the woodland floor. During the Revolutionary War, most of the trees were cut for firewood or cleared for crops to provision the British troops who bivouacked here, but it's possible a few were spared the ax. Hickory was especially prized for its quality as firewood and charcoal briquettes that were used to smoke meats. My husband Joe and I have birded here many times with the Brooklyn Botanic Garden bird group, led for many years by bird artist John Yrizarry, who grew up near the park and birded the area for fifty-plus years. Our birding forays always took us into the Midwood section, where we were likely to find rich bird life in the densely wooded area. Always the raconteur, John would entertain us with tree stories as well as bird lore. Every time we passed a particular spot, he would tell us of the great oak that stood there for as long as he could remember, and according to legend bore the scar of a bullet fired in the Revolutionary War. He mourned the year that oak came crashing down — a fatality of a storm — taking a piece of history with it.

What explains our reverence for old trees, and our sadness at their fall? Is it that they mark time, living beyond our individual lives, and connect us to history? Is it that a great tree connects us to a place? Biologist Bernd Heinrich, in *The Trees in My Forest*, likens the planting of an oak sapling by him and his son on his property in Vermont to the deliberate creating of history: "We see permanence in the hills we get to know. They do not visibly change, but we can grow up with trees and see them change with us. Since they can outlive us, they connect us to the future and to the places where they grow."[2]

In New York City, trees were once used by surveyors to mark property boundaries. Henry Stiles, in his nineteenth-century history of Brooklyn, recounted a number of tree stories. A seventeenth-century surveyor of a land grant between Bushwick and Newtown in Brooklyn drew the boundaries by a "mark in a certain white oak tree west . . . to a mark in a walnut tree . . . to a chestnut tree . . . and from that tree to a mark in a small tree at the creekside." The name Bushwick speaks of its sylvan origins: the Dutch word Boswijck means place of woods. A white oak with three notches made by Indians stood at the bend of an old Indian path in Flatbush until blown down in the early 1800s, to be replaced by a stone monument that marked "the most southerly angle of the city of Brooklyn." An eighteenth-century map of downtown Brooklyn depicts a tulip tree marking a boundary corner. It was located atop a hill near the waterfront, since leveled and now the site of the Brooklyn wharves. Stiles described it as "an immense Magnolia, which, when in blossom, perfumed the air for a great distance around." (It was common to refer to the tulip tree as a magnolia because of its large, magnolia-like flowers.) Old Brooklyners still living at the time of Stiles's history remembered the great tree as a favorite picnic site for New Yorkers who rowed across the East River from Manhattan to Brooklyn to spend a day underneath its shade. It was also favored by fishermen, much to its misfortune. At the base of the tree was a cavity large enough for a man to stand in; a careless fisherman

Fig. 8.2. Oak tree, Alley Pond Park. (Photo by Ben Cooper.)

built a fire in this cavity to cook his breakfast one morning and burned the tree down to a stump. As the story goes, the stump valiantly continued to put out leaves until it finally died.[3]

In the graveyard of the Presbyterian Church in Basking Ridge, New Jersey, stands a great white oak of six hundred years. When the church was founded in 1717, the tree was already three hundred years old and an object of reverence. As its pastor Reverend Alfred Tisdale, Jr., remarked to *New York Times* reporter Richard Lezin Jones in an interview, "The church grew up around the tree and the town grew up around the church. . . . We see ourselves as stewards of this ancient oak."[4] The Basking Ridge Oak is more fortunate than the 450-year-old tulip tree that stands neglected in an out-of-the-way corner of Alley Pond Park. Known as the Queens Giant, it is deemed by the park service the city's tallest tree. As of 2002, its girth was measured at 19 feet, and its height at 134 feet; similar to the now gone Brooklyn tree, it has a door-sized blackened cleft at its base.[5]

For some, like Bernd Heinrich, trees are our breath. They absorb the carbon dioxide we exhale, and we inhale their oxygen. Old growth forest, he writes, "is not our 'environment.' It is us." For those who hear the language of trees, like Cherokee Johnie Leverett (Standing Woman), the "great trees . . . securely connect ground and sky, Heaven and Earth," and each encounter with a tree in an old growth forest is with a living, breathing organism imbued with spirit, a vital being whose severing from earth by human hands leaves one bereft.[6]

The trees of the deciduous forest evolved over a span of 50 million years, according to Rutherford Platt. Fossils dating back to 70 million years ago in Arundel County, Maryland, include fifty species of pine, as well as willow, poplar, beech, elm, mulberry, sassafras, even a rare gingko and cycad. Most of these were "keynote trees" of the deciduous forest that would weather the Ice Age. Some would emerge unchanged, while others would evolve into new species. Sycamore, for example, retained its ancient characteristics: "Look twice at an old sycamore and you will see how it bears the imprint of antiquity. Its bark is smooth, but unlike the smooth bark of the more recent cherries and birches it is inelastic. It rips off as the trunk expands, exposing whitish inner bark. Also the trunk and main limbs are heavy in proportion to the twigs — a massive central axis with short slender branches. This is the style of very ancient trees." Other trees "modernized": beech, including oaks; birch, willow, walnut, elm, maple and ash — all generated many new species. The forest as a whole ecosystem also modernized: "The outstanding feature of the modernization of the original all-wood deciduous forest was not the addition of a few new species of conservative hardwoods, but the eruption of little trees, bushes, ferns and wild flowers. . . . These were birch, aspen, scrub oak, blue beech, hop hornbeam, witch hazel, sassafras, alder, redbud and dogwood," many of them referred to by foresters as "weed trees." In addition, "the rose family staged an extraordinary performance. Under prodding by the Ice Age, it generated a host of little trees, including wild cherry, crab-apple, plum, mountain ash and hawthorn." This diverse understory included the hazelnut bush, hollies, laurels, viburnums, sumac, sweet pepperbush, honeysuckles, and heaths — which "transformed the dark and ancient fastness into the lively, varied wilderness which men found on this continent."[7]

It was this forest that astounded Europeans long used to a deforested land.

When the Dutch and English first explored the northeastern coast of America, they reported large sizes and numbers of trees. In 1609, the year Hudson nosed his ship the *Half Moon* into New York Bay and sailed up the river that would be named after him, the captain noted in his log that along the Great River were stands of "all kinds of timber suitable for shipbuilding." Dutch colonial chronicler Wassenaer described oaks "of very close grain" and "thick as three or four men." In 1629, the traveler Isaac de Rasieres described New Netherland as full of "oaks, elms, walnuts and fir trees. Also wild cedar and chestnut trees." Van der Donck, who settled in the colony in the 1640s, listed the trees he found, often noting their utilitarian value: "The oak trees are very large; from sixty to seventy feet high without knots, and from two to three fathoms thick, being of various sizes. There are several kinds of oak, such as white, smooth bark, rough bark, grey bark and black bark." Hickory was also abundant, making "excellent firewood, surpassing every other kind. . . . When it is dry, it keeps fire and sparkles like matches. Our women prefer nut-coals to turf for their stoves, because they last longer, and are not buried in ashes. This kind of wood is found all over the New Netherlands in such abundance, that it cannot become scarce in the first hundred years with an increased population." Nutten Island (Governor's Island) was named for its abundant hickory trees, which were quickly harvested for fuel to supply Fort Amsterdam. Van der Donck also noted chestnut, beech, ash, linden, sycamore, maple, tulip-tree, "birch, yew, poplar, sapine, alder, willow, thorn trees, sassafras, persimmon, mulberry, wild cherry, crab."[8]

The erroneous impression Europeans received back home from these accounts was of a vast virgin forest — in fact, at least in the mid-Atlantic region, it was more of a patchwork of woodlands, wetlands, and fields long shaped by human hands, as we'll see — but to the wood-hungry Europeans, the North American forests were a new supply source of lumber. The reports by ship captains and merchants were often exaggerated to justify the expense of such voyages to the investors by pointing to the great riches the newly discovered continent had to offer, if Europeans were quick to exploit them — and exploit

them they did, with the same disregard for conservation they had shown in
Europe.

During the sixteenth and seventeenth centuries, fuel shortages in England and Europe were common; centuries of cutting trees with little thought
of conservation had denuded much of the land of forest cover. By the end of
the seventeenth century, a mere one-eighth of England was still wooded, a
fact that moved John Evelyn to declare, in *Sylva: A Discourse of Forest Trees*,
that timber was diminished not only from glass and iron works "but from the
disproportionate spreading of tillage, caused through that prodigious havoc
made by such as lately professing themselves against root and branch . . .
[who] were tempted not only to fell and cut down, but utterly to extirpate,
demolish and raze as it were, all those many goodly woods and forests, which
our ancestors left standing for the ornament and service of their country."
The landowner's retort to the sentiments of Evelyn was expressed by Samuel
Pepys in his diary of May 5, 1667, to wit: trees are "an excrescence of the
earth provided by God for the payment of debts."[9]

Shipbuilding, which became an essential industry during the years of capi-
talist expansion and empire building, drastically depleted old-growth forests.
To build a single warship, for example, the English felled two thousand
century-old oaks.[10] According to British naval historian Robert Albion, in
Elizabethan England's Duffield Forest alone, "59,412 large oaks and 32,820
small ones standing in 1560 were reduced to 2,864 large and 3,032 small
trees in 1587."[11] Shipbuilding consumed a number of different kinds of wood.
Shipbuilders sought "great" timber—preferably 80- to 120-year-old white oak
at least fifteen inches in diameter—and "compass" or curved timber. Young
oak was used for the planks; old oak, elm, beech, and fir for the hulls; black
oak for the underwater timbers; rot-resistant cedar and chestnut for outside
timber; tall white pine, forty yards in length and forty inches in diameter, for
single-stick masts; spruce for topmasts and spars; and pitch pine for pitch and
turpentine.[12]

When the English arrived in the Northeast, they found forests of two-
hundred-foot-tall white pine—prime reserves of "mast" timber. It was not
long before these reserves—like those of Europe—soon became depleted.
The 1711 "Act for the Preservation of White and Other Pine Trees," passed
by the English Parliament to preserve mast trees for the Royal Navy, set aside
royal preserves from Maine to New Jersey. Stricter acts were passed in 1721

and 1729, but they failed to achieve their aim. The American colonists openly flaunted the laws, citing the rights of private property, and cut down possibly five hundred trees for every one cut for the navy. Even the royal agents got into the act, as noted in a letter of 1747 to the admiral: the agents are "great destroyers of the woods under the color of masting . . . for all or most of them are concerned in Saw Mills and they take their contracts to have greater liberty to log, and sell masts to private persons as cut off private property."[13]

It is ironic that the original meaning of "Holland" was "land of forests" — a meaning lost to the Dutch of the seventeenth century. Forests had disappeared from the Low Countries centuries before, as population pressures forced the clearance of large tracts of land. The rise of such industries as iron and glassworks further depleted wood reserves. The construction of houses, windmills, factories, and warehouses required wood, as did the manufacturing of farm implements, industrial machines, and tools.[14]

The first sawmill in New Amsterdam was built in 1628 for the purpose of exporting lumber to the "Fatherland." A cargo of timber was shipped out of New Amsterdam as early as 1626, but the oak and hickory timber was far outweighed by furs. The shipment included 7,246 beaver pelts, 675 otter, 48 mink, and 36 wildcat. By 1640 however, once the fur trade had diminished, lumbering became a more lucrative enterprise. Lumber was needed not only for naval supplies and shipbuilding, but also for cooperage: in 1648, for example, sixty thousand white oak staves for wine barrels were carried on one Bristol ship from the American colonies to Spain, Portugal, the Canaries, and Madeira, where the staves were exchanged for wine.[15]

In addition to foreign trade, there was an extensive local trade in timber. Distillers, brewers, shipbuilders, and fishermen all needed casks, hence the huge demand for oak staves. Ash and oak were fashioned into farm implements; black walnut, wild cherry, and red maple for furniture; burlwood for bowls. Van der Donck noted that hickory was "useful for many purposes, it grows straight and is tough and hard. We now use it for cogs and rounds in our mills and for threshing flails, swivel-trees, and other farming purposes." The tanning industry preferred the bark of young white oak, which was found only in coastal areas south of Boston. And of course trees were cut for the construction of the settlers' houses and fences, white and red cedar being particularly valued for fences and shingles.[16]

To the American colonist, wood seemed "free for the taking" — one had simply to cut it, split it, and ship it — never mind questions of conservation or land-use rights. And cut it they did, with an abandon fueled by the illusion that the American forests were infinite. Van der Donck was so convinced that trees would always be in plentiful supply that he encouraged colonists to go ahead and destroy the woods for tillage — they "can do nothing better." He based this belief on his observation that his Indian neighbors had cleared the land for tillage, and twenty years after the fields were abandoned, the woodland had grown back so thickly "that it was difficult to pass through it on horseback."[17]

Connecticut farmer Jared Eliot reported on the effects of the early settlers' wasteful land-clearing practices in his 1760 manual, *Field Husbandry:* "Their unacquaintedness with the Country, led them to make choice of the Worst Land for their Improvement, and the most expensive and chargeable Methods of Cultivation: they tho't themselves obliged to stub all Straddle, and cut down or lop all great trees; in which they expended much Cost and Time, to the prejudice of the Crop and impoverishing the Land."[18] Peter Kalm, a student of Linnaeus who was collecting plant specimens of the New World, documented what happened. He traveled to the region in the mid-eighteenth century and left a meticulous account of what he observed. In New Jersey, he noted the extirpation of cedars from the swamps, because both red and white cedars were highly esteemed for their rot-resistant qualities. The demand for white cedar shingles, for example, extended from New York to the West Indies, and colonists were profligate in exploiting that demand. "Thus the inhabitants are very busy here, not only to lessen the number of these trees, but even to extirpate them entirely. They are here (and in many other places) in regard to wood, bent only upon their present advantage, utterly regardless of posterity. By this means many cedar swamps are already quite destitute of cedars, having only young shoots left; and I plainly observed, by counting the circles around the stems, that they do not grow up very quickly, but require a great deal of time before they can be cut for timber." To make fenced enclosures, Kalm noted their lazy method: "The people do not cut down the young trees, as is common with us [Swedes], but they fell here and there thick trees, cut them in several places, leaving the pieces as long as is necessary, and split them into poles of the usual thickness; a single tree affords a multitude of poles."[19]

The Middle Atlantic region at the time of European Contact was a patch-work of parkland-type forest, meadows, wetlands, and clearings — a land-scape already shaped by the Native Americans who had culled trees, burned underbrush, and cultivated land for millennia. Dutch plantation owner David de Vries, for instance, described sixty acres on the North River (the Hudson) of "maizeland, where there were no trees to remove; and hay-land lying all together, sufficient for 200 cattle." English settler Silas Wood reported that the western part of Long Island was "bare of timber" because the Indians practiced annual burning. It seemed, in the words of a New Jersey colonist, "that I may yoke a plow where I please."[20] Indeed, the American Indians had long practiced land management. When they wanted land for crops, they cleared the fields either by the slash-and-burn method or by the practice of girdling, whereby the tree was stripped of its lower bark and left to stand until dead, with crops interplanted between the stumps. They also practiced an-nual, controlled burning to keep woodlands free of underbrush and mead-ows free of weeds — creating favorable habitat for such browsers as deer, elk, and hare, as well as wild foods such as strawberries and raspberries that grew in the clearings. When the fields were no longer arable, usually after eight to ten years, they were abandoned. In time, a succession forest took root: in the Northeast, white pines would establish themselves in dry soils, while red maple and red cedar favored wetter soils.[21]

In one respect, Native Americans were not that different from the Euro-peans in their utilitarian view of trees. Trees were sources of food, fuel, tools, and construction materials. For instance, Van der Donck describes how the Lenapes stripped the bark off chestnut trees to cover their houses, and fash-ioned the wood of the tulip tree to make canoes, hence their name for the tree, canoe-wood. Unlike the Europeans, however, the Indians did not cut trees for profit; moreover, they cultivated a more spiritual relationship to nature. Trees were alive and imbued with spirit; great trees and ancient forests inspired awe and veneration — hardly typical of the prevailing European mindset (although pre-Christian Europeans possessed a sacred relationship with nature). Perhaps their living on the land for millennia had taught a hard lesson about preserving for future generations. They used without destroy-ing, sparing great trees; to harm them would have been like killing their el-ders. Why had the ancient American forests been preserved, if not for an en-vironmental ethic that was implicit in the Indians' relation to nature? Writes contemporary Mahican Steve Comer: "Europe-descended Americans . . . have lived in this forest for less than 400 years, not nearly long enough, in my view, to grow the psychic roots that would provide a collective sense of innate belonging. Sadly, the prevailing mindset produces the exact opposite. The willing participants of mainstream society think of their natural surroundings only in terms of exploitative use. . . . The forest is our teacher and will in due time tell us all we need to know."[22]

The Indians of the Middle Atlantic region preserved the arability of their croplands and ensured the continuance of healthy woodlands so that these habitats would continue to provide them the wild plant and animal species they needed to thrive. With the arrival of Europeans, the forests would be degraded, fragmented, and often eradicated. The loss of unbroken forest habitats decimated the species that depended on them. The Europeans' wasteful forestry practices and "carelessness for futurity" appalled Kalm: "We can hardly be more lavish of our woods in Sweden and Finland than they are here: their eyes are fixed upon the present gain, and they are blind to futurity."[23]

Euro-American agricultural practices seriously degraded and fragmented forests. Ecological historian William Cronon informs us that New England colonists, erroneously judging the fertility of the soil by the abundance and variety of trees, cleared stands of "hickories, maples, ashes, and beeches," and planted their crops in rich woodland humus. The benefits were short-lived, however; once the forest was removed, the nutrients in the soil were rapidly depleted. The trees had provided the humus, retained water and nutrients, and anchored the soil; crops, particularly the single-culture crops planted by the Europeans, simply used up water and nutrients.[24] Further, European domestic animals were allowed to graze in the remaining woodlands, where the undergrowth had been burned off by the colonists (following the Indian method), with destructive consequences. The animals ate up the tender shoots of sprouting trees, making it impossible for trees to grow into maturity. They trampled and compacted the soil, which rendered the habitat inhospitable to plant life and reduced the soil's water-retaining capacity, as noted by eighteenth-century naturalist John Bartram:

> Above 20 years past when the woods was not pastured and full of high weeds
> and the ground light, then the rain sunk much more into the earth and did
> not wash and tear up the surface (as now). The rivers and brooks in floods

would be black with mud but now the rain runs most of it off on the surface, is collected into the hollows which it wears to the sand and clay which it bears away with the swift current down to the brooks and rivers whose banks it overflows.[25]

Forest hydrologist Richard Lee lists the ecological consequences of grazing in forest lands: "serious disturbance to watershed stability . . . , range deterioration, soil compaction, reduced infiltration, and increased overland flow, erosion, and sedimentation." The catastrophic effects of deforestation was not news to the colonists; Lee points out that even "Medieval and Renaissance governments established 'protection forests' for the express purpose of controlling avalanches, mountain torrents, shifting sands, erosion, and siltation."[26] For example, a 1543 English "Act for the Preservation of Woods" forbade farmers "from turning woodland more than two furloughs from their dwellings into pasture or tillage," and kept cattle out of young woods.[27] Such preservation acts, it seems, did little to stem the tide of deforestation.

The onset of the Industrial Revolution in the United States stepped up the rate of destruction. In the nineteenth century, the conversion of steam to energy required fuel. The steam that powered factories, steamboats, and rail trains was produced by the burning of wood until coal began to be mined. Hudson River historian Robert Boyle sums up the ecological impact of steam production on the woodlands of the Hudson Valley: "As early as 1825, the thirteen steamers on the Hudson and the ferries in the harbor used one hundred thousand cords of wood in the eight months of the year that the river was free of ice. Wood was cut on the top of the Palisades and slid down the cliffs to deep water. Thus the name High Gutter Point on the New York–New Jersey state line." The iron industry also required enormous amounts of wood fuel, continues Boyle, "and the end result was that much of the [Hudson] valley was clear cut every thirty or forty years."[28]

The production of pig iron required enormous quantities of wood both in the form of firewood and charcoal. So-called iron plantations were located in ample woodland—at least four square miles were needed for each furnace. Iron was smelted in a chimney-shaped stone or brick blast furnace, typically twenty feet high and twenty to twenty-four feet square at the base, which was built into a low hillside, insulated by sand or broken stone, with a stone or slate or firebrick core, its top and bottom open. The core was on a hearth, and the fire was kindled below. Into the top opening was dropped crushed ore, charcoal, and limestone "flux," filling the furnace, and an air blast produced by bellows through a pipe intensified combustion, separating the iron from the slag. In the blast furnace, during a "blast" of sixteen to eighteen weeks (and later, with the advent of more heat-resistant core materials, seven to eight months), the furnace was continually fed fuel. Charcoal was made mainly from pine as the preferred wood, with one and a half cords producing 80 bushels of charcoal; 120 bushels were required to smelt one ton of pig iron. One iron plantation at the New Jersey–New York border employed fifty-five woodcutters, ten master colliers and forty collier's helpers to cut and trim logs, pile them into a cone, cover the pile with damp earth and leaves, and kindle and burn the pile for three to ten days to produce charcoal. A cone consisted of twenty-five to thirty cords of wood to produce one thousand to fifteen hundred bushels of charcoal. To produce 360 tons of hollowware, for example, 2,130 cords of wood were converted into 1,420 loads of charcoal. The total iron production in the colonies in 1775 was estimated at 30,000 tons, most for domestic use.[29]

In 1864, George Perkins Marsh sounded the clarion call of conservation with his publication of *Man and Nature*, an overnight classic that anticipated the environmental movement by a century. The book offers a historical view of the ecological devastation wrought by civilized man since the days of the Romans, with particular focus on deforestation. Marsh, a native Vermonter, had witnessed the razing of forests in his home state as the United States became more industrialized, and described how such deforestation rippled through the whole system of nature. He noted how the denuded soil was "alternately parched" in summer and "seared" in winter, with rain and melting snow no longer absorbed but running off. "The face of the earth is no longer a sponge," he lamented, "but a dust heap." Man had disturbed the natural harmonies and upset the balance of nature, inflicting ever more damage with his ever more powerful technology. "Man is everywhere a disturbing agent," he declared, and the establishment of his dominion over earth and sea is nothing short of a revolution:

> Wherever he plants his foot, the harmonies of nature are turned to discord. The proportions and accommodations which insured the stability of existing arrangements are overthrown. Indigenous vegetable and animal species

are extirpated, and supplanted by others of foreign origin, spontaneous production is forbidden or restricted, and the face of the earth is either laid bare
or covered with a new and reluctant growth of vegetable forms, and with
alien tribes of animal life.[30]

Marsh was the first to call on Americans to replant forests and set aside forest preserves for the sake of restoring the "disturbed harmonies" rather than
solely for industrial use. He cited the precedents set by European countries such
as Italy, where he was deeply impressed by the successful restoration of forests
in Tuscany. As a diplomat in the Lincoln administration (he was ambassador
to Italy), his voice was heard and heeded. His influence led to Lincoln's sign-
ing of the first conservation legislation in 1864, in the middle of a wrench-
ing Civil War, giving Yosemite Valley permanent protection as a state park.
This set the precedent for the preservation of Yellowstone as a national park, the
first of its kind, in 1872, and of the Adirondacks as a mixed-use state park in
1892. It was at this time that a clause was written into the New York State
constitution promising to keep a portion of the state "forever wild."[31]

From pollen studies we can reconstruct the forest of the Northeast just before European contact. For at least five thousand years, 95 percent of the land
had been covered by forest, extending to the edge of the sea in some places
and onto many islands. Clearings increased to the south, in the Middle Atlantic region, and were both natural and artificial: grasslands, river meadows,
coastal marshes, sand plains, and swamps alternated with planting fields and
parkland forest. Estimates of the extent of old-growth eastern forest prior to
European Contact range from 822 million acres to 950 million acres. That
compares to a survey of remaining old-growth forest in the Northeast conducted in 1993 by Mary Byrd Davis, who reckoned 1.5 million acres "of forest, woodland, and savannah" were left, with a few hundred thousand added
since her survey.[32]

Statistics can't begin to convey the reality of the degradation and loss of
our forests. It was a reality made palpable to me when I encountered a felled
Atlantic white-cedar tree in New Jersey's Meadowlands, the once great wetlands that extended unbroken for miles along the Hackensack River, about
a half hour's drive from Manhattan. I was visiting a preserve managed by the
New Jersey Department of Environmental Preservation, on the site of a closed
landfill. The tree had been laid to rest on a path that winds around an artifi-

cial lagoon, its weathered, bleached gray trunk and gnarled roots eloquently attesting to the history detailed on a sign next to it. It was 350 years old at the time it was cut, and is a relic of the old cedar forest that once grew in abundance in the Meadowlands. It was dug up and salvaged when the state constructed the superhighway that now fragments the wetlands.

The loss is about more than individual trees, but entails a whole ecosystem. The Atlantic white cedar grows in glacial kettle holes, thriving in boggy, acidic soil—which also supports unique plants such as orchids, starflower, goldthread, and skunk cabbage. The trees grow in dense stands, with an understory of sweet pepperbush, sheep laurel, swamp white azalea, blueberry, winterberry, and inkberry. Birds attracted to this habitat include cedar waxwings, northern saw-whet owl, alder flycatcher, northern waterthrush, hermit thrush, black-throated green warbler, and Canada warbler.

Fig. 8.3. 350-year-old Atlantic white-cedar trunk, DeKorte Environmental Center, Hackensack Meadowlands. (Photo by Betsy McCully.)

The cedar woodland of the Meadowlands is forever gone, replaced by a sad history of degradation as the region was first clear-cut, then industrialized and polluted, then used as a landfill and dumping ground. Now, efforts are underway to restore at least a portion of the former vast wetland, but replanting of wetland grasses is easy compared to reforestation. As Kalm had noted over two centuries ago, cedars grow slowly and take a long time to reestablish themselves, far beyond an individual lifetime.

The best we can do is to preserve the forest remnants that are left. In New York City these are precious few. Examples include the Midwood section of Prospect Park, a section of the New York Botanical Gardens in the Bronx, a portion of Hunter's Island in Pelham Bay, and Alley Pond Park and Forest Park in Queens. All have been degraded to one extent or another, and all have been overgrown by alien species or weed trees. The New York City Parks Department, under the tenures of previous commissioner Henry Stern and current commissioner Adrian Benepe, has undertaken a heroic effort to restore as much as possible of the old woodlands on park land. The Prospect Park Plan, for instance, was implemented in 1995. Directed by Edward Toth, who heads the Parks Department's land management office, its goal is to restore 250 acres of woodland. The effort entails uprooting and discouraging alien species while encouraging the growth of native seedlings. Hickories, for example, do not transplant well, so their reestablishment depends on the success of seedlings taking root and thriving—a process that takes perhaps fifty years.[33]

It takes a long view to stay committed to reforesting the land. It takes an environmental ethic that has to be taught, passed down from one generation to the next. It takes a parent and child like Bernd Heinrich and his son planting a tree together, or together paying homage to a great tree. It takes stories of trees, both living and fallen, told by the elders to take root in the memories of the young. It takes a longtime memory of a place where one has roots, or puts down roots. It's that kind of connection that gets us to hear the voices of the wild, to desire to heal the earth and, in the process, ourselves.

9

Urban Flyway

New York City is along the migratory corridor of Neotropical birds, and Central Park is one of their prime havens. From a birds-eye view, the park must appear like a green oasis in a concrete desert, drawing down thousands of birds to rest and feed before continuing on their long journeys during spring and fall migrations. They are accompanied by hordes of birders hoping for what is known as a "fallout" of warblers, especially in spring, when the birds are in their colorful breeding plumage. Conditions have to be just right: a stiff southwest wind carries birds north, and rain or low cloud cover pushes them down to the ground. During the first and second weeks of May, it's possible for a dawn-to-dusk birder to see as many as twenty-five warbler species and a hundred bird species in a single day, mostly concentrated on the Point, a wooded spit of land that juts into Central Park's Rowboat Lake.[1]

One Saturday morning in May 2002, I joined a group of birders from the Brooklyn Botanic Garden led by my husband, Joe Giunta, in search of spring migrants. The day started out drizzly, following days of rainy weather and southwest winds — a perfect setup for a fallout. We were not to be disappointed. We gathered beneath an overpass off West Seventy-second Street by Strawberry Fields, waiting for the rain to let up. As soon as it cleared, we headed for the Ramble. We were hardly the only group in the park. Hundreds of people were pouring in — tourists, bikers, joggers, walkers, and birders — all out to enjoy a lovely spring day. Sunlight sparkled on wet leaves and birds stirred to life. Their songs brightened the air and their colors flashed in the trees. A Canada warbler displayed his distinctive black necklace set against bright yellow plumage; a red and black American redstart opened and closed his tail like a Japanese fan; a Blackburnian warbler swelled his flame-orange throat as he sang; a yellow Wilson's warbler donned his black cap; a black-and-white warbler crept along tree trunks and branches; a blue and gold northern parula flitted among the tree tops; a black-throated blue warbler sported his signature white "handkerchief" — and lucky for us that day, a gray and gold prothonotary warbler, a southern bird, made a rare regional appearance. What we could not see in the dense canopy, we heard: the "sweet, sweet, sweet" song of the yellow warbler; the ascending trill of the prairie warbler; the measured question-and-answer phrases of the red-eyed vireo; the rich, warbling notes of Baltimore orioles and scarlet tanagers. It was a feast for the eyes and a symphony for the ears, imprinted in our memories for life. Most of all, it was a rare privilege to witness the Neotropicals' spring rites of passage, winging their way to their northern breeding grounds as they had every spring for millennia.

When humans first entered our region around eleven thousand years ago as the last glacier retreated northward, they found an abundance of bird species common to forest, plains, and wetlands. Archaeological sites from the early Holocene (around ten thousand years ago) have unearthed bones of loon, grebe, heron, crane, rail, passenger pigeon, turkey, grouse, quail, and woodcock. Birds were hunted for food, their bones shaped into tools and flutes, and feathers worn as ornaments.[2]

Birds have always played an important role in the ritual and mythology of the American Indians. A great blue heron, for example, was found buried with an Iroquois woman at a prehistoric burial ground along the Genesee River near Avon in upstate New York. Archaeological sites in the Northeast have yielded polished, bird-shaped objects called birdstones, which may have been worn as ornaments or used as weights on hunting spears.[3]

One Iroquois myth relates the tale of a hunter who would kill a deer in order to lure an eagle to the kill, shoot it, and take its feathers. As retribution, the Mother of all Eagles seized the hunter and took him to her eyrie. When Mother Eagle left her nest to find food, the hunter managed to tie up the beaks of her eaglets with a leather thong. Upon seeing her eaglets' predicament, and unable to free them herself, she made a pact with the hunter: she would free him if he would untie her eaglets' beaks and promise never to shoot an eagle again without her permission. He agreed, and his descendants kept his word.[4]

When Europeans first began exploring these shores, they wrote glowing reports of the flora and fauna they encountered, giving them names that corresponded to the European species they knew. Van der Donck describes wild swans — perhaps whistling swans — "so plentiful that the bays and shores where they resort appear as if they were dressed in white drapery," their nightly chatter keeping awake those settlers who lived near their nesting grounds. Nicolaes van Wassenaer, a popularizer of the Dutch enterprise in the New World, describes an Edenic place of astonishing plenty, awaiting the arrival of the European to reap her bounty:

> In their waters are found all sorts of fowls, such as cranes, bitterns, swans, geese, ducks, widgeons, wild geese, as in this country. Birds fill also the woods so that men can scarcely go through them for the whistling, the noise, and the chattering. Whoever is not lazy can catch them with little difficulty. . . . Pigeons fly wild; they are chased by the foxes like the fowls. . . . 'Tis surprising that storks have not been found here, since it is a marshy country. Spoonbills, ravens, eagles, sparrow hawks, vultures are numerous and are quickly shot or knocked down by the natives.[5]

Unlike their Indian counterparts, Euro-American hunters quickly decimated local birds, as they were hunted far beyond the need for meat. Peter Kalm, a Swedish naturalist who traveled through New York, New Jersey, and Pennsylvania in the mid-eighteenth century, reported that old-timers remembered when the waterways were so filled with waterfowl, a man could easily kill eighty ducks in a single morning with a shotgun, whereas now he was lucky to see a single duck, crane, or wild turkey. The hunter's taking of eighty ducks struck Kalm as extremely wasteful. He was quick to discern the cause of such "diminution":

> Before the arrival of the *Europeans* [Kalm's emphasis], the country was uncultivated, and full of great forests. The few Indians that lived here seldom disturbed the birds. They carried on no trade among themselves, iron and gunpowder were unknown to them. One hundredth part of the fowl, which at that time were so plentiful here, would have sufficed to feed the few inhabitants. . . . But since the arrival of great crowds of Europeans, things are greatly changed: the country is well peopled, and the woods are cut down: the people increasing in this country, they have by hunting and shooting in part extirpated the birds, in part scared them away: in spring the people still take both eggs, mothers and young indifferently, because no regulations are made to the contrary. And if any had been made, the spirit of freedom which prevails in this country would not suffer them to be obeyed.[6]

It should be noted that Kalm's characterization of the American Indians is somewhat erroneous. The Indians actively managed the land for farming and hunting purposes, and traded goods over an extensive trading network. Nonetheless, Kalm's point about most Euro-Americans' wasteful hunting practices and disregard for conservation is indisputable.

The passenger pigeon was once celebrated in a Seneca dance as a harbinger of spring and abundant food, according to early accounts. We know that the passenger pigeon depended on mast (beechnuts in particular) as its main source of food, and hence on old-growth deciduous forest habitat. It was once an abundant fall migrant, migrating inland through beech-oak forests from its northern breeding grounds, its great flocks darkening the September skies. In 1672, John Josselyn reported that these migrating flocks "had neither beginning nor ending, length nor breadth, and so thick I could see no Sun." Passenger pigeons were viewed by the farmers as a scourge and thus shooting them was considered a service. Peter Matthiessen, in his book *Wildlife in America*, relates a story of the pigeons who inflicted damage on Plymouth crops in 1643, when thousands of the birds "descended . . . with such violence as to cause a serious threat of famine" — but it was the pigeons who staved off famine, serving as an alternate food when crops failed five years later.[7]

In the fall of 1813, Audubon witnessed a flyover of passenger pigeons in Ohio that seemed unending. He wrote in his journal: "The air was literally filled with pigeons; the light of noonday was obscured as by an eclipse; the dung fell in spots, not unlike melting flakes of snow; and the continued buzz of wings had a tendency to lull my senses to repose." He also marveled at how the birds defended themselves against a hawk attack by forming a compact ball (much as starlings do today): "In these almost solid masses, they darted forward in undulating and angular lines, descended and swept close over the earth with inconceivable velocity, mounted perpendicularly so as to resemble a vast column, and, when high, were seen wheeling and twisting within their continued lines, which then resembled the coils of a gigantic serpent." His admiration for their aerial acrobatics gave way to sheer wonder when he saw how subsequent flocks would trace in the air the exact same "angles, curves, and undulations" performed by the preceding flock warding off the hawk. Audubon, who estimated their numbers to be in the billions, could not conceive that they were ever in danger of extinction, despite the mass slaughter of them he observed, concluding only "that nothing but the gradual diminution of our forests can accomplish their decrease."[8]

The pigeons were easily picked off by anyone who could aim a rifle at the sky and pull the trigger — and this the settlers did, far beyond the need for meat or feathers. James Fenimore Cooper dramatizes an annual pigeon shoot in *The Pioneers*, set in central New York in the late 1700s. Every spring, when pigeons migrated by the hundreds of thousands, a whole village turned out to shoot the birds down from the skies. Cooper's old protagonist Natty Bumpo, known as Leather-stocking, comes out to join one of the shoots, but the scene of carnage disturbs him. Hundreds of twitching pigeons litter the fields. When one of the sportsmen rolls out a cannon to fire into the flocks, it is too much for Leather-stocking. He indignantly cries out: "This comes of settling a country! Here have I known the pigeons to fly for forty long years, and, till you made your clearings, there was nobody to scare or to hurt

Fig. 9.1. Louis Agassiz Fuertes, "Passenger Pigeons." (From Elon Howard Eaton, *Birds of New York*, New York State Education Department, New York State Museum Report 63, v. 3, part 2: 1914.)

them. . . . But now it gives me sore thoughts when I hear the frighty things whizzing through the air." When a farmer retorts that he'd feel differently if it were his crops the pigeons ate, Leather-stocking makes clear it is the manner of killing he deplores: "It's wicked to be shooting into flocks in this wastey manner. . . . I don't like to see these wasty ways that you are all practysing, as if the least thing was not made for use, and not to destroy." Leather-stocking then demonstrates his own efficiency as a hunter by taking down a single pigeon in one clean shot, and declares it quite enough for a man's dinner. His parting words condemn the settlers' prodigal ways, whether slaughtering pigeons or hacking trees to leave "dark and charred stumps" just as they leave wounded birds in the fields.[9]

Pigeons were killed by the thousands for the market. Audubon describes seeing schooners piled with pigeons caught along the Hudson unloading at the wharf in New York in 1805, when they fetched a penny a bird on the market. In March of 1830, pigeons fetched four cents each in New York's bird market. Young pigeons were especially esteemed as squabs, and these were gotten by cutting down or shaking the trees where the pigeons nested in huge colonies. The young birds were thereby "violently hurled to the ground," in a process that destroyed far more than the market hunters took.[10]

As late as the 1870s, hundreds could still be shot in a day; but by the 1880s, the passenger pigeon had become rare. The last known record in the New York City region was of "an immature male shot at Englewood, New Jersey, June 23, 1896," according to Frank Chapman in his 1906 guide, *Birds of the Vicinity of New York City*; the last New York State sighting was in 1907, when John Burroughs spotted a large flock in Kingston; and the last passenger pigeon known was a captive bird called Martha, who made the Cincinnati Zoo her home until her death in 1914.[11]

A similar fate met the heath hen. J. P. Giraud, in his 1844 book, *The Birds of Long Island* (the first book on New York birds), recounts its demise:

> Thirty years ago, it was quite abundant on the brushy plains in Suffolk County, which tract of country is well adapted to its habits — but being a favorite bird with sportsmen, as well as commanding a high price in the New York markets, it has been pursued, as a matter of pleasure and profit, until now it is very doubtful if a brace can be found on the Island. On a recent ex-

cursion over its former favorite haunts, I could find no trace of it. In con-
versation with several of the elder residents, they spoke of the "Heath Hen"
as being very abundant some twenty or thirty years since, but now consider
it entirely extinct.[12]

The heath hen is now classified as the eastern subspecies of the greater
prairie-chicken (also called pinnated grouse) of the Midwest. Like its western cousin, it was famous for its mating dances, which involved drumming
that could be heard for miles — hence its Latin name *Tympanuchus cupido
cupido*. In spring, the males would gather at a lek, or mating ground, around
sunrise. They would inflate their bright orange throat sacs like bellows to
produce a hooting sound, whir their wings, vibrate their erect tail feathers,
stamp their feet, and leap in the air to attract females in a spectacular
courtship ritual.[13]

The last heath hen on Long Island was shot in 1836; a colony of three
hundred or so survived on Martha's Vineyard until 1932.[14]

Like passenger pigeons, wild turkeys feed on mast (beech nuts, acorns,
and the like that have fallen to the ground) in heavily forested land. A highly
desirable game bird, it was hunted nearly to extinction by the mid-1800s,
and was extirpated from New York State by 1844. A small stock survived in
south-central Pennsylvania, which slowly expanded its range as farms reverted
to woodland and forests recovered from logging during the mid-twentieth
century. The turkey was deliberately reintroduced in New York State beginning in 1959; by 1995, Stephen W. Eaton reports in *Bull's Birds of New York
State* that "they had bred within sight of Long Island Sound in Westchester
County, were wandering through suburban backyards, and were even being
seen in the Bronx." In 2003, a *New York Times* article reported several sightings in Manhattan — one on a ledge of an Upper West Side high-rise, another in the branches of a London plane tree in Chelsea, and several days
later in the same area, on the lawn of the General Theological Seminary of
the Episcopal Church.[15]

The millinery trade of the nineteenth century pushed a number of species to the brink of extinction. Women's hats were often adorned not merely
with plumes but with whole, stuffed birds such as warblers, saw-whet owls,
hummingbirds, and red-headed woodpeckers. One hat might sport ten

warblers. The name egret is derived from the French word for plume, *l'aigrette*, and indeed the ornamental white plumes displayed by great and snowy egrets during mating season were in especially great demand.[16]

In 1844, Giraud reported that the snowy heron (the contemporary name for the snowy egret) was a "not uncommon breeder" on Long Island. Known to gunners as "White Poke," it was observed in salt marshes and mudflats "wading about in the shallow water, in search of small crabs, lizards and worms." In the same report, Giraud noted that the great white heron (great egret) was being killed in "large numbers . . . for the value of their plumes, which are prized as ornaments." Sightings of the egrets on Long Island became increasingly scarce. In his 1906 guide, Chapman noted that on May 30, 1885, William Dutcher observed just three snowy egrets at Sayville, Long Island, one carrying a stick in its mouth. It would be a long time before egrets would again breed in the region. Chapman concluded that the snowy egret is "now an exceedingly rare bird breeding in a few isolated localities in Florida."[17] By 1910, the snowy egret was considered extirpated from North America, and the great egret nearly exterminated.

The egrets were mostly hunted in Venezuela and Florida to supply the millinery trade in New York and London, with New York cornering about 90 percent of the market. In the egret nesting season of 1892, a single shipment of 130,000 "scalps" — bird skins with feathers attached — was sent to the New York millinery market. Allan Cruickshank, in an article published in 1948, described the slaughter: "Men fought and sometimes killed each other to maintain control over colonies of snowy egrets. When the eggs hatched and the instinct to care for the hungry young was strongest, the killers descended on the colonies. They shot each bird as it attempted to return to its helpless young." In this manner, adults were decimated and the young left to die.[18]

Alarmed at the egrets' imminent demise, George Bird Grinnell led the fight to stop the slaughter of the beautiful birds. Boston society women like Harriet Hemenway joined forces with him, boycotting bird hats and raising the consciousness of other women. Helen Winslow's declaration was typical: "The place for dead birds is not above a pretty woman's face." This group became the core of the first state Audubon Society, founded in 1896 in Massachusetts. Other states followed suit. In January 1905, William Dutcher filed papers with New York State to incorporate the National Association of Audubon Societies for the Protection of Wild Birds and Animals.[19]

Under President Theodore Roosevelt, several bird sanctuaries and wild-life refuges were created to protect endangered birds. The persistent efforts of the Audubon societies to protect birds from market hunting sometimes met deadly resistance. In 1905, a poacher murdered Audubon warden Guy Bradley as he was patrolling a bird sanctuary in Monroe County, Florida. Three years later, another warden, Warren McLeod of Charlotte Harbor in South Carolina, was murdered in similar fashion. These cold-blooded murders had the effect of galvanizing the conservation movement and of winning new converts. Audubon Society members in New York, led by president of the society, T. Gilbert Pearson, introduced and successfully lobbied for the passage of the Audubon Plumage Bill, which was signed into law by New

Fig. 9.2. Great white egret. (Photo by Ben Cooper.)

York governor Charles Evan Hughes in 1910. This law banned possession for sale, offering for sale, and sale of the plumage of wild birds.[20]

While this ban helped close down the New York market in plumes, it did nothing to prevent their slaughter or sale elsewhere. And of course, the scarcer the egrets became, the hotter the market in their plumes — and the more intense the hunt for them. In the year 1914, for instance, 21,528 ounces of egret plumes were sold in the London market alone, representing the slaughter of 130,000 adult birds, and this number does not take into account the untold deaths of their orphaned offspring due to starvation in the nest. The plumes brought thirty-two dollars an ounce on the international market. Not until the passage of the Federal Migratory Bird Treaty Act in 1918 did the egrets begin their slow recovery.[21]

When John Bull published his *Birds of the New York Area* in 1964, he noted how the egrets had greatly increased in numbers in the coastal salt meadows. "Only those active observers who have been in the field for the past 30 years or so can appreciate the phenomenal comeback this heron has made," he wrote. "Even as recently as the early 1930s the report of a Snowy Egret in the New York City region was enough to send an observer rushing to the spot in hopes of seeing it. Today the Snowy is the most numerous of the native 'white' herons, at least on the outer coast, and is more deserving of the appellation 'common' than its larger relative." By the time Bull published his *Birds of New York State* in 1974, the snowy was "the most numerous breeding heron on the south shore of Long Island, even outnumbering the formerly abundant Black-crowned Night Heron."

Black-crowned night herons were decimated by a combination of pesticides, wetland pollution, and habitat loss. They have slowly recovered, but not as dramatically as other herons. Robert E. Marcotte, in the 1998 edition of *Bull's Birds of New York State*, reported that nesting herons on Long Island "still average only about half what they were, ranging from 1105 pairs at 17 colonies in 1992 to 1887 pairs at 23 colonies in 1993." Like other colonial nesting waterbirds, black-crowned night herons usually prefer to roost and nest in trees somewhat removed from human traffic. But there are exceptions to the rule. In Nassau County, for instance, my husband and I have observed a black-crowned night heron pair nesting year after year in a tall tree in a suburban backyard. In Bay Ridge, Brooklyn, while taking sunset walks on the esplanade beneath the Verrazano Bridge, we have heard the hoarse croaks of the black-crowns calling, and looked up to see their chunky neck-less bodies and outspread wings silhouetted against the pink sky as they headed for their roost beneath the bridge.

Another waterbird severely impacted by pesticides and other chemicals is the double-crested cormorant. Cormorants were decimated between the 1950s and 1970s as a result of DDT, mercury, and PCBs in the Great Lakes where they bred. Passage of strong antipollution legislation in the seventies enabled the cormorants to recover, and since then they have rapidly increased and spread from the Great Lakes southward. The first ever reported nesting on Long Island was at Fishers Island in 1977. In the New York City region, they rebounded "from 585 breeding pairs in 1985 to 3528 pairs in 1995," according to a survey conducted by New York City Audubon and the New York State Department of Environmental Protection. Their nesting grounds include islands in Arthur Kill, where a 2002 census found 1,203 nests. Shooters Island, once a duck hunters' haunt, then a thriving shipyard, and later a graveyard for abandoned vessels, is in its latest incarnation a rookery for dozens of cormorants who nest in the decayed docks, hulls, and pilings. As of 2004, thirty-one active nests were confirmed on this island. According to the same survey, North and South Brother Islands in the East River support 350 active breeding pairs of cormorants.[22]

For years during my walks along Sheepshead Bay, I have observed the comical cormorants, who winter on this bay. They perch on buoys and old fishing boats, stretching their wings to dry like laundry on a clothesline. I enjoy the sight of these birds here, but I know they are not so appealing to some fishermen, fish farmers, and even conservationists. Since their recovery, they have increased so much on the Great Lakes that they are viewed as marauders of fish stocks and competitors with other nesting species. In 1989, the Canadian government authorized the killing of ten thousand nesting double-crested cormorants on the Saint Lawrence River, and the U.S. legislature passed laws in 1997 and 1998 that permitted the killing of nesting cormorants in the Great Lakes region. According to Brinkley and Humann (2001), the grounds for such extermination programs are open to question. The authors cite studies that have shown the cormorants taking fish of little commercial value. They also express surprise that such programs are aimed against the birds when they so recently recovered from decimation due to pesticides and are still threatened by oil spills and fish nets.[23]

The passage of the Clean Water Act in 1972 may well have enabled cormorants, herons, and other colonial nesters to breed successfully in once polluted wetlands. This landmark legislation lowered the level of fecal matter and other organic pollutants that sewage treatment plants could release into the water, thereby raising its level of oxygen, which in turn enabled the birds' prey species to survive—and provide good eating to adults and offspring. As a result, waterbirds were able to roost even on islands in a heavily trafficked waterway like Arthur Kill, a narrow fifteen-mile channel between Staten Island and New Jersey. That is, until oil spread its deadly calm over the waters.[24]

The Exxon oil spill of 1990 saturated the waters and marshes of Arthur Kill with 567,000 gallons of heating oil, killing hundreds of birds and thousands of fish and other aquatic organisms. On the night of January 1, a pipeline ruptured and oil leaked into the waters; high winds and tides quickly spread the oil throughout the channel, its tributaries, and wetlands. After the accident, wildlife rehabilitators collected eight hundred dead and injured birds; of the still living birds, less than half were able to return to the wild. Most of the affected birds were gulls and ducks. Because the spill occurred in the winter, when herons and other waders are few, it diminished but luckily did not destroy these birds. However, the oil killed one-fifth of the cordgrass that makes up the primary vegetation of the wetlands and provides important habitat to wading birds. It also suffocated invertebrates and other prey species of birds. When wading birds returned to breed in the spring, they were adversely affected by the conditions created by the oil spill. Most hard-hit were snowy egrets, whose reproductive rate declined until 1993. Since then, the wading birds of Arthur Kill have made a comeback. In 1995, a census conducted by New York City Audubon counted 2,051 breeding pairs of herons and ibises on five islands in Arthur Kill and the East River (known as the Harbor Herons Complex). The herons included such previous rarities as the yellow-crowned night heron, green-backed heron, and little blue heron.[25]

Rachel Carson, in her landmark book published in 1962, *Silent Spring*, alerted us to the perils of the indiscriminate use of pesticides. The book documents the insidious poisoning of the earth and its creatures, including ourselves, as a result of the use of chemicals to kill agricultural pests. At the time she wrote the book, there was a deluge of alarming reports of mass bird and fish kills. Birds were literally dropping dead from the skies. Where chemicals were extensively and repeatedly sprayed over a wide area, whole regions grew silent of birdsong and empty of bird life. At the time of her writing, she reported that five hundred new chemicals a year were being produced and applied:

> These sprays, dusts, and aerosols are now applied almost universally to farms, gardens, forests, and homes — non-selective chemicals that have the power to kill every insect, the "good" and the "bad," to still the song of birds and the leaping of fish in the streams, to coat the leaves with a deadly film, and to linger on in soil. . . . Can anyone believe it is possible to lay down such a barrage of poisons on the surface of the earth without making it unfit for life? They should not be called "insecticides," but "biocides."[26]

While Carson's main focus was on agricultural applications, she also noted the uses of pesticides to beautify roadsides, parks, and suburban lawns. It was astounding to her that homemakers could buy such lethal chemical products and be trusted to apply them, unaware of their deadly impact on the environment. These toxins washed into waterways, built up in soil and animal tissues, and posed health risks to humans in the form of cancers and outright death from poisoning.

Rachel Carson wrote her book while fighting a personal battle with breast cancer. She bravely withstood attacks by chemical industry spokesmen on her work and her character, and continued to raise her voice to educate the public about pesticides. The last years of her life were not spent in vain. Her book galvanized grassroots groups to push for legislation to ban DDT and other pesticides. In 1970, the Environmental Protection Agency was established by an act of Congress, and domestic production and application of DDT was halted.

Roger Tory Peterson echoed Carson's concerns in his "Foreword" to Bull's *Birds of the New York City Region,* published in 1964, the same year Carson died of cancer. Already, he gloomily reported, ospreys had declined drastically since 1950 on eastern Long Island and Gardiners Island, and he feared complete extirpation from the region "before the successor to this book is written." The population of breeding ospreys on Long Island had plummeted from five hundred nests in 1940 to seventy-five by 1950. He noted that the peregrine falcon was gone from the Hudson Valley, compared to pre-1950s reports of a dozen nesting pairs. The peregrine once had perhaps fifty nest sites throughout the eastern half of New York State, but by the early sixties it had disappeared from New York. Declines of breeding pairs of both ospreys and peregrines were caused by DDT's effect of thinning their eggshells, combined with habitat loss and the human practice of stealing their young and eggs, as well as sport hunting.[27]

Since the ban on DDT, populations of ospreys and peregrines have recovered. Their recovery has been aided by state and federal laws that protect birds of prey from sport hunting and breeding-habitat disturbance. In addition, since the 1970s, nesting platforms for osprey have been erected throughout Long Island, which was their traditional breeding ground (primarily on the eastern end, with historical accounts listing three hundred nest sites in the early nineteenth century). As of 1994, 247 pairs were counted on Long Island — a great success story. As of this writing, pairs of ospreys and their offspring have been reported at sites on the western end of Long Island, including Jamaica Bay, Hempstead Lake, and along the Southern Parkway in Nassau County. It is thrilling to hear the whistling calls of a pair of ospreys as they circle together over their nesting platform.[28]

Peregrines have been deliberately reintroduced into the urban landscape of New York City by the New York State Department of Environmental Conservation (NYDEC) since 1972. By 1983, peregrine nests were established on the Throgs Neck Bridge and the Verrazano Narrows Bridge. During the nineties, new nests were established throughout the New York City region. Now, reports Barbara Allen Loucks in the 1998 edition of *Bull's Birds of New York State*, New York City "has the largest urban population in the world, with some nesting pairs only a kilometer apart."[29] Peregrines hunt by nosediving (the technical term is stooping) at speeds of perhaps one hundred miles per hour, catching their unsuspecting prey in flight. Typical prey include pigeons (rock doves), jays, and starlings. Joe and I used to observe a pair of peregrines at the defunct Coney Island parachute jump. They loved to nest high on this rusting steel tower and hunt for rodents and small birds in the weedy vacant lot beneath them. Sadly, the Coney Island pair disappeared when the parachute jump was taken down to build a new baseball stadium. The pair at the Jones Beach tower in Nassau County, however, still reigns over their park dominion, where rock doves and starlings are plentiful. We have observed them through a spotting scope as they preened or rested on a high ledge of the brick observation tower.[30]

Like the peregrine and osprey, the bald eagle was also susceptible to the adverse effects of DDT. Yet even before the widespread use of DDT after World War II, as noted by Peter Nye in *Bull's Birds of New York State,* eagles had been severely decimated by habitat loss and sport shooting. J. P. Giraud, in *Birds of Long Island,* reported in 1844 that sixty to seventy eagles were shot in a single winter season on Long Island. Such sport hunting reduced their numbers on Long Island, but they continued to breed successfully upstate. Eighty known nesting sites were continuously used from at least the early 1800s into the mid-twentieth century. Continued illegal sport shooting combined with habitat loss drastically reduced nesting pairs of eagles from eighty to twenty. DDT dealt a near-death blow to the species. By 1970, one breeding pair was left in New York State.[31] New Jersey had also been a prime breeding territory, where fifteen successful nests just south of New York City were reported in 1957. By 1961, only one out of seven nests monitored by biologists was successful. The banning of DDT aided the comeback of bald eagles, but they would not have made such a spectacular recovery if it were not for the captive breeding and release program initiated in 1976 by the New York State Department of Environmental Conservation. In 1996, according to Peter Nye, nineteen of twenty-nine breeding pairs in New York State successfully fledged thirty-seven young. In an interview with Peter Nye conducted in 2004 by Anthony dePalma of the *New York Times,* Nye expressed growing dismay at the habitat destruction he witnessed in an aerial survey of prime eagle breeding territory in upstate New York, where housing developments with cruelly ironic names like Eagle's Nest Estates were clear-cutting wooded hillsides to make way for second homes. "The question now is whether, by 2050, the habitat they need is still going to be here to support them or will we keep whittling away at it so that the habitat disappears?" Nye's concern is parental: it was he who nursed and released eaglets collected from Alaskan nests to repopulate New York.[32]

In the brutally cold winter of 2004, New Yorkers were startled to see bald eagles hitching rides on ice floes in the Lower Hudson. As reported by Joseph Berger in the *New York Times,* urban park rangers spotted mature male, female, and immature eagles riding ice floes, soaring, and perching at points along the Hudson near Manhattan's shores. In a winter that froze up many waterways, the eagles were pursuing their prey fish southward where the water was still open. The return of the bald eagle to our region is cause for rejoicing.

The red-tailed hawk is another raptor that has adapted in surprising ways to our urban habitats. Highways are prime hunting grounds for this hawk, who may often be seen perched on a street light overarching the highway watching for prey in the median. This hawk prefers to nest in wooded areas next to open fields, but one pair has now taken to urban living — much to the delight of experienced birdwatchers. The book by Marie Winn, *Red-Tails in Love,* and most recently the film *Pale Male,* chronicle the life of a male red-tail who took up apartment living in Manhattan. Dubbed Pale Male for his unusually light coloration, the hawk successfully mated and bred with three females in succession over a period of twelve years, producing twenty-seven offspring. (Red-tails are monogamous, seeking a new mate only when the former mate has died.) In 1993, Pale Male wooed his first mate, Chocolate, to the twelfth-floor window ledge of a luxury apartment building at 927 Fifth Avenue. The two built an unlikely nest on a set of anti-pigeon spikes installed on the ledge. After two nesting failures, the pair successfully bred beginning in 1995, fledging three chicks. It was the first known breeding of red-tails in an urban site. Ornithologists from the American Museum of Natural History and the birdwatching community of Central Park have monitored the doings of this red-tail family for years now, acting as protective guardians of their fates. In December of 2004, Pale Male and his current mate, Lola, gained world fame and advocacy when their nest was unceremoniously dismantled by the building's co-op board. The eviction of the hapless hawks was bitterly opposed by several of the building's residents, Mary Tyler Moore being the most vociferous. Reaction among the birding community, led by E. J. Adams of the New York City Audubon, was swift and was supported by birders and wildlife advocates worldwide. An agreement was negotiated with the co-op board, and the nesting platform was rebuilt in time for the pair to start a new nest. Unfortunately, this nest was not successful (they laid eggs, but they never hatched), perhaps due to the tremendous stress they were subjected to during their eviction.[33]

Migratory species of owls such as the long-eared and saw-whet are known to winter in Central Park (and other city parks with coniferous woodland, particularly Pelham Bay), but only one owl species has bred here. The eastern screech owl prefers broken forested habitat with water and open space — hence they have benefited from low-density suburban development, as long as there are mature trees with cavities that serve as nesting holes, or human-constructed nest boxes. The screech owl was known to nest in Central Park as late as the publication of *Bull's Birds of New York City* in 1964. By the 1990s it had disappeared. According to E. J. McAdams, an urban park ranger before he became the current executive director of New York City Audubon, the New York City Parks Department decided to reintroduce the owls to the park based on their conclusion that the screech owl was nonmigratory and therefore had no way of returning to the park on its own. They also hoped the owls would provide a natural check on the rat population. In 1998, they released six owls into the park, of which one survived. Working with wildlife ecologist Bill Giuliano of Fordham University, E. J. and his team released eighteen more in the fall of 2001. In April 2002, they were overjoyed to discover two fledglings with their mother roosting and hunting by the lake; their mother was the only survivor of the 1998 release. In March of 2003, two baby owls were found on the ground, rescued, and taken to a wildlife rehabilitation center, then released back into the park on April 30. Since then, no more owls have been released. Several owls dispersed to locations outside the park. The East Harlem owl, for instance, has been observed roosting at a construction site at 108th Street and Madison Avenue. The owls have a hard time thriving in the park, perhaps the result of the owls eating poisoned rodents, and because of human harassment — one man was actually caught trying to net an owl. But they have persisted. In the breeding seasons of 2004 and 2005, birders have reported two breeding pairs of screech owls in the park. In May 2004, Joe and I observed a screech owl roosting in a tree cavity in the Ramble, its mottled gray feathers perfectly blending with the gray bark of the tree.[34]

In countless spots where we drop crumbs and uneaten leftovers — city parks, outdoor cafes, open trash cans — English sparrows and pigeons can be found milling around. Neither species is native to North America. The first eight pairs of the misnamed sparrows, which are really weaver finches, were released in Brooklyn in 1851; fifty more pairs were released the following year, and another fifty in 1853. They soon multiplied, thriving on grain-flecked mounds of horse manure that filled city streets and lots in the days before the automobile. In 1892, four thousand were reported at a single pool in Central Park. Their numbers declined with the advent of the automobile, but they quickly adapted. They are aggressive birds who hog feeder stations and usurp nesting boxes intended for bluebirds. The pigeon, or rock dove, was first introduced to North America by the French in the early 1600s and has become a ubiquitous urban denizen, although it is also known to inhabit farmland.[35]

Starlings were introduced as early as 1844, but their numbers did not take off until a misguided bird lover, hoping to populate New York City with the birds of Shakespeare, released eighty starlings in Central Park in 1890 and forty more in 1891. The number of starlings now rival the population of the United States, their hordes proving a bane to farmers whose fruit trees are stripped by the voracious birds, and usurping the nest sites of native cavity-nesting birds. Donald Windsor, in *Bull's Birds of New York State*, attributes their success to their ability "to readily exploit opportunities offered by humans through both agricultural and urban developments." Indeed, the subdivision of farms and woodlands into suburban housing tracts provides ideal habitat for the starling. I personally observed a roost of perhaps twenty thousand starlings in a subdivision in Sterling Forest, Orange County, during the Orange County Christmas Bird Count in December 2003. Yet despite the overwhelming impression that starlings are thriving, statistics derived from Christmas Bird Counts over the past forty years in the United States prove the contrary: they have declined significantly.[36]

Suburban sprawl has favored some species while discouraging others. Consider the Canada geese who have found park and golf course greens quite to their liking. Once, the geese migrated southward from their breeding grounds in Canada; now huge numbers of them have become year-round residents, their large droppings fouling the greens. A number of other species prefer the edge habitats created by suburban lawns and golf courses adjacent to woodlands. Wintering sparrows such as the white-throated and white-crowned find nutritious food in grasses gone to seed. These and other birds are also drawn to an increasing number of backyard birdfeeders, including the black-capped chickadee, cardinal, blue jay, titmouse, dark-eyed junco, downy woodpecker (if suet is available) — and possibly a sharp-shinned or Cooper's hawk who predates them. Indeed, the backyard feeding stations may be contributing to the sharp-shinned hawk's comeback. Backyard birdwatchers who dislike the hawk's visits should recall that it was once a threatened species due to sport hunting in the early twentieth century and pesticide spraying since 1950. The sharp-shin was shot for sport in huge numbers during the years 1917 to 1920. The shooters used owl decoys to draw down the birds during their fall migration, shooting them by the hundreds. On a single day — September 19, 1920 — 406 were shot. The 1998 *Bull's Birds of New York State* reports a large increase of wintering "sharpies" in New England.

Christmas Bird Counts in New York City are tallying increasing numbers of sharpies, the maximum being seventeen in southern Nassau County in 1994.[37]

Such success stories as the comeback of egrets and eagles underscore the vital importance of conservation. Beginning with the movement to stop the feather trade and the organization of the first Audubon societies, persistent efforts by people on behalf of birds has helped endangered populations recover and protected threatened populations. Indeed, according to New York State Breeding Bird Survey data, as summarized by Charles R. Smith of Cornell in 1998, more breeding bird species are increasing in abundance or remaining stable than are declining. Populations of Neotropical migrants are remaining stable or increasing. Most breeding bird species on the decline are habitat-specific, such as grassland birds. Declines are due to human disturbance, but increases are due to human intervention.[38]

Human intervention efforts on behalf of wildlife now focus on restoring and preserving habitats as the key to protecting threatened species. Habitat degradation and fragmentation have severely impacted bird populations worldwide. In the 1980s, BirdLife International initiated the Important Bird Area program (IBA), identifying sites across the globe deemed vital to maintaining viable bird populations. Sites were selected based on their importance as critical breeding, feeding, wintering, or migratory stopover areas. In 1995, the National Audubon Society collaborated with the American Bird Conservancy to adopt IBA. As of 2005, they selected 1,600 sites nationwide, of which 127 are in New York State, and 35 in New York City. Audubon's 2004 Breeding Bird Survey found a 30 percent reduction in the populations of the four hundred bird species they monitored, an alarming decline that underscores the urgent need for habitat protection. History shows that the populations of birds once deemed common can be pushed to the brink of extinction.[39]

The passenger pigeon will never again darken the skies with its endless flocks, nor will the heath hen drum his feet on Long Island's pine barren heath. What has been destroyed can never be created again.

10

Weathering

When the northeaster of 1992 hit, powerful winds pushed the waters of Lower New York Bay into the cul-de-sac created by western Long Island and New Jersey, forcing them to back up and flood shoreline communities. It was December 11, a night of astronomical significance as the earth, moon, sun, and planets lined up in a phenomenon known as Syzygy. Just two nights before, I had witnessed a spectacular lunar eclipse while crossing Sheepshead Bay on the wooden footbridge: the huge orb of the moon hung low in a clear black sky, the shadow of the earth projected on it, slowly swallowing the moon. On the day of December 10, the weather shifted, bringing rain and warm temperatures and high winds. That night, the wind grew so fierce it shook our house and tore off pieces of siding, which crashed down to our driveway with a loud metallic crackling, rousing my family out of bed. Still, we dismissed it as just another winter storm. The next morning, when we stepped outside, we were flabbergasted to see the ocean pouring over the esplanade wall, tossing huge boulders onto the street like beach balls, and coursing down the street like a river. It was white and wild and seething. It roared and hissed, pounding away at the sea wall. Water was pouring in everywhere: it sloshed over the Sheepshead Bay footbridge and overflowed into adjacent streets; it poured over sidewalks and lawns, and slithered down sloping driveways; and as the tide rose, the flood waters rose — one, two, three, four feet — stranding cars and pedestrians, inundating basements and garages. Homeowners stood on their stoops unable to go farther because water was lapping over their front steps. The sands of Brighton Beach and Coney Island disappeared under the waves that frothed and foamed under the boardwalk. The winds howled, ripping off roofs and branches, conspiring with the sea to pound the shore and bring piers and houses crashing down. Seawalls began to crumble and give way before the ocean's onslaught.

Several high tides came and went before the storm abated. Our house was spared but many others were flooded, wherever the water gathered and pooled. The seawall that protected our community held, but huge chunks had been torn away, and the esplanade buckled and gaped. The worst fear of our community—that the waters of Sheepshead Bay and the Lower New York Bay would unite, drowning Coney Island—did not materialize. Other communities did not fare so well. Surveying the damage, I found myself awed and sobered by our encounter with a nature that is powerful and indifferent to human life. A biblical passage came to my mind about building homes on sand.

The winter of 1992–93 brought three northeasters pounding the Atlantic Coast. Northeasters are common in winter, deriving their energy from the jet stream, a west-to-east current of air that sends a high-pressure system colliding with a more southerly low-pressure system, generating a classic cyclone of counterclockwise winds. Over the last several decades, the jet stream has shifted its winter path over North America. It used to follow a shallow arc across the continent; now, it traces an S-curve that dips into the South, drawing up warm moist air into the Northeast and eastern Canada. The result of this shift is more severe winter storms, as the continual feeding of warm air from the south intensifies and often prolongs the storm system. It is not clear whether the shift is due to global warming or natural causes such as a cyclical change in ocean currents. Causes of climate change are debatable, but effects are undisputed: record rains and snowfalls, hurricane-force winds and monstrous waves, coastal flooding and erosion.[1]

There is no question that the world is warmer than it was during the deep freeze of the last ice age, presumably ended over ten thousand years ago—although some scientists argue we are now in the early stages of a new glaciation. Twenty-two thousand years ago, in the depths of the last Ice Age, the world was nine degrees Fahrenheit colder than now and the sea level 350 feet lower along the Atlantic Coast. By twelve thousand years ago, the sea level had risen to just one hundred feet below the present level, and by six thousand years ago it reached its present level. Slowly, steadily over the millennia, the sea has been gaining ground, drowning the Atlantic Coastal Plain that once extended miles out over the continental shelf.[2]

One of our most cherished beliefs about nature is her balance and equilibrium, a kind of steady state that we humans disrupt. In fact, change is the way of nature. Any study of nature—whether of planet earth, the evolution of life, the history of continents and oceans, climate and atmosphere—discloses the dynamics of change. But it is change on a timescale that dwarfs our human lives, even the very existence of the human species. We cannot perceive the continents drifting, though we may see clear evidence of the rifting and suturing of continents, and feel our earth quake. We experience the daily and seasonal changes in the weather, but may not notice the slow shifts in the sun's angle from season to season, nor the even slower changes in climate. We see the ocean swells but cannot observe the ocean rising, nor understand the implications of climate change, until a storm surge sweeps the beach away. Shaken by nature's destructive power, we go about shoring up sea walls and dams, and blindly continue to build homes on barrier islands and low-lying coastlines.

Unfortunately, there are those who argue that if change is the way of nature, then why should we be so concerned about the inevitable? What difference does it make if there are a few species more or less? What difference if we are adding carbon dioxide to the atmosphere, when it has been in higher concentrations before? And what difference that the polar ice caps are melting and seas rising? It will take centuries, we assume, before the sea will encroach on our properties, and besides — we have always solved the problems of nature with technology.

The difference is the human factor. We are no longer the hunter-gatherers of the ice age; we may have hunted some species to extinction even then, and in the last ten millennia, through our agricultural and city-building practices, we have altered landscapes. But never before has our population been so large, never before have we so altered the very composition of our atmosphere, never before have we so fragmented our earth and disrupted ecosystems and decimated species — that we now face an unprecedented global catastrophe brought on by human interference with nature. Stephen Schneider, a University of California Berkeley professor and author of *Laboratory Earth: the Planetary Gamble We Can't Afford to Lose*, writes: "What appears to be unprecedented is the combination, or synergism, of potentially very rapid rates of human-induced change at the same time that nature has been fragmented and assaulted with a host of chemical agents or transplanted 'exotic' species that do not naturally occur where they are introduced by humans."[3] In the past, global temperature changes were measured out over millennia — perhaps one degree per one thousand years; now, degrees of global warming can be measured out in centuries. The speed of human-induced change far outpaces the natural cycles of climate change. Species that once had centuries and millennia to adapt to environmental change — usually by migrating with shifting climate zones — now have decades, and their migrations are often blocked by habitat fragmentation. Already we are in the midst of an extinction that rivals the great extinction at the close of the Cretaceous, which decimated the dinosaurs.[4]

Over the last century along the New York coastline, the ocean has risen ten inches. In the twenty-first century, it is projected to rise another twenty-two inches. Ocean waters expand because of warmer temperatures, melting ice caps and glaciers, and greater rainfall. As measured in Albany, New York, the temperature over the last century rose one degree Fahrenheit, and rainfall for the state increased by 20 percent. In the twenty-first century, temperatures in New York are predicted to climb four degrees in winter and spring months, and two to eight degrees in summer and fall months; precipitation will increase 10 to 20 percent.[5] Coastal cities like New York, even if its citizens build sea walls and dykes, will be subjected to the ravages of monstrous storms. Timing, of course, is everything: take a spring tide, a full or new moon, and have the storm hit with its full force at high tide, and we're sunk.

We have speeded up nature's clock. The most recent findings in climate studies point to a rate of climate change far more rapid than at first predicted. Based on ice-core borings in Greenland and Antarctica, deep-sea borings, cores of ancient pollen preserved in peat bogs, and analysis of tree rings, scientists have been able to reconstruct the story of the last ice age from its onset around 1.5 million years ago, through its nine glacial episodes punctuated by rapid warming intervals. Ice borings taken at the Vostok station in Antarctica reveal rising levels of carbon dioxide and methane gases during the warming phases, a phenomenon still little understood, that accelerated the melting of the polar ice sheets. In all four interglacial episodes, carbon dioxide rose from 180 parts per million to 300 parts per million. This compares to the current level of 365 parts per million.[6] Most significantly, warming took place far more rapidly than once thought — the climate flipping like a light switch rather than gradually like a dimmer — and the current warming trend has been accelerated by the human factor.

Since the industrial revolution, greenhouse gases have spiked dramatically. Greenhouse gases such as carbon dioxide and methane are found naturally in the earth's atmosphere, serving to trap the sun's energy and warm the earth in a benign fashion. With industrialization, the burning of fossil fuels like oil and coal has released more greenhouse gases into the atmosphere — increasing carbon dioxide levels, for instance, by 30 percent. At the same time, rural populations have expanded into marginal lands, razing forests that absorb carbon dioxide. By the end of the twenty-first century, if the trend continues, the level of carbon dioxide could rise between 30 and 150 percent. Rising levels of greenhouse gases have pushed up global mean surface temperatures between 1.6 and 6.3 degrees Fahrenheit.[7] This is more than "ten times faster than what has been the average rate of natural sustained global temperature change from the end of the last ice age to the present interglacial," claims Schneider.[8] Melting ice caps and glaciers are releasing freshwater into the oceans, raising sea levels. In the past century, the global sea level rose four to ten inches, and during the present century, the level is predicted to rise three times as fast — perhaps another eight to twelve inches by 2050, if not earlier.[9] All this is happening at a time when the human population has spread over the globe, crowding into marginal land areas such as low-lying coastal areas, barrier islands, and flood-prone river deltas, where large numbers of people are vulnerable to weather-related catastrophes.[10]

Still we believe we will find a technological solution to avert disaster. We build seawalls, groins, jetties, and other hard structures to break the onslaught of the sea. We construct levees to protect us from river floodwaters. We pump sand to replenish shores ravaged by winter storms. We discuss erecting dikes to stop the encroachment of the sea. Hey, didn't those old hands at dikes, the Dutch, save their country from being claimed by the sea? A little history lesson may give some perspective on the problem we face now.

Much of the Netherlands was once a vast floodplain, with the Rhine, Meuse, Waal, and Maas rivers draining to the sea. The first polders, which are below sea-level lands reclaimed for farmland, were created by draining coastal and river delta lands, and building dikes to hold back the sea. Keep in mind that they had experienced catastrophic floods and storm surges that claimed the lives of tens of thousands of people. The Elizabeth's Day Flood of November 1421, for instance, inundated five hundred square kilometers and killed ten thousand people; and a storm of 1570 breached the seawall and claimed one hundred thousand lives. Necessity breeds invention, as they say, and the Dutch became acknowledged masters of hydraulic technology. Wind-powered pumping mills were in use in Alkmaar in the early 1400s, and were refined by the late 1500s into more powerful pumping machines. The technology was perfected in the 1600s by Jan Adriaansz Leeghwater for the purpose of drainage: the *wipmolen*, situated behind the dikes, pumped water from the soil and transported it by means of "bucket chains" to canals. Leeghwater (the literal translation of his name is "Empty Water") sought to win the war with the sea through his ambitious schemes for land reclamation. Historian Simon Schama describes Leeghwater's projects: "At the inland sea, [he] deployed a battery of forty-three windmills with a lift of four feet and a system of encircling ring dykes to reclaim 17,500 acres of the richest alluvial soil, both for direct farming and the creation of urban estates for the urban patriciate whose capital made it possible." In the Beemster drainage project, for example, undertaken in 1607–1608 and completed in 1612, 123 investors reaped a 17 percent return in the form of rent on the new farms.[11]

Between 1590 and 1640, 200,000 acres were reclaimed and twenty-seven lakes pumped dry. The irony in all this feverish land building was that the Dutch were also cutting extensive tracts of peat, exposing the land to inundations that formed vast shallow lakes such as the Harlemmermeer, which grew from 2,600 hectares in 1531 to 16,000 hectares in 1700. In fact, the total land lost to peat dredging in the seventeenth century "far exceeded that won in *droogmakerijen*" or drainage projects, according to Audrey Lambert, author of *The Making of the Dutch Landscape* (1985). Moreover, the system of dikes and dams, "by constraining the waters too closely, made floods more destructive. Truly the Dutch were the engineers of their own disasters."[12]

Fast forward to the twentieth century. Twenty-seven percent of the country's land mass lies below sea level, supporting 60 percent of the population, who are protected from floodwaters by a network of dikes fifteen hundred miles long. In 1953, the North Sea broke through sea dikes in Zeeland, killing eighteen hundred people, a disaster that prompted calls for the government to strengthen and repair the dikes. They complied as they always have, spending close to $3 billion over three decades bolstering the seawalls ($2.4 billion was spent on constructing a new seawall in 1986).[13] The aggressive strategy the Dutch had followed for centuries to hold back the waters was challenged in the 1990s, when the proposal was put forward to dismantle some of the river dikes and let the land revert to wetlands and floodplain forest. Why? There were both environmental and economic reasons. It was becoming clear that not only was it costly to continually pump the low-lying farmlands and maintain the hard structures — $400 million a year, not counting billions spent on sea dikes—but runoff from the farms was polluting the aquifer, and continual pumping was actually depressing the lowlands further (as much as two feet in the last century), making them more vulnerable to flooding. Agronomist Maarten Peren, interviewed by Marlise Simons for the New York Times, acknowledged: "We've become like a big artificial park, where every centimeter is dammed in, sprayed, fertilized, grazed or cultivated or else it's paved and inhabited."[14] The government's "master plan for nature," adopted in 1990, aims to return 600,000 acres (comprising one-tenth of reclaimed farmland) to nature, creating green corridors, restoring ecosystems, and hopefully attracting native wildlife and flora that had been extirpated (one-third of bird species had disappeared since 1950, for example). The government is now buying up farms in the lowest-lying lands, dismantling dikes, and unleashing the rivers to flood their banks. Mildrecht, for example, lies twenty feet below sea level and is a prime candidate for flooding. This farm region was created at the end of the nineteenth century out of shallow lagoons that had themselves been created when the peat bogs were cut centuries before.[15]

In the winter of 1995, floodwaters again threatened to breach the river dikes, as 100,000 people fled rising river waters. The New York Times reported: "The few roads still open in flooded regions were jammed with cars, trucks, tractors and bicycles, many of them heavily laden with suitcases and furniture. Dozens of towns were submerged, populated only by livestock huddling on isolated patches of dry land."[16] Prime Minister Wim Kok pointed with pride to the Dutch "reputation for its defenses against the sea," but admitted that "now the danger from the great rivers seems greater than many have thought." Environment Minister Margaretha de Boer insisted that "this is not just a Dutch problem, it's a European problem. The absorbent effect of the land has been lost in many areas, so water descends on us much more quickly."[17] As Europe becomes more and more densely populated—and the Netherlands is the most densely populated country—land clearing for developments has robbed river-front lands of the capacity to act as a sponge for floodwaters. A biologist with the Foundation for Nature and the Environment, Marijke Brunt, bristled at suggestions that the floods were the fault of environmentalists who blocked dike-strengthening projects. "The true causes lay further away, in Germany and France, where deforestation is increasing runoff from streams and artificially increasing the flow of the Rhine," she claimed.[18] Indeed, river waters were inundating these countries along Holland's borders as well. As in 1953, the floods of 1995 galvanized the public to call for a strengthening of river dikes. But environmentalists argued that such hardening projects would have the opposite effect, by funneling the floodwaters and forcing them to rise ever higher. (The older dikes, in contrast, were constructed of mud.) The environmental argument prevailed, with the result that wherever possible, rivers are allowed to overflow their banks and be absorbed by a restored floodplain.[19]

Along our Atlantic Coast, a similar debate rages over how to control coastal flooding and beach erosion. According to *New York Times* journalist Cornelia Dean, author of *Against the Tide: The Battle for America's Beaches*, people who have homes and businesses to protect will naturally call for hardening of the defenses against the sea. The traditional thinking, implemented by the Army Corps of Engineers, is to construct seawalls and groins to protect beach communities from the ravages of storm surges. ("Groin" is an engineering term for rock barriers that extend into the water perpendicular to the beach, designed to trap sand; a more common term is "jetty.") It is the same thinking that advocates the construction of river levees to contain the rivers. But such hardening of shorelines causes more problems than it solves; building a groin to protect one community on the South Shore of Long Island may keep their beach from eroding but will starve the beaches downcurrent. Dean gives a capsule history of Westhampton Beach as an example.[20]

Westhampton Beach is a barrier island that lies between Shinnecock Inlet and Moriches Inlet on Long Island's South Shore. Both inlets were cut by storms, Moriches in 1931 and Shinnecock in the hurricane of 1938. The inlets were kept artificially open, blocking the natural flow of sand carried east to west by the littoral current, with the result that beaches to the west were being starved. Severe beach erosion prompted a study undertaken by the Army Corps of Engineers to figure out how to prevent further erosion. The corps released a report in 1960 outlining several steps to take: pump in 34 million cubic yards of sand to replenish the beach; plant dune grass to stabilize it; move or raise buildings affected by coastal flooding; and build "as many as fifty groins to hold the new sand in place."[21] Because of pressure by local residents, the first eleven groins were built in Westhampton Beach, an action characterized by critics as a bad move that protected Westhampton Beach homes but put homes downcurrent in jeopardy. A cry went out for more groins to the west, which only transferred the erosion even farther down-current. In 1970, Suffolk County withdrew its financial support of the West-hampton project, and the building of groins ceased. However, homeowners continued to build their homes on sand, counting on federal flood insurance to bail them out should a storm flood their property. Meanwhile, erosion continued. During the Halloween northeaster of 1991, the barrier island was cut in two by the sea. The three northeasters of 1992–1993 dealt further blows to the waterlogged community. Residents incorporated themselves into the town of West Hampton Dunes and filed suits against the county, state, and federal governments on the grounds that the erosion-control proj-ect had destroyed their beaches. They won their suit in 1994, and under the terms of settlement, 4.5 million cubic yards of sand were pumped in to cre-ate a new beachfront; as a salve to taxpayers, a portion was opened up to the public. The cost? Thirty-two million dollars. And that's only the upfront cost. The settlement also required the governments to continue to protect the beaches for thirty years.[22]

Does the pumping of sand and building of groins solve the problem of beach erosion? No, says Dean, it only forestalls the inevitable encroachment of a rising sea:

> West Hampton Dunes is a dismal example of what happens when people disregard the realities of the coast, build an unstable landform, and then try to avoid the inevitable consequences of armoring the beach. To suit their own purposes, they jettied inlets rather than letting them close naturally to restore the natural flow of sand. When erosion worsened, as it inevitably would, they built groins. When the groins made the problem even worse, they turned to federal, state, and local governments — that is, to the taxpayers. The taxpayers, in turn, find themselves committed to spending tens of mil-lions of dollars to protect the property of people who, in many cases, had every reason to know that they were building or buying in an unsafe place.[23]

The point is, hardening of the coast does not work except in highly local-ized ways, creating problems for adjacent beach communities and worsen-ing the erosion overall. It was a fact recognized as early as 1923, notes Dean, when an engineer observed how the groins built at Coney Island had caused more erosion than they had halted:

> Taken as a whole, the beach had been eroded, losing at some points substantial amounts. The groynes did in some cases perform the service of preventing further erosion, but that is all that can be claimed for them. As a rule, each groyne that was put in place by an upland owner made a small amount of sand in one interior corner or the other but always at the expense of the adjacent owners' land by shutting off the natural sand supply. The best protection that an extended natural beach can have is the sand itself. Almost every beach taken as a whole appears to be injured by jetties or groynes.

The beach replenishment project at Coney Island was the first such project in the United States. In 1921, engineers dredged sand from fifteen hundred feet offshore and pumped 1.5 million cubic yards of it onto Coney's existing beach to widen it 330 feet and accommodate a planned boardwalk; to maintain it, they also built a series of groins. The project cost $4 million, but over the decades, millions of dollars more have been pumped into maintaining the artificial beach.[24] The cost of such a reshaping of the shore was more than taxpayer dollars; it constituted a destruction of the dune habitat that had once characterized Coney Island's seaward side, and that did a far better job of protecting the shore from erosion.

The South Shore of Long Island was once comprised of a continuous line of dunes studded by marshes. A geologist of the mid-nineteenth century, William Mather, described a coastline covered with "sand hills" on which grew myrtle (*Myrica cerifera*), red cedar (*Juniperus virginianus*), beach grass (*Bamma arenaria*), and "a small creeping vine." Coney Island's seaward side was covered with "a labyrinth of sand dunes, formed by wind, which present almost every imaginable shape that such a material can assume." The dunes were five to thirty feet high, "with a few straggling tufts of beach-grass, and clumps of bushes half-buried in the drifted sand." He noted how the glacial-era ponds and pools of the eastern end of Coney were gradually silting up, becoming salt marshes between the upland and the beach. The sandy beach was created by the action of the littoral current, ferrying sand east to west and depositing it in overlapping sandbars. Coney Island, he noted, was "mostly alluvial," and was "rapidly washing away on its south side, where it is exposed to the full force of the ocean swell." Indeed, the beach that was once a mile broad was now half that, and the dunes near Ocean House (a hotel) that had once been covered with bushes and small pines, were now exposed to the ravages of northeasters. At the time Mather wrote, Coney Island was not yet connected to Long Island, but was separated from Long Island by a creek that wound through a salt marsh. "Mr. Wyckoff," he wrote, "who has lived for many years on the island, remembers when this creek was a broad inlet; but it has been gradually filled up with silt, organic alluvions, and drift sand, until it is reduced to its present size."[25]

Walt Whitman loved the once secluded beach of Coney Island, which he described as "the long bare unfrequented shore that I had all to myself . . . and where I loved after bathing to race up and down."[26] The poet would not feel alone for long. Indeed, he could not have accessed Coney Island until a bridge and road had been built by a private company in 1823; Shell Road was the first road to the island, and Coney Island House the first hotel. By the 1840s, three hundred carriages rode the toll road to little Coney, bearing tourists drawn to its five miles of beaches, and duck hunters drawn to the marshes. Most visitors were affluent if not wealthy New Yorkers who could afford private carriages; they included the likes of Daniel Webster, Henry Clay, John C. Calhoun, Jenny Lind, Washington Irving, Herman Melville, and Reverend Lyman Beecher. By 1847, a small ferry carried passengers from the city of New York to the pier of Gravesend Bay, a form of cheap transport that brought in more working-class people.[27] Development of Coney Island as a resort and later as a playground for the masses was swift once Austin Corbin built a railway to connect New York City with Manhattan Beach, bought out private landowners, and built two hotels, the Oriental and the Manhattan Beach. In similar fashion, William A. Engeman bought out landowners in Brighton Beach. The Brighton Beach Bathing Pavilion was built in 1878, the Brighton race track in 1879, the Sheepshead Bay racetrack in 1880, Steeple Chase in 1897, and Luna Park (the amusement park) in 1903. It was just a matter of time when the boardwalk and artificial beach would be built to accommodate fifty thousand people a day at the height of summer.[28] Today, the little sand island supports thousands of year-round residents in Manhattan Beach, Brighton Beach, Coney Island, and Seagate.

The boardwalk of Coney Island is weathering in the sun and salt air, its planks worn thin and splintery by the shoes of thousands of beachgoers and residents. The beach, exposed to the combined powers of sea and wind, is rapidly eroding. Each winter, northeasters pound the shore, waves seething under the boardwalk, sucking away the sand; each year, it is replenished with dredged sand. Who will win? Geologist Nicholas K. Coch, known as Dr. Doom, predicts disaster for New York when the next big hurricane makes a direct hit. He points to the hurricane of 1893, which surged over a barrier island off the seaward side of Far Rockaway, named Hog Island because it was shaped like a pig's back. The island had risen from the sea only decades before, a whimsical creation of sand. No sooner had it appeared,

Fig. 10.1. 1954 Hurricane Carol striking Connecticut coast. (NOAA Photo Library Historic National Weather Service Collection. www.photolib.noaa.gov/historic/nws.)

than developers rushed to get a piece, and a new beach resort was born. The 1893 hurricane swept away bathing houses, pavilions, and restaurants; a northeaster of 1902 drowned the island entirely. Today, says Coch, far more people live along the coast, and that portends disaster: "Now we have millions of people to offer to the God of the Sea."[29]

In August 2005, Hurricane Katrina slammed into the Gulf Coast. New Orleans, much of which is built below sea level and has been protected by levees since the 1700s, was flooded as the Mississippi River breached the levees. Hundreds of people were killed and thousands of homes and other buildings were destroyed. Just a year before, the U.S. Army Corps of Engineers and climate forecasters warned of catastrophe if the levees were not built higher, and if development continued to destroy the protective wetlands and barrier islands of the gulf. A decade earlier, the disastrous Mississippi floods of 1993 had prompted scientists to argue for restoring wetlands along river banks, because they act like sponges to absorb floodwaters. In a *New York Times* article in 1995, William K. Stevens wrote:

> The 1993 floods brought into focus long-standing criticisms of Federal flood-control policy, which has relied largely on the building of levees, flood walls, dams and other public works to channel flood water and keep it away from towns and farms. There is widespread disagreement that tightly corseting a flood in this way only forces the water ever-higher and increases its velocity and destructiveness. A Federal task force last year urged that the Army Corps of Engineers abandon its preference for engineering solutions and that greater reliance be placed on natural means of flood control.[30]

Unfortunately, a change in thinking did not translate into effective actions. Wetlands protecting the Gulf Coast continued to be eroded over the next decade, and development on barrier islands proceeded apace. The worst-case scenario came to pass. Hurricane Katrina left in its wake scenes of devastation and human misery that shocked Americans. The catastrophe prompted a number of articles and letters in the *New York Times* to examine not only our hurricane preparedness, but also reignited the debate over how we would protect coastal communities along the Atlantic seaboard from a similar hurricane. Should we shore up these communities? Are hard structures the answer? Or will these structures merely exacerbate the problem and provide only short-term solutions to a much more intractable long-term problem?

Old-timers recall the devastation of the hurricane of 1938, also known as the Long Island Express. This category 3 hurricane (sustained winds of between 111 and 130 miles per hour) swept over Long Island's East End on September 21, claiming the lives of fifty East Enders and killing hundreds more in Rhode Island, which took the full brunt of the storm. It demolished coastal homes and left sixty-three thousand people homeless. Storm surges reached ten to twelve feet. Today, Long Island's South Shore is far more heavily populated. A direct hit on Long Island by a category 4 hurricane at high tide during a full moon, for example, would inundate a barrier island like Long Beach. Gregory J. Caronia, director of Nassau County's Office of Emergency Management, calculates that the tidal surge could be as high as twenty-one feet in Long Beach, twenty-four feet in Hempstead Harbor, and thirty feet in Little Neck Bay. The Far Rockaways, the spit of land that protects Lower New York Bay, would be washed away, and Lower Manhattan would be under water. All those expensive projects to replenish beaches and rebuild dunes would crumble like sand castles at high tide. According to an interview conducted by John Rather of the *New York Times*, Army Corps of Engineers project manager Clifford Jones admitted that their beach replenishment efforts would not protect the shore from the ravages of a category 4 hurricane.[31]

It doesn't necessarily take a devastating category 4 hurricane to render incalculable damage. Lesser storms, including winter northeasters, pose a continual threat to our shores. Extraordinarily heavy rains during the month of October 2005, coupled with a northeaster, caused extensive erosion of beaches and barrier islands along the Mid-Atlantic Coast, rendering the coast more vulnerable to winter storms. On Long Island, primary dunes protecting communities on the East End, for example, were eaten away, undermining the foundations of homes and buildings built along these dunes. Once again, heated arguments arose over whether or not to shore up the beaches in order to protect expensive homes built by people who know the risk of living at the water's edge. Residents claim, with some justification, the right to pump in sand, even at their own expense, since their beaches were starved by groins erected farther east. They ask to install hard structures of their own, but the state of New York now refuses to allow such coastal hardening. But whether residents protect their beach-front communities with soft methods such as sand replenishment, or hard methods such as groins and seawalls, the ongoing process of coastal erosion cannot be halted.

Cornelia Dean tells the story of a house built in the 1870s in Wainscott, on Long Island's South Shore. It originally was protected by three lines of dunes. The hurricane of 1938 demolished the first line, and through successive storms over the decades, the second line crumbled into the sea. Now the house perches at the edge of the beach, and the primary dune that offered a last line of defense is giving way before the ocean's onslaught.[32]

Attempts to stabilize beaches and dunes go against nature, which is dynamic and fluid. The climate is changing and the seas are rising. Should we be building at all on shifting sands?

Coney Island, like all the barrier islands and wetlands along the South Shore of Long Island, was created only in the last instance of geological time: a mere two thousand years.[33] Islands rise and islands disappear, creations of a willful sea. Wind and water shape and shift the sands, sculpting shorelines, giving and taking away as they always have. And as they always have, humans make their homes by the sea, forever drawn to its restless beauty.

Notes

Introduction: Coming Home

1. Kirkpatrick Sale, *Dwellers in the Land: The Bioregional Vision* (1985; Santa Cruz, Calif.: New Society Publishers, 1991).

2. Peter Berg, "A Metamorphosis for Cities: From Gray to Green," *City Lights Review* 4 (n.d.). Reprint courtesy of Planet Drum, San Francisco.

1. Bedrock New York

1. Charles Merguerian and John Sanders, *Geology of Manhattan and the Bronx* (New York: New York Academy of Sciences, Section of Geological Sciences, Field Trips 1990–1991). Unless otherwise noted, my primary source for the reconstruction of New York City's geological history prior to the ice age is the series of field-trip notes by Merguerian and Sanders of Hofstra University published under the auspices of the New York Academy of Sciences. Additional sources are Les Sirkin, *Western Long Island Geology* (Watch Hill, R.I.: Book and Tackle Shop, 1996); Bradford B. Van Diver, *Roadside Geology of New York* (Missoula, Mont.: Mountain Press, 1985); and David C. Roberts, *Geology of Eastern North America* (Boston: Peterson Field Guides, Houghton Mifflin, 1996). Although predating plate tectonic theory, John Kieran's *Natural History of New York City* (Boston: Houghton Mifflin, 1959) also provides a good description of New York City's bedrock geology.

2. Charles Merguerian and Mickey Merguerian, "Geology of Central Park — From Rocks to Ice," www.dukelabs.com/Abstracts%20and%20Papers/CMMM2004.htm.

3. Charles Merguerian and John E. Sanders, *Staten Island and Vicinity* (New York: New York Academy of Sciences, Section of Geological Sciences: September 29, 1991, Field Trip), 25–28.

4. Merguerian and Sanders, *Geology of Manhattan and the Bronx*, 27–28.

5. Charles Merguerian, "Tunnel Vision: Subterranean Paradise or Name That Quake," Hofstra University Distinguished Faculty Lecture Series, September 27, 2000. www.dukelabs.com/Abstracts%20and%Papers/CM2000b.htm.

2. The Teeming Shore

1. Much of the description of life on the shores of New York City is based on information from William H. Amos and Stephen H. Amos, *Audubon Society Nature Guides: Atlantic and Gulf Coasts*, Chanticleer Press Edition (New York: Alfred A. Knopf/Borzoi Book, 1988), and Rachel Carson, *The Edge of the Sea* (1955; Boston: Houghton Mifflin, 1983).

2. Lynn Margulis et al., eds., *Handbook of Protoctista* (Boston: Jones and Bartlett, 1990).

3. Carson, *The Edge of the Sea*, 169–173.

4. Ibid., 53.

5. Lynn Margulis and Dorion Sagan, *Microcosmos: Four Billion Years of Microbial Evolution* (New York: Summit Books, 1986), 60–64.

6. Charles Merguerian and Charles E. Sanders, *The Geology of Manhattan and the Bronx* (New York: New York Academy of Sciences, Section of Geological Sciences, Field Trip 1990–1991: April 21, 1991), 14.

7. Stephen Jay Gould, *Wonderful Life: The Burgess Shale and the Nature of History* (New York and London: Norton, 1989), 47.

8. Ibid., 99.

9. Ibid., 145–151. Gould's italics.

10. Ibid., 30–31.

11. Russell D. White, *The Legacy of Invertebrate Paleontology at Yale University* (New Haven: Peabody Museum of Natural History/Yale University, 1999), reprint accessed at www.peabody.yale.edu.

12. Derek E. G. Briggs and Gregory D. Edgecombe, "The Gold Bugs," *Natural History*, November 1992, 37–42. Briggs is the current Curator of Invertebrate Paleontology at the Peabody Museum; investigation of the Beecher Trilobite Bed is ongoing.

13. William A. Shear, "One Small Step for an Arthropod," *Natural History*, March 1993, 47–51; Linda VanAllen Hernick, *The Gilboa Fossils*, New York State Museum, Circular No. 65, 2003. My reconstruction of fossil discoveries at Gilboa are based on both the Shear article and Hernick book.

14. Hernick, *Gilboa Fossils*, 62–77.

15. Harlan P. Banks and J. D. Grierson, *Lycopods of the Devonian of New York State*, Paleontographica Americana 4, no. 31 (1963), cited in ibid.

16. Shear, "One Small Step for an Arthropod," and Hernick, *Gilboa Fossils*, 77–85.

17. My reconstruction of vertebrate evolution is based on information provided at the American Museum of Natural History, Hall of Vertebrates. On "living fossils," see Niles Eldridge, *Fossils: The Evolution and Extinction of Species* (Princeton: Princeton University Press, 1991), 92–94. See also Richard Fortey, *Life: A Natural History of the First Four Billion Years of Life on Earth* (New York: Alfred A. Knopf, 1997), 160.

18. Philip Whitfield, *From So Simple a Beginning: An Illustrated Exploration of the 4-Billion-Year Development of Life on Earth*, Foreword by Roger Lewin (New York: Macmillan, 1993), 38; and Fortey, *Life*, 166–185.

19. Fortey, *Life*, 149.

20. Ibid., 202–209.

21. William B. Gallagher, *When Dinosaurs Roamed New Jersey* (New Brunswick: Rutgers University Press, 1997).

22. http://paleo.amnh.org/projects/newyork/index.html.

23. Thomas R. Holtz, Jr., "All in the Family," *Natural History* 114, no. 4 (May 2005): 40.

24. Gallagher, *When Dinosaurs Roamed New Jersey*, 67.

25. Ibid., 92–94, 35–39.

26. Philip J. Hilts, "Expedition to Far New Jersey Finds Trove of Amber Fossils," *New York Times*, January 30, 1996, sec. C10; Jeff Poling, "New Jersey Has Treasure Trove of Amber," www.ucmp.berkeley.edu.

27. Richard Monastersky, "Closing in on the Killer," *Science News* 141 (January 25, 1992): 56–58.

28. Amos and Amos, *Audubon Society Nature Guides: Atlantic and Gulf Coasts*, 94–96.

29. Gould, *Wonderful Life*, 43n.

30. David Everitt, "Eons May Be Running Out for the Horseshoe Crab," *New York Times*, June 6, 2004, sec. 14.

31. J. William Schopf, *Major Events in the History of Life* (Boston: Jones and Bartlett Publishers, 1992), 168–169.

3. At the Glacier's Edge

1. I have reconstructed the events and life of ice age New York based on the following sources: Charles Merguerian, *The Narrows Flood — Post-Woodfordian Meltwater Breach of the Narrows Channel, NYC*, in G. N. Hanson, chair, Tenth Annual Conference on Geology of Long Island and Metropolitan New York, April 12, 2003, State University at Stony Brook, NY., Long Island Geologists Program with Abstracts (www.dukelabs.com/Abstracts%20and%20Papers/CM2004.htm); Les Sirkin, *Western Long Island Geology* (Watch Hill, R.I.: Book and Tackle Shop, 1996); E. C. Pielou, *After the Ice Age: The Return of Life to Glaciated North America* (Chicago and London: University of Chicago Press, 1991); Robert H. Boyle, *The Hudson River: A Natural and Unnatural History*, exp. ed. (New York and London: W. W. Norton, 1969, 1979), 157–158.

2. Pielou, *After the Ice Age.*

3. Quoted in Charles Merguerian and John Sanders, *Glacial Geology of Long Island* (New York: New York Academy of Sciences, Section of Geological Sciences, Field Trips, 1990–1991), 19–21; L. D. Gale, *Diary of a Geological Survey of the Island of New York*, Part 4 of W. W. Mather, *Geology of New York* (Albany: Carroll and Cook, 1843), 581–604.

4. Quoted in Merguerian and Sanders, *Glacial Geology of Long Island*, 19–21.

5. Edward Lurie, *Nature and the American Mind: Louis Agassiz and the Culture of Science* (Chicago: University of Chicago Press, 1960), 85; Louis Agassiz, *Geological Sketches* (Boston, 1866); Ernst Mayr, *One Long Argument: Charles Darwin and the Genesis of Modern Evolutionary Thought* (Cambridge, Mass.: Harvard University Press, 1991), 16; Peter J. Bowler, *Evolution: The History of an Idea*, rev. ed. (Berkeley: University of California Press, 1989), 128; Mather, *Geology of New York.*

6. Sirkin, *Western Long Island Geology*, 19–45.

7. Merguerian and Sanders, *Glacial Geology of Long Island*, 18, 26.

8. Merguerian, *Post-Woodfordian Meltwater Breach of the Narrows Channel*; Boyle, *The Hudson River.*

9. Pielou, *After the Ice Age*, 168–175.

10. Ibid., 229.

11. Ibid., 129; Rutherford Platt, *The Great American Forest* (Englewood Cliffs, N.J.: Prentice Hall, 1965; 1969), 44–49. The Pine Barrens of New Jersey are actually preglacial, a coastal refugia south of the glacier that harbored plants dating to the Miocene. See John W. Harshberger, *The Vegetation of the New Jersey Pine-Barrens* (1916; New York: Dover, 1970).

12. Platt, *The Great American Forest*, 49–50.

13. Pielou, *After the Ice Age*, 251–266.

14. Ibid., 254–265; Brian M. Fagan, *Ancient North America: The Archaeology of a Continent* (New York and London: Thames and Hudson, 1991), 77–82. Martin continues to vigorously defend his theory. See Paul Martin, *Twilight of the Mammoths: Ice Age Extinction and the Re-wilding of America* (Berkeley and Los Angeles: University of California Press, 2005).

15. Pielou, *After the Ice Age*, 251–266.

16. Fagan, *Ancient North America*, 81–82.

17. Anne-Marie Cantwell and Diana diZerega Wall, *Unearthing Gotham: The Archaeology of New York City* (New Haven and London: Yale University Press, 2001), 44; Margaret Mittelbach and Michael Crewdson, *Wild New York* (New York: Crown, 1997), 38; Pielou, *After the Ice Age*, 140.

18. Sirkin, *Western Long Island Geology.*

19. Ibid., 127–133.

20. Ibid.

21. *New York Walk Book*, 6th ed. (New York–New Jersey Trail Conference, 1998), 47; Robert Grumet, *The Lenapes* (New York: Chelsea House, 1989), 90.

4. Land of the Lenapes

1. Hitakonanu'laxk (Tree Beard), *The Grandfathers Speak: Native American Folk Tales of the Lenape Peoples* (New York: Interlink Books, 1994), 76–77. I have condensed and adapted the author's version of the story. All the quotes are his.

2. E. C. Pielou, *After the Ice Age: The Return of Life to Glaciated North America* (Chicago and London: University of Chicago Press), 141, 215.

3. Brian M. Fagan, *Ancient North America: The Archaeology of a Continent* (New York and London: Thames and Hudson, 1991), 77–81, 109. "Archaeological footprints" is his term.

4. Dena F. Dincauze, "The Earliest Americans: The Northeast," *Common Ground: Archaeology and Ethnography in the Public Interest*, Spring/Summer 2000, National Park Service Online Archive. www.nps.gov.

5. Anne-Marie Cantwell and Diana diZerega Wall, *Unearthing Gotham: The Archaeology of New York City* (New Haven and London: Yale University Press, 2001), 39–45.

6. Fagan, *Ancient North America*. Fagan cites the theory of Joseph Caldwell, who in 1958 coined the term "Primary Forest Efficiency" to define the "adaptive shift toward more efficient exploitation of woodland environments" (307). Only in the West, on the Great Plains, did a traditional big-game hunting culture persist, centered on the bison that roamed the plains, survivors of the mass extinction because of their ability to adapt to short-grass feeding in a more arid environment (123). See also Pielou, *After the Ice Age*, 262, 289. Traditional hunter-gatherer societies also persisted in the boreal and tundra regions of the northern part of the continent.

7. I have relied on two main sources for my reconstruction of the lifeways of the Eastern Woodland peoples: Herbert Kraft, *The Lenape: Archaeology, History and Ethnography* (Newark: New Jersey Historical Society, 1986), and Brian Fagan, *Ancient North America*.

8. See also Fagan, *Ancient North America*, 109.

9. Pielou, *After the Ice Age*, 289, on the period of global warming called the hypisthermal; Dean Snow, "Late Pre-History of the East Coast," in Bruce G. Trigger, ed., *Handbook of the North American Indians: The Northeast* (Washington, D.C.: Smithsonian Institution Press, 1978).

10. Cantwell and Wall, *Unearthing Gotham*, 55–57.

11. Fagan, *Ancient North America*, 357–358. Fagan cites Bruce Smith, "The Independent Domestication of Indigenous Seed-Bearing Plants in Eastern North America," in William F. Keagan, ed., *Emergent Horticultural Economies of the Eastern Woodlands* (Carbondale, Ill: Center for Archaeological Investigations, Southern Illinois University, 1987), 3–48. See also Bruce Smith, *Rivers of Change: Essays on Early Agriculture in Eastern North America* (Washington, D.C., and London: Smithsonian Institution Press, 1992), 3–31, 273. Smith asserted that domestication of wild plants in eastern North America was an independent development. He cautioned, however, that such plant domestication "should not be conflated with the initial development of agriculture — substantial human investment in, and reliance on, food production economies." He also noted that "along the Atlantic and Gulf coastal plains and across the northern latitudes, forager economies based almost exclusively on wild species of animals and plants (with some *Cucurbita* cultivation) persisted until the A.D. 800 to 1100 shift to maize-centered agriculture."

12. Smith, *Rivers of Change*, 267–291; John Barrat, "Indians Cultivated First Gourd in the United States," *Smithsonian Runner*, March–April 1993; Bert Salwen, in *Handbook of the North American Indians: The Northeast*, ed. Trigger; William W. Newcomb, Jr., "The Culture and Acculturation of the Delaware Indians," *Anthropological Papers*, no. 10 (1956), Museum of Anthropology, University of Michigan, Ann Arbor.

13. Smith, *Rivers of Change*.

14. Kraft, *The Lenape*, 41–54; Robert S. Grumet, *The Lenapes* (New York and Philadelphia: Chelsea House, 1989), 14.

15. Hitakonanu'laxk (Tree Beard), *The Grandfathers Speak*, 7–9.

16. Grumet, *The Lenapes*, 25; Hitakonanu'laxk, *The Grandfathers Speak*, 5–6. The designation of Munsee-speaking distinguishes them from the Unami-speaking Lenapes, also called "Down the River People," who lived along the Delaware to the south, and the Unalaxtako people who lived along coastal New Jersey to the south. All Lenapes spoke variants of Eastern Algonquin, which was the common tongue of people who lived on the Atlantic Coastal Plain from Canada to the Carolinas.

17. The Lenape culture has been designated as something of a "backwater" compared to their more sophisticated neighbors (Grumet, lecture, American Museum of Natural History, February 1994). Cantwell and Wall protest that we are applying a Western standard of comparison, which labels highly organized and stratified societies as more "advanced." "The coastal peoples were not huddled in an isolated backwater at the edge of a continent," they assert. Indeed, they had contact with these societies through trade. Perhaps, they suggest, the Lenapes had no reason to change since they were thriving in "the rich estuarine environment" of the region (91–92).

18. David de Vries, "Voyages," in J. Franklin Jameson, ed., *Narratives of New England* (New York: Scribner's, 1909; New York: Barnes and Noble, 1937), 162.

19. Grumet, "Sunksquaws, Shamans, and Tradeswomen: Middle Atlantic Coastal Algonkian Women during the 17th and 18th Centuries," in Mona Etienne and Eleanor Leacock, eds., *Women and Colonization: Anthropological Perspectives* (n.p., n.d.), 56; Kraft, *The Lenape*, 154; David de Vries, *Voyages from Holland to America, 1632–1644*, trans. Henry C. Murphy (1853; reprint, New York: Kraus Reprint Company, 1971). See also Newcomb, "The Culture and Acculturation of the Delaware Indians."

20. Newcomb, "The Culture and Acculturation of the Delaware Indians"; Grumet, *The Lenapes*, 16–17; Ives Goddard, "Delaware," in *Handbook of the North American Indian: The Northeast*, 217.

21. Bert Salwen, in *Handbook of the North American Indian: The Northeast*, 161–163; Roger Williams, *The Complete Writings of Roger Williams*, vol. 1 (New York: Russell and Russell, 1963), 60.

22. Fagan, *Ancient North America*, 356–360; Smith, *Rivers of Change*, 289; Richard Ford, *Prehistoric Food Production in North America* (Ann Arbor, Mich.: Museum of Anthropology, University of Michigan, 1985); Kraft, *The Lenape*, 118. Cantwell and Wall suggest that maize was not the mainstay of their diet, citing a 1994 archaeological study based on bone chemistry undertaken by Patricia Bridges of Queens College (*Unearthing Gotham*, 110–114).

23. William Cronon, *Changes in the Land: Indians, Colonists and the Ecology of New England* (New York: Hill and Wang, 1991), 50–51. On the use of fire in agriculture, see also Percy Wells Bidwell and John Falconer, *History of Agriculture in Northern United States 1620–1860* (Washington, D.C.: Carnegie Institution, 1925); and Carl O. Sauer, *Agricultural Origins and Dispersals* (1952; Hanover and London: University Press of New England, 1986).

24. Hitakonanu'taxk, *The Grandfathers Speak*.

25. Grumet, "Sunksquaws," and *Lenapes*, 15; see also Anthony F. C. Wallace, "Women, Land and Society: Three Aspects of Aboriginal Delaware Life," *Pennsylvania Archaeologist* 17 (1947): 1–35.

26. Bidwell and Falconer, *History of Agriculture*, 8; Grumet, *Lenapes*, 18; Cronon, *Changes in the Land*, 48; Kraft, *The Lenape*, 118, 62. According to Bidwell and Falconer, girdling was a common practice. Grumet attributes to the Lenapes this particular method of clearing a field. The slash-and-burn technique was practiced by the southern New England Indians, as described by Cronon. According to this method, women piled brush at the base of the tree and set fire to it, killing the tree; they would then strip the bark and plant corn between the stripped trees, which were left to fall in their own time.

27. Kraft, *The Lenape*, 138; Newcomb, "The Culture and Acculturation of the Delaware Indians," 13; Hitakonanu'laxk, *The Grandfathers Speak*, 11.

28. Kraft, *The Lenape*, 141; David de Vries, *Voyages from Holland to America, 1632–1644*, trans. Henry C. Murphy (1853; reprint, New York: Kraus Reprint Company, 1971); Newcomb, "The Culture and Acculturation of the Delaware Indians"; Salwen, in *Handbook of the American Indian: The Northeast*; Grumet, *The Lenape*; Hitakonanu'laxk, *The Grandfathers Speak*.

29. Robert Grumet, "Sunksquaws," 5; Lee Allen Peterson, *Edible Wild Plants*, Peterson Field Guides (Boston: Houghton Mifflin, 1977); E. Barrie Kavasch, *Guide to Northeastern Wild Edibles* (Surrey, British Columbia, and Blaine, Washington: Hancock House Publishers, 1994).

30. Gaynell Stone Levine, "The Lore of the Long Island Indians," *Readings in Long Island Archaeology and Ethnohistory* 4 (Stony Brook, N.Y.: Suffolk County Archaeological Association, 1980), 265.

31. James A. Duke and Steven Foster, *Eastern/Central Medicinal Plants*, Peterson Field Guides (Boston and New York: Houghton Mifflin, 1990), xii.

32. Mrs. John King Van Rensselaer, *The Goede Vrouw of Mana-ha-ta, 1609–1760* (New York: Charles Scribner, 1898), 74.

33. Barrie Kavasch, *Native American Earth Sense: Herbaria of Ethnobotany and Ethnomycology*, ed. Alberto C. Meloni (Washington, Conn.: Birdstone Publishers, the Institute of American Indian Studies, 1996), 49–70.

34. Kraft, *The Lenape*, 182.

35. Kavasch, *Native American Earth Sense*. Trudie Lamb Richmond quoted in ibid., 36.

36. Kraft, *The Lenape*, 162–169; Hitakonanu'laxk, *The Grandfathers Speak*, 32–40. I have adopted the spelling for Lenape terms used by Hitakonanu'laxk.

37. Grumet, *The Lenapes*, 13–16, 25–26; see also Robert Grumet, *Place Names of New York City* (1981), and Rev. John Heckewelder, "Indian Tradition of the First Arrival of the Dutch at Manhattan Island, Now New York," in Henry C. Murphy, ed., *Collections of the New York Historical Society*, 2d series, vol. 1 (1841), 71–74.

38. Grumet, *The Lenapes*, 14–15; Wallace, "Women, Land and Society," 14.

5. Staking Claim

1. David de Vries in J. F. Jameson, ed., *Narratives of New Netherland, 1609–1664* (1909; reprint, New York: Barnes and Noble, 1959), 223.

2. Adriaen Van Der Donck, *The Description of New Netherlands*, ed. Thomas F. O'Donnell (Syracuse, N.Y.: Syracuse University Press, 1968), 7–9.

3. Jacques Habert, *When New York Was Called Angouleme: A History of the Discovery of New York Bay* (New York: Transocean Press, 1949). See also Samuel Eliot Morison, *The Great Explorers: The European Discovery of America*, abridged ed. (New York: Oxford University Press, 1986), 150.

4. Daniel M. Friedenberg, *Life, Liberty, and the Pursuit of Land: The Plunder of Early America* (Buffalo, N.Y.: Prometheus Press, 1992), 54.

5. Henri and Barbara Van der Zee, *A Sweet and Alien Land: The Story of Dutch New York* (New York: Viking, 1978), 12.

6. Kirkpatrick Sale, *The Conquest of Paradise: Christopher Columbus and the Columbian Legacy* (1990; New York: Plume Penguin, 1999), 290.

7. Oliver Rink, *Holland on the Hudson: An Economic and Social History of New York* (Cooperstown: New York State Historical Association; Ithaca, N.Y.: Cornell University Press, 1986), 215; William Cronon, *Changes in the Land: Indians, Colonists, and the Ecology of New England* (New York: Hill and Wang, 1983), 99.

8. Cronon, *Changes in the Land*, 92–99; Francis Jennings, *The Invasion of America: Indians, Colonialism, and the Cant of Conquest* (Chapel Hill: University of North Carolina Press, 1975), 71, 88, 95; Robert S. Grumet, "Children of Muhheahkkunnuck: A Lower River Indian History," in *Many Trails: Indians of the Lower Hudson Valley*, gen. ed. Catherine Coleman Brawer (Katonah, N.Y.: Katonah Gallery, 1983), 19.

9. Michael Kammen, *Colonial New York: A History*, History of the American Colonies Series (New York: Scribner, 1975; reprint, Millwood, N.Y.: KTO Press, 1978), 91.

10. Percy Wells Bidwell and John Falconer, *History of Agriculture in Northern United States 1620–1860* (Washington, D.C.: Carnegie Institution, 1925), 42–45.

11. Cronon, *Changes in the Land*, 136.

12. John Newton Phelps Stokes, *The Iconography of Manhattan Island, 1498–1909* (1928; reprint, New York: Arno Press, 1967), vol. 4, 92–120.

13. Rink, *Holland on the Hudson*, 52.

14. Friedenberg, *Life, Liberty and the Pursuit of Land*, 53–66. Those who held on to their lands continued to acquire more, as documented by Friedenberg. The patroon Van Rensselaer, for example, expanded his original 700,000 acres in Columbia County into one million acres through a number of slick deals. After New Netherland became the royal colony of New York, the English retained the Dutch land tenure system, with royal governors granting huge tracts of land to their cronies, keeping one-third of each grant for themselves. By 1697, writes Friedenberg, the Van Rensselaers, Van Cortlandts, Philipses, and Livingstons owned among them 1.6 million acres—most of "Westchester, Dutchess, Albany, Putnam, Columbia and Rensselaer" counties. These and other "land barons" of the Hudson "were

enmeshed through marriage, politics, landholdings, and commerce in a net that imitated the feudal pattern of European countries." Some of the seeds of the American Revolution were sown here, he argues, when the "river lords" resisted any attempts by the English government to curb their land hunger.

15. Kammen, *Colonial New York*, 36.

16. Ibid., 44.

17. Grumet, "Children of Muhheahkkunnuck," 21; Grumet, *Native American Place Names in New York City* (New York: Museum of the City of New York, 1981), 33, 47; Allen W. Trelease, *Indian Affairs in Colonial New York: The Seventeenth Century* (Ithaca, N.Y.: Cornell University Press, 1960), 62–63; Kammen, *Colonial New York*, 45.

18. Kammen, *Colonial New York*, 36.

19. R. P. Bolton, *New York City in Indian Possession*, vol. 2 of Indian Notes and Monographs, 2d ed. (New York: Museum of the American Indian Heye Foundation, 1975), 11–21; William Newcomb, Jr., "The Culture and Acculturation of the Delaware Indians," University of Michigan Museum of Anthropology, Anthropological Papers, no. 10 (1956); Grumet, *Native American Place Names in New York*, 23; Grumet, "Children of Muhheahkkunuck," 20.

20. Rink, *Holland on the Hudson*, 217; David de Vries, *Voyages from Holland to America, 1632–1644*, trans. Henry C. Murphy (1853; reprint, New York: Kraus Reprint Co., 1971), 208; Grumet, "Children of Muhheahkkunuck," 19.

21. Jameson, *Narratives of New Netherland*. According to Jameson in a footnote to the reprint of the de Vries account of the massacre, de Vries cribbed his account from an anticompany tract printed in Antwerp in 1649; such borrowing was common practice.

22. Trelease, *Indian Affairs in Colonial New York*, 65–83; Rink, *Holland on the Hudson*, 215–221; de Vries in Jameson, *Narratives of New Netherland*, 228; Grumet, "Children of Muhheahkkunuck," 20.

23. Van der Donck, *A Description of the New Netherlands*; Ada Van Gastel, "Van der Donck's Description of the Indians: Additions and Corrections," *William and Mary Quarterly* 47, no. 3 (July 1990): 411–421.

24. Robert S. Grumet, *The Lenapes* (New York: Chelsea House), 44.

25. Ibid., 44–46.

26. *Documents Relating to New Netherland, 1624–1626*, ed. and transl. A.J.F. Van Laer (San Marino, Calif.: Huntington Library, 1924), 39.

27. Jasper Danckaerts and Peter Sluyter, *Journal of a Voyage to New York*, March of America Facsimile Series 27 (1867; reprint, New York: Kraus Reprint Company, 1971); Charles T. Gehring and Robert Grumet, "Observations of the Indians from Jasper Danckaert's Journal, 1679–1680," *William and Mary Quarterly* 44, no. 1 (1987): 104–120. I have used Gehring and Grumet's translation of Danckaerts on the Indians.

28. Grumet, *The Lenapes*, 13, 33–34; Pastorius and Morton quoted in Newcomb, "The Culture and Acculturation of the Delaware Indians." According to Alfred Crosby, the pestilence that hit New England before the Pilgrims arrived was possibly bubonic plague, or typhus. Its spread was limited to the coast between Narragansett Bay and the Kennebec River. For some reason it swept through native populations like wildfire, killing nine out of ten, but leaving Europeans among them unscathed. The 90 percent depopulation rate may have been the direct result of infection, or the indirect result of the disease, as it weakened men and women to such an extent they could not tend the fields or attend the hunt. Starvation inevitably followed. Alfred W. Crosby, *Ecological Imperialism: The Biological Expansion of Europe, 900–1900* (Cambridge: Cambridge University Press, 1986; reprint, Canto Edition, 1993), 110–113.

29. Newcomb, "The Culture and Acculturation of the Delaware," 112.

30. Grumet, *The Lenapes*, 50.

31. Ibid., 61; Grumet, *Place Names*, 31. See also Ellice B. Gonzales, "Tri-Racial Isolates in a Bi-Racial Society: Poosepatuck Ambiguity and Conflict," in Frank W. Porter III, ed., *Strategies for Survival: American Indians in the Eastern United States* (New York: Greenwood Press, 1986), 113–137.

32. Grumet, *The Lenapes*, 63–83, 102; Lydia Wyckoff and Curtis Zunigha, "Delaware: Honoring the Past and Preparing for the Future," *Native Peoples* 7, no. 3 (Spring 1994): 56–62. For a detailed account of the series of removes westward and northward undertaken by the Lenapes through the eighteenth and nineteenth centuries, see Grumet, *The Lenapes*, 49–93, and Ives Goddard, "The Delaware," in Bruce Trigger, ed., *Handbook of the North American Indian*, vol. 15 (Washington, D.C.: Smithsonian Institution Press), 213–239.

6. Muddied Waters

1. Robert Grumet, *Native American Place Names in New York City* (New York: Museum of the City of New York, 1981), 22.

2. Les Sirkin, *Western Long Island* (Watch Hill, R.I.: Book and Tackle Shop, 1996), 8–9; William H. Amos and Stephen H. Amos, *Atlantic and Gulf Coasts* (New York: Knopf, 1988), 79–97.

3. Robert H. Boyle, *The Hudson River: A Natural and Unnatural History* (1969; New York: W. W. Norton, 1979), 23.

4. John and Mildred Teal, *Life and Death of a Salt Marsh* (New York: Ballantine Books, 1969), 122–154.

5. Rachel Carson, *The Edge of the Sea* (Boston: Houghton Mifflin, 1983), 148–150.

6. Carson, *The Edge of the Sea*, 143–145; Amos and Amos, *Atlantic and Gulf Coasts*; Teal and Teal, *Life and Death of the Salt Marsh*, 122–154; Peter Alden and Brian Cassie, *National Audubon Society Field Guide to the Middle Atlantic States* (New York: Knopf/Chanticleer Press, 1999).

7. Amos and Amos, *Atlantic and Gulf Coasts*.

8. Teal and Teal, *Life and Death of a Salt Marsh*; Audubon quoted in Paul R. Ehrlich et al., *The Birders' Handbook: A Field Guide to the Natural History of North American Birds* (New York: Simon and Schuster/Fireside Books, 1988), 99.

9. Tom Anderson, *This Fine Piece of Water: An Environmental History of Long Island Sound* (New Haven and London: Yale University Press, 2002), 129.

10. Adriaen Van der Donck, *Description of New Netherland*, ed. Thomas O'Donnell (New York: Syracuse University Press, 1968), 18; J. F. Jameson, ed., *Narratives of New England, 1609–1664* (New York: Scribner's, 1909; New York: Barnes and Noble, 1959); Peter Kalm, *Travels into North America*, trans. John Reinhold Forster (Barre, Mass.: Imprint Society, 1972); William Woods quoted in William Cronon, *Changes in the Land: Indians, Colonists, and the Ecology of New England* (New York: Hill and Wang, 1983), 22; Jaspar Dankers and Peter Sluyter, *Journal of a Voyage to New York* (Brooklyn, 1867; Ann Arbor: University Microfilms, March of America Facsimile Series, 1967).

11. Van der Donck, *A Description of the New Netherlands*, 18.

12. Simon Schama, *The Embarrassment of Riches: An Interpretation of Dutch Culture in the Golden Age* (Berkeley and Los Angeles: University of California Press, 1988), 38; Fernand Braudel, *Civilization and Capitalism*, trans. Sian Reynolds (New York: Harper, 1981), 358; J. A. van Houtte, *An Economic History of the Low Countries* (New York: St. Martin's, 1977), 8; Keith Lindley, *Fenland Riots and the English Revolution* (London: Heinemann Educational Books, 1982), 19–23.

13. Lindley, *Fenland Riots*, 2.

14. Quoted in Jameson, *Narratives of New Netherland 1609–1664*, 100.

15. Jared Eliot, *Essays upon field Husbandry in New England and Other Papers (1748–1762)*, Studies in the History of American Agriculture Series, ed. Harry J. Carman, Rexford G. Tugwell, and Rodney H. True (New York: Columbia University Press, 1934).

16. Kalm, *Travels into North America*.

17. George Reiger, *Wanderer on My Native Shore: A Personal Guide and Tribute to the Ecology of the Atlantic Coast* (New York: Simon and Schuster, 1983), 65–91; Anderson, *This Fine Piece of Water*, 82–99; New York State Committee on Regional Plan of New York and Its Environs, *Regional Survey of New York and Its Environs: Physical Conditions and*

Public Services, compiled by Harold Maclean Lewis, vol. 8 (1929); Garry F. Mayer, ed., *Ecological Stress and the New York Bight: Science and Management* (Columbia, S.C.: Estuarine Research Foundation, 1982).

18. Anderson, *This Fine Piece of Water,* 118–126; "Clean Water for Today: What Is Wastewater Treatment?" (Alexandria, Va.: Water Environment Federation, n.d.).

19. George Rafter and M. N. Baker, *Sewage Disposal in the United States* (New York: Van Nostrand; London: Sampson Low, 1900), 71–72; Lewis, comp., *Regional Survey of New York.*

20. Lewis, comp., *Regional Survey of New York*; Martin V. Melosi, *Garbage in the Cities: Refuse, Reform, and the Environment, 1880–1980* (College Station: Texas A&M University Press, 1981), 42.

21. U.S. Public Health Service Report cited in *Hudson River Ecology: Symposium on Hudson River Ecology* (Tuxedo, N.Y.: New York Hudson River Valley Commission, 1966), 230.

22. Egbert Viele, *Topography and Hydrology of New York* (New York, 1865); John Duffy, *A History of Public Health in New York City, 1866–1966,* vol. 2 (New York: Russell Sage Foundation, 1973), 117.

23. *Regional Survey of New York,* 106–8.

24. Anderson, *This Fine Piece of Water,* 157–158; New York City, Sanitation Department, *Annual Report,* 1929–1930. See also John Waldman, *Heartbeats in the Muck: A Dramatic Look at the History, Sea Life, and Environment of New York Harbor* (New York: Lyons Press, 1999), 81–87.

25. Rafter and Baker, *Sewage Disposal in the United States,* 349–381; Franz, "History of Mollusks in New York Harbor," in Mayer, ed., *Ecological Stress and the New York Bight,* 189.

26. John Cronin and Robert F. Kennedy, Jr., *Riverkeepers: Two Activists Fight to Reclaim Our Environment as a Basic Human Right* (New York: Scribner, 1997), 156.

27. Boyle, *The Hudson River,* 282–302; Andrew C. Revkin, "Toxic Chemicals from 70's Still Pollute Hudson, Study Says," *New York Times,* July 24, 1998; http://www.riverkeeper.org.

28. Cronin and Kennedy, *Riverkeepers,* 154, 232–233.

29. Ibid.; New York State Department of Environmental Conservation and the New York State Department of Health, *Health Advisory on Eating Sport Fish,* 2004.

30. "Clean Water for Today: What Is Wastewater Treatment?"; Ron Bourque, "A Trip to the Sewage Plant," *Urban Audubon* 18, no. 8 (November 1997).

31. Anderson, *This Fine Piece of Water,* 112, 115, 122, 125. His statistics on nitrogen levels in the Long Island Sound are based on a study conducted by Paul Stacey of the Connecticut Department of Environmental Protection, U.S. Geological Service data, and EPA studies carried out in the 1990s.

32. Charlie Le Duff, "Last Days of the Baymen," *New York Times,* April 20, 1997, sec. 13; Reiger, *Wanderer on My Native Shore,* 71–76.

33. Waldman, *Heartbeats in the Muck,* 65.

34. *The New York State Audubon Advocate,* Spring 1998.

35. Kalm, *Travels into North America,* 151.

36. Stephen Marshall, "The Meadowlands before the Commission: Three Centuries of Human Use and Alteration of the Newark and Hackensack Meadows," *Urban Habitats* 2, no. 1 (2004): http://www.urbanhabitats.org. I have relied on Marshall's account to reconstruct the history of land use in the Meadowlands. See also www.meadowlands.state.nj.us.

37. Susan Bass Levin, "The New Jersey Meadowlands Commission's Visionary Master Plan," *New Jersey Audubon* 31, no. 1 (Spring 2005): 18; Pete Bacinski, "Embracing the Hackensack Meadowlands," *New Jersey Audubon* 31, no. 1 (Spring 2005): 17.

38. David M. Herszenhorn, "Fighting Over the Ugliest Wilderness," *New York Times,* March 16, 1998, sec. B1; Levin, "Visionary Master Plan."

7. Footprints

1. Carole Neidich, "Hempstead Plains: Long Island's Vanishing Prairie," New York City Audubon Society (www.nycas.org/issues/hempstead); the Web article was adapted from

"The Hempstead Plains and the Birdfoot Violet," *Long Island Forum* 43, no. 6 (2002): 108–115; John C. Kricher and Gordon Morrison, *Ecology of Eastern Forests*, Peterson Field Guides (Boston and New York: Houghton Mifflin, 1988), 90; www.prairie.org.

2. The list of native plants growing in Hempstead Prairie (or Hempstead Plains grassland) is based on Carol Reschke's "Ecological Communities of New York State" (1990), revised by Edinger et al. (2002). Reschke's revised survey of "Terrestrial Communities" in New York State can be viewed online at the Web sites of the New York State Nature Conservancy/Natural Heritage Program (www.nynhp.org) and New York State Department of Environmental Conservation (www.dec.state.ny.us).

3. Alfred Crosby, *Ecological Imperialism: The Biological Expansion of Europe, 900–1900* (1986; Cambridge and New York: Cambridge University Press/Canto, 1993), 156–158, 165. See also Crosby, *Germs, Seeds, and Animals: Studies in Ecological History* (Armonk, N.Y., and London: M. E. Sharpe, 1994).

4. Crosby, *Ecological Imperialism*, 155.

5. Ibid., 157–158.

6. Torrey, *Flora of New York State* (New York: Lyceum of Natural History of New York, 1843).

7. France Royer and Richard Dickinson, *Weeds of the Northern United States and Canada* (Renton, Wash., and Edmonton, Alberta: Lone Pine Publishing and University of Alberta Press, 1999), 164.

8. Ibid.

9. Crosby, *Ecological Imperialism*, 149.

10. Brian Fagan, *The Long Summer: How Climate Changed Civilization* (New York: Basic Books, 2004), 121. According to Fagan, grains were first domesticated in the Fertile Crescent around 10,000 B.C.; cereal cultivation spread to Europe around 5600 B.C.

11. Crosby, *Ecological Imperialism*, 288–290.

12. Bruce Smith, *Rivers of Change: Essays on Early Agriculture in Eastern North America* (Washington, D.C., and London: Smithsonian Institution Press, 1992), 267–291.

13. Adriaen Van der Donck, *A Description of the New Netherlands*, ed. Thomas F. O'Donnell (Syracuse, N.Y.: Syracuse University Press, 1968), 28.

14. Carlos Westey and Lloyd G. Carr, "Surviving Folktales and Herbal Lore among the Shinnecock Indians of Long Island," *Journal of American Folklore* 58 (1945): 113–23. See also Herbert C. Kraft, *The Lenape: Archaeology, History, and Ethnography* (Newark: New Jersey Historical Society, 1986), 180. Today, we are seeing a resurgence of herbal medicine among Americans, as indicated by the publication of a number of modern herbals, or guides to medicinal wild plants, including those sources cited in this chapter.

15. Roger Tory Peterson, "Editor's Note," in Steven Foster and James A. Duke, *Eastern/Central Medicinal Plants* (Boston and New York: Houghton Mifflin, 1990), v.

16. Mrs. John King Van Rensselaer, *The Goude Vrouw of Mana-ha-ta: At Home and in Society, 1609–1760* (New York: Charles Scribner's, 1898), 12.

17. John Torrey, *Catalogue of Plants Growing in the Vicinity of the City of New York* (New York: Lyceum of Natural History of New York, 1819). Torrey inscribes this catalog to Dr. Mitchill, and cites his predecessors in botanical study.

18. Ibid.

19. Ibid., 158.

20. Lynn White, "The Historical Roots of Our Ecological Crisis," *Science* 155, no. 3767 (March 10, 1967): 1203–1205.

21. Quoted in Percy Wells Bidwell and John Falconer, *History of Agriculture in the Northern United States, 1620–1860* (Washington, D.C.: Carnegie Institution, 1925), 70.

22. Daniel Denton, *A Brief Description of New York* (1670; Ann Arbor, Mich.: University Microfilms, 1967).

23. New York State Nature Conservancy/Natural Heritage Program (www.nynhp.org); New York State Department of Environmental Conservation (www.dec.state.ny.ns); and Invasive Plant Council of New York State (www.ipcnys.org).

24. www.nycaudubon.org/projects/gramp.

25. www.massaudubon.org/Birds_&_Beyond/grassland.

26. George R. Robinson, Mary E. Yurlina, and Steven N. Handel, "A Century of Change in the Staten Island Flora: Ecological Correlates of Species Losses and Invasions," *Bulletin of the Torrey Botanical Club* 121, no. 2: 119–129. On the relation between local extirpation and global extinction events, they cite L. Roberts, "Extinction Imminent for Native Plants," *Science* 245: 1508.

27. George R. Robinson and Steven N. Handel, "Forest Restoration on a Closed Landfill: Rapid Addition of New Species by Bird Dispersal," *Conservation Biology* 7, no. 2 (June 1993): 271–277; Heather Millar, "Let a Billion Flowers Bloom," *Sierra Magazine* (November–December 2005): 44–46; the Center for Urban Restoration Ecology, http://www.i-cure.org; New York Metropolitan Flora Project, http://www.bbg.org/sci/nymf.

8. Forests for Trees

1. Not to be confused with the famous Bunker Hill of Massachusetts, where a decisive Revolutionary War battle was fought. There are many Bunker Hills, which simply refer to places where American or British soldiers bivouacked.

2. Bernd Heinrich, *The Trees in My Forest* (New York: Cliff Street Books/HarperPerennial, 1997), 76.

3. Henry R. Stiles, *A History of the City of Brooklyn*, 3 vols. (1867; Bowie, Md.: Heritage Books Reprints, 1993), 2: 42, 316; 1: 389.

4. Richard Lezin Jones, "Please Forgive Gnarled Limbs: Its Age is 600," *New York Times*, November 12, 2003.

5. Corey Kilgannon, "In Obscurity, the Oldest and Tallest New Yorker," *New York Times*, March 27, 2004, sec. B1.

6. Heinrich, *The Trees in My Forest*, 24; Johnie Leverett (Standing Woman) and Steve Comer, "Old-Growth Forests: A Native American Perspective," in Mary Byrd Davis, ed., *Eastern Old Growth Forests: Prospects for Rediscovery and Recovery* (Washington, D.C.: Island Press, 1996), 108.

7. Rutherford Platt, *The Great American Forest* (Englewood Cliffs, N.J.: Prentice Hall, 1969), 43–49.

8. Hudson quoted in Johan de Laet, *New World*, 1625, in J. Franklin Jameson, *Narratives of New Netherland, 1609–1664* (1909; New York: Barnes and Noble, 1959), 49; Wassenaer, *Historisch Verhael*, in ibid., 81; Isaac de Rasieres, in ibid., 270; Adriaen Van Der Donck, *A Description of New Netherlands*, ed. Thomas F. O'Donnell (Syracuse, N.Y.: Syracuse University Press, 1968), 19–23.

9. Fernand Braudel, *Structures of Everyday Life: The Limits of the Possible*, vol. 1 of *Civilization and Capitalism* (French edition, 1979; New York: Harper, 1981), 367; Charles F. Carroll, *The Timber Economy of Puritan New England* (Providence, R.I.: Brown University Press, 1973), 11; Evelyn quoted in Robert G. Albion, *Forests and Sea Power: The Timber Problem of the Royal Navy, 1652–1862* (1926; reprint, Hamden, Conn.: Archon Books, 1965), 131; see also 97, 113.

10. Carroll, *Timber Economy*, 9.

11. Albion, *Forests and Sea Power*, 123.

12. Braudel, *Structures of Everyday Life*, 363; Carroll, *Timber Economy*, 9; Albion, *Forests and Sea Power*, 7–32; Carolyn Merchant, *The Death of Nature: Women, Ecology, and the Scientific Revolution* (San Francisco: Harper, 1989), 65; William Cronon, *Changes in the Land: Indians, Colonists and the Ecology of New England* (New York: Hill and Wang, 1983), 109.

13. Albion, *Forests and Sea Power*, 249–260.

14. John R. Stilgoe, *Common Landscape of America* (New Haven and London: Yale University Press, 1982), 171. See also J. A. Van Houtte, *An Economic History of the Low Countries, 800–1800* (New York: St. Martin's Press, 1977).

15. Michaelius, in Jameson, *Narratives of New Netherland*; John Newton Phelps Stokes, *The Iconography of Manhattan Island, 1498–1909*, 6 vols. (1928; reprint, New York: Arno Press, 1967), 4: 65; Carroll, *Timber Economy*, 69.

16. Carroll, *Timber Economy*, 24, 78, 123–124; Peter Kalm, *Travels in North America*, ed. Adolph B. Benson, rev. ed. (New York: Wilson-Erickson, 1937), 212–213, 291; Van der Donck, *A Description of New Netherland*, 19.

17. Van Der Donck, *A Description of New Netherland*, 22.

18. Percy Wells Bidwell and John Falconer, *History of Agriculture in the Northern United States, 1620–1860* (Washington, D.C.: Carnegie Institution, 1925), 9.

19. Peter Kalm, "The Prodigality of American Farmers," in David B. Greenberg, comp. and ed., *Land That Our Fathers Plowed* (Norman: University of Oklahoma Press, 1969), 228.

20. Bidwell and Falconer, *History of Agriculture*, 6–7.

21. Ibid., 6; Robert Grumet, *The Lenapes* (New York and Philadelphia: Chelsea House, 1989), 18; Ives Goddard, "Delaware," in *Handbook of the North American Indian: The Northeast*, ed. Bruce Trigger (Washington, D.C.: Smithsonian Institution Press, 1978), 216; Cronon, *Changes in the Land*, 13, 30, 53; J. C. Kricher, *A Field Guide to the Ecology of Eastern Forests of North America*, Peterson Field Guide Series (Boston and New York: Houghton Mifflin, 1988), 125.

22. Leverett and Comer, "Old Growth Forests: A Native American Perspective" in Davis, ed., *Eastern Old Growth Forests*, 105.

23. Kalm, "The Prodigality of American Farmers," 4.

24. Cronon, *Changes in the Land*, 114–116.

25. Ibid., 147.

26. Richard Lee, *Forest Hydrology* (New York: Columbia University Press, 1980), 245.

27. Carroll, *Timber Economy*, 13.

28. Robert Boyle, *The Hudson River: A Natural and Unnatural History*, exp. ed. (New York: W. W. Norton, 1979), 62.

29. Neu, "Hudson Valley Extractive Industries before 1815," in Joseph R. Frese and Jacob Judd, *Business Enterprise in Early New York* (Tarrytown, N.Y.: Sleepy Hollow Press, 1979), 133–165; J. Leander Bishop, *A History of American Manufactures from 1608 to 1860*, 3 vols. (1868; New York and London: Johnson Reprint Company, 1967), 2: 472–535.

30. George Perkins Marsh, *Man and Nature*, ed. David Lowenthal (1864; reprint, Cambridge, Mass.: Belknap Press/Harvard University Press, 1965).

31. John Elder, "Forever Wild," *Wild Earth*, Spring 2003, 58–61.

32. Davis, ed., *Eastern Old Growth Forests: Prospects for Rediscovery and Recovery*, 18.

33. Douglas Martin, "Urban Backyard to Be Revitalized," *New York Times*, April 9, 1995, Metro sec.

9. Urban Flyway

1. Michael F. Burger and Jillian M. Liner, *Important Bird Areas of New York* (New York: Audubon New York, 2005); Marie Winn, *Redtails in Love* (1998; New York: Random House/Vintage Books, 1999), 71.

2. David W. Steadman, "From Glaciers to Global Warming: Long-Term Changes in the Birdlife of New York State," in Emanuel Levine ed., *Bull's Birds of New York State* (Ithaca, N.Y., and London: Cornell University Press/Comstock Publishing Associates, 1998), 56–71.

3. C. F. Wray, "The Bird in Seneca Archaeology," *Proceedings of the Rochester Academy of Sciences*, 11 (1964): 1–56, cited in Steadman, "From Glaciers to Global Warming"; Esther K. Braun and David P. Braun, *The First Peoples of the Northeast* (Lincoln, Mass.: Moccasin Hill Press, 1994), 66.

4. Cottie Burland, *North American Indian Mythology*, rev. by Marion Wood (1965; New York: Peter Bedrick Books, 1985), 71.

5. J. F. Jameson, ed., *Narratives of New Netherland, 1609–1664* (1909; New York: Barnes and Noble, 1959), 71–72.

6. Peter Kalm, *Travels into North America*, trans. John Reinhold Forster (Barre, Mass.: Imprint Society, 1972), 150–151.

7. W. N. Fenton, "The Maple and the Passenger Pigeon in Iroquois Indian Life," *New York State Education Department School Bulletin*, March 1955, cited in Steadman, "From

Glaciers to Global Warming"; John Josselyn, cited in Peter Mathiessen, *Wildlife in America* (1959; New York: Viking, 1967), 56.

8. John James Audubon, "The Passenger Pigeon," in Roger Tory Peterson, ed., *The Bird-watcher's Anthology* (New York: Harcourt Brace, 1957), 141–145.

9. James Fenimore Cooper, *The Pioneers, or The Sources of the Susquehanna: A Descriptive Tale,* 1st ed. (New York: Wiley, 1823), chapter 3.

10. John James Audubon, "The Passenger Pigeon," in Joseph Wood Krutch and Paul S. Eriksson, eds., *A Treasury of Bird Lore* (Garden City, N.Y.: Doubleday, 1962), 283–284.

11. Frank Chapman, *The Birds of the Vicinity of New York City: A Guide to the Local Collection in the Department of Ornithology* (New York: American Museum of Natural History, 1906); Steadman, "From Glaciers to Global Warming," 67. As Steadman notes, both white settlers and Seneca Indians would encamp at passenger pigeon nesting sites and engage in mass shootings; the last known site was reported in 1868 at the Pennsylvania–New York border near Ceres, Allegheny County.

12. J. P. Giraud, Jr., *Birds of Long Island* (New York: Wiley, 1844), 195–196.

13. Chris Elphick, John B. Dunning, Jr., and David Allen Sibley, eds., *The Sibley Guide to Bird Life and Behavior* (New York: Alfred A. Knopf, 2001), 238–241. See also Ernest Thompson Seton, "The Dance of the Prairie Chickens," in Peterson, ed., *The Birdwatchers Anthology,* 358–361.

14. Stanley R. Lincoln, "Greater Prairie Chicken," in Levine, ed., *Bull's Birds of New York State,* 1998.

15. Stephen W. Eaton, "Wild Turkey; *Meleagris gallopavo,*" in Levine, ed., *Bull's Birds of New York State,* 1998, 213–215; *New York Times,* May 23, 2003.

16. John H. Baker, "Fifty Years of Progress: The National Audubon Society," *Audubon Magazine,* January–February 1955.

17. Chapman, *Birds of the Vicinity of New York,* 28.

18. Baker, "Fifty Years of Progress: The National Audubon Society," and H. Cruickshank, "Snowy Egrets at East River Rookery," both in Krutch and Erikson, eds., *A Treasury of Bird Lore,* 351–358.

19. Baker, "Fifty Years of Progress"; David J. Miller, "Celebrating National Audubon Society's Centennial," *New York State Conservationist* 60, no. 2 (October 2003): 2–3.

20. Charles M. Brookfield, "The Guy Bradley Story," *Audubon Magazine,* July–August 1955, in Krutch and Eriksson, eds., *A Treasury of Bird Lore,* 359–363.

21. Brookfield, "The Guy Bradley Story," and H. Cruickshank, "Snowy Egrets at East River Rookery," 1948, in Krutch and Eriksson, eds., *A Treasury of Bird Lore,* 356–358.

22. John Bull, "Double-crested Cormorants Breeding at Fishers Island," *Kingbird* 31:83 (1981); L. Sommers, M. Alfieri, K. Meskill, and R. Miller, "Long Island Colonial Waterbird and Piping Plover Survey" (NYSDEC, 1996), cited in Levine, ed., *Bull's Birds of New York State,* 1998, 119; Brinkley and Humann, in Elphick et al., *The Sibley Guide to Bird Life and Behavior,* 164; *Audubon,* June–July, 2003; Burger and Liner, *Important Bird Areas of New York,* 269, 296.

23. Brinkley and Humann, in Elphick et al., *The Sibley Guide to Bird Life and Behavior,* 164.

24. Jane Brody, *New York Times,* September 8, 1998.

25. Joanna Burger, *Oil Spills* (New Brunswick, N.J.: Rutgers University Press, 1997), 61–69; Brody, *New York Times;* www.nycaudubon.org.

26. Rachel Carson, *Silent Spring,* 40th Anniv. ed. (1962; New York: Houghton Mifflin/Mariner Books, 2002), 7–8.

27. P. R. Spitzer, "Osprey Egg and Nestling Transfers: Their Value as Ecological Experiments," in S. A. Temple, ed., *Endangered Birds: Management Techniques for Preserving Threatened Species* (Madison: University of Wisconsin Press, 1978), 171–182, cited in Barbara Allen Loucks, "Osprey," in Levine, ed., *Bull's Birds of New York State,* 1998, 178; Barbara Allen Loucks, "Peregrine Falcon," in Levine, ed., *Bull's Birds of New York State,* 1998, 203–206.

28. Loucks, "Osprey," 178–180.

29. Loucks, "Peregrine Falcon," 204.

30. Ibid.

31. Peter G. Nye, "Bald Eagle," in Levine, ed., *Bull's Birds of New York State*, 1998, 182–185.

32. John Bull, *The Birds of New York City*, 1964; Bull, *The Birds of New York State*, 1974; Nye, "Bald Eagle"; *New York Times*, January 31, 2004.

33. Winn, *Red-Tails in Love*.

34. E. J. McAdams, "Wilderness on 68th Street," *Topic Magazine* 3 (Winter 2003): 141–146.

35. Donald A. Windsor, "House Sparrow," in Levine, ed., *Bull's Birds of New York State*, 1998, 574; and Windsor, "Rock Dove," in Levine, ed., *Bull's Birds of New York State*, 1998, 316.

36. Windsor, "European Starling," in Levine, ed., *Bull's Birds of New York State*, 1998, 447–448; Geoffrey S. LeBaron, "Trash Birds and the Christmas Count," *Birding* 36:4 (August 2004): 389–390.

37. Bull, *Birds of New York City*, 1964; C. D. Duncan, "Changes in the Winter Abundance of Sharp-shinned Hawks in New England," *Journal of Field Ornithology* 67: 171–199 (1996), cited by Windsor, "Sharp-shinned Hawks," in Levine, ed., *Bull's Birds of New York State*, 1998, 188.

38. Charles R. Smith, "The Role of the Federation in Conservation of New York Birds: The Past Twenty Years," in Levine, ed., *Bull's Birds of New York State*, 1998, 50–51.

39. Burger and Liner, *Important Bird Areas of New York State*, v.-3.

10. Weathering

1. William K. Stevens, "Fewer Northeasters Pound U.S., but Punch Is More Powerful," *New York Times*, October 29, 1996, sec. C4.

2. Les Sirkin, *Western Long Island Geology* (Watch Hill, R.I.: Book and Tackle Shop, 1996); E. C. Pielou, *After the Ice Age: The Return of Life to Glaciated North America* (Chicago and London: University of Chicago Press, 1991).

3. Stephen H. Schneider, *Laboratory Earth: The Planetary Gamble We Cannot Afford to Lose* (New York: Basic Books, 1993), 50–51.

4. Richard Leakey and Roger Lewin, *The Sixth Extinction: Biodiversity and Its Survival* (New York: Doubleday, 1995; London: Weidenfeld and Nicolson, 1996), 241.

5. U.S. Environmental Protection Agency, "Climate Change and New York," report 230-F-97-008ff (September 1997). The report cites the Hadley Climate Model of the Intergovernmental Panel on Climate Change. http://yosemite.epa.gov/oar/globalwarming.nsf/content/us-newyork.html.

6. Brian Fagan, *The Long Summer: How Climate Changed Civilization* (New York: Basic Books/Perseus Books Group, 2004), 23–25.

7. "Climate Change and New York," U.S.E.P.A. 230-F-97–008ff (September 1997).

8. Schneider, *Laboratory Earth*, 51.

9. National Oceanic and Atmospheric Administration, "Global Warming," 2001; www.ncdc.noaa.gov/oa/climate/globalwarming.html#Q9.

10. Fagan, *The Long Summer*, 250.

11. Simon Schama, *The Embarrassment of Riches: An Interpretation of Dutch Culture in the Golden Age* (Berkeley and Los Angeles: University of California Press, 1988), 34–44; Dirk J. Struik, *The Land of Stevin and Huygens*, rev. ed., Studies in the History of Modern Science, vol. 7 (Dordrecht, Boston, London: Reidel, 1981), 68–69; Fernand Braudel, *Structures of Everyday Life: The Limits of the Possible*, vol. 1 of *Civilization and Capitalism* (New York: Harper, 1981), 358.

12. Audrey M. Lambert, *The Making of the Dutch Landscape: An Historical Geography of the Netherlands*, 2d ed. (London: Academic Press, 1985), 187–189, 122.

13. Marlise Simons, "Dutch Floods Came in the Back Door," *New York Times*, February 5, 1995, sec. 1.

14. Marlise Simons, "Dutch Do the Unthinkable: Sea Is Let In," *New York Times*, March 7, 1993, sec. 1.

15. Ibid.

16. Stephen Kinzer, "100,000 Dutch Flee the Worst Flooding in Four Decades," *New York Times*, February 1, 1995, sec. A.

17. Ibid.

18. Kinzer, "As Dike Cracks in Holland, Fear Rises with the Flood," *New York Times*, February 2, 1995, sec. A.

19. Simons, "Dutch Floods Came in the Back Door."

20. Cornelia Dean, *Against the Tide: the Battle for America's Beaches* (New York: Columbia University Press, 1999).

21. Ibid., 37.

22. Ibid., 36–42.

23. Ibid., 43.

24. Ibid., 97.

25. William W. Mather, *Geology of New York* (Albany, N.Y.: Carroll and Cook, 1843), 19–32.

26. Quoted in Oliver Pilat and Jo Ransom, *Sodom by the Sea* (New York: Doubleday, 1941), 19.

27. Ibid., 15–19.

28. Ibid., 315.

29. Norimitsu Onishi, "The Little Island That Couldn't," *New York Times*, March 18, 1997, sec. B1.

30. William K. Stevens, "Restoring Wetlands Could Ease Threat of Mississippi Floods," *New York Times*, August 4, 1995, sec. C1.

31. John Rather, "Dreading a Replay of the 1938 Hurricane," *New York Times*, August 28, 2005. Caronia's forecast is based on National Oceanographic and Atmospheric Administration "Slosh" maps (slosh stands for "sea, lake and overland surges from hurricanes"). See also www.nassaucountyny.gov/agencies/OEM.

32. Cornelia Dean and Peter Beller, "Calling the Ocean's Bluff," *New York Times*, November 3, 2005, sec. F.

33. M. R. Rampino and J. E. Sanders, "Evolution of the Barrier Islands of Southern Long Island, New York," *Sedimentology* 28, no. 1 (1981): 37–47; and Rampino and Sanders, "Episodic Growth of Holocene Tidal Marshes in the Northeastern United States," *Geology* 9, no. 2 (1981): 63–67. Both articles are cited in Charles Merguerian and J. E. Sanders, *The Glacial Geology of Long Island* (New York: New York Academy of Science, 1990).

Index

Page numbers in italics indicate illustrations.

About the Author

Betsy McCully is an associate professor of English at Kingsborough Community College of the City University of New York, where she has taught for ten years. She earned her doctorate in American literature in 1989 at George Washington University in Washington, D.C.

Betsy McCully has lived in New York City for two decades, where she has raised a son, tended a garden, and taught generations of students. over the years, she has walked the city's streets and hiked the trails of its many parks. She now lives with her husband, Joe Giunta, on Long Island.